1990

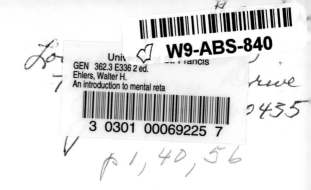
p 1, 40, 56

AN INTRODUCTION TO
MENTAL RETARDATION:
A PROGRAMMED TEXT

Second Edition

$9.95
tax   .50
postage 1.25
$ 11.70 (total)

AN INTRODUCTION TO MENTAL RETARDATION: A PROGRAMMED TEXT

Second Edition

Walter H. Ehlers
Florida State University

Curtis H. Krishef
Florida State University

Jon C. Prothero
Florida State University

CHARLES E. MERRILL PUBLISHING COMPANY
A Bell & Howell Company
Columbus Toronto London Sydney

1300 Alum Creek Drive
Columbus, Ohio 43216

Published by
CHARLES E. MERRILL PUBLISHING COMPANY
A Bell & Howell Company
Columbus, Ohio 43216

The book was set in Century.
The Production Editor was Linda Hillis.
The cover was prepared by Will Chenoweth.
Cover photograph from Bernstein Photo.

International Standard Book Number: 0-675-08526-8

Library of Congress Catalog Card Number: 76-49380

2 3 4 5 6 — 82 81 80 79 78

Printed in the United States of America

Foreword

Mental retardation is a complex subject. Because practically any statement about the condition requires some qualification, it is difficult to introduce readers to the subject without sacrificing accuracy for simplification.

The authors of *An Introduction to Mental Retardation: A Programmed Text* have avoided that pitfall. They have presented the material with clarity, accuracy—and practicality. And they have resisted the professional temptation to plunge too deeply into any one aspect of the subject at the expense of the total picture.

It is not enough to describe the condition; it is necessary also to describe ways in which retarded people and their families can be helped toward better lives. This book attempts to do both.

We hope that the students who use this textbook will be introduced not only to the subject of mental retardation, but also to the humanity of those individuals who happen to be retarded, and who need the help of informed and caring people.

Fred J. Krause
Executive Director,
President's Committee
on Mental Retardation

Washington, D.C.

Preface

We hope that you will like this revised edition which incorporates some of the new concepts that have come to the fore since publication of our original text. Many colleagues, friends, and readers have contributed suggestions which were helpful. Wherever possible these ideas were added or concepts expanded so that hopefully we would have a more valuable book. In some cases though we had to regretfully set aside an excellent suggestion since its addition would have moved the text out of its realm as an introductory one. We definitely feel that a basic introductory text serves a real need for many different persons and in many settings. Those persons just entering the fields of special education, social workers in agencies that serve the retarded, teachers and others involved in staff training projects—need a beginning text. We recognize the need also to move beyond this text to greater depth in a number of areas, including diagnosis, treatment, and services. To meet this need we have a selected bibliography at the end of each lesson which should help students and instructors move beyond the basic content of this introductory text.

We would like to repeat what we said in the preface to the first edition, that the contents of this text have been tested with students in the Department of Habilitative Sciences, in special education classes, and in both the undergraduate and graduate programs of the School of Social Work at Florida State University. We have either taught the classes in which the material was used, or in some instances worked closely with the teaching staff using the materials. Analyses of student reactions were made after each lesson. A final evaluation of student reaction was made at the end of each course to determine whether students really had profited from and preferred to use a programmed text. Unsigned questionnaires used in this evaluation process indicated a high degree of acceptance. Students who had never read anything on mental retardation before beginning the course felt that they had a good solid base from which to advance their knowledge.

In keeping with the beginning learner format there are few footnotes in this text to slow down the reader. The authors feel that this is especially important both in the beginning narrative section of each lesson, and even more so in the programmed material which follows. Although references are not introduced throughout each lesson, they are available to the interested student at the end of each lesson. Since the selected references pertain directly to the chapter in which they are found, it is a simple matter to find references which will provide a more detailed explanation for any item in question.

It should also be noted that this programmed text has at least four opportunities in each lesson to learn and reinforce knowledge. First, the narrative text acts as an introduction to the general subject; second, the list of objectives make clear what is expected; third, the programmed text moves the student step by step through the complexities of a particular knowledge area; fourth, a series of review questions allows for personal testing and provides immediate feedback to the question, "Have I really learned what is presented in this lesson?"

As we mentioned earlier, this text has been used and tested in manuscript and first edition form at Florida State University with the help of colleagues in other departments and in the School of Social Work. To all of them we wish to publicly acknowledge our thanks and appreciation.

In respect to this revised edition, our very special thanks and appreciation to Dr. Reuben Altman, Coordinator, Programs in Mental Retardation, University of Missouri-Columbia and to Dr. Thomas A. Burton, Division for Exceptional Children, University

of Georgia for their scholarly analysis and their helpful suggestions, many of which were incorporated into this edition. We are
grateful to them for their careful reading and pointing out of
errors and needs with which we need to deal.

And, finally, we want to express our sincere thanks and
appreciation to the Department of Health, Education and Welfare,
Social Rehabilitation Services, for grant #20-p-20009 which
partially supported Walter H. Ehlers and Jon C. Prothero during a
portion of the research and writing of this book.

Instructions for the User

This book must be read differently from traditional text books. It is really an instructional program which may be used as a "self-instructional" text or in a class in which there is a teacher and in which you as the student may be referred to other readings, instructional films, slides, slide tapes, and other material.

Each lesson in this book is made up of four parts which should be read and in which instruction should be followed as directed. First, the narrative should be read as you would a traditional text. This material introduces the theme or area of discussion. Second, the listing of objectives specifies exactly what you are expected to be able to do at the conclusion of the lesson. Third, the programmed lesson reintroduces the content which appeared in the narrative in a question-and-answer format. The answers appear in a separate section in a "scrambled" fashion so it is important to follow the instructions given after each question. This format may bother you at first, but if you follow the directions, reading only the answer item number indicated, you will find that reading this portion is interesting and exciting. The fourth and last section of the lesson permits a review of the questions and is a way for you to find out if you have a good grasp of the material that has been presented.

In order to use this book effectively, you will need to follow all directions carefully. Fill in the spaces in pencil wherever you are asked to do so. Then check your answers against the ones given in the programmed text. If this course is being taught with an instructor in charge, you may want to raise any questions you have with the instructor privately or in class so that a particular point may be clarified. Doing so will provide the most effective learning process. It is also recommended that you not wait more than a day between your study sessions. Material gets "cold" under these circumstances, and waiting can result in your spending more time than is necessary in order to learn the material.

We sincerely hope you will not only enjoy reading this "different" book but will also find that it successfully aids you in remembering the basic facts regarding mental retardation.

DEFINITION

Mental retardation refers to significantly subaverage general intellectual functioning existing concurrently with deficits in adaptive behavior and manifested during the developmental period. (From: Herbert J. Grossman, ed., *Manual on Terminology and Classification in Mental Retardation.* Washington, D.C.: AAMD, 1973.)

Contents

UNIT 1

LESSON ONE
An Introduction to the
Concept of Mental Retardation

Recent changes in thinking and revised classification systems in retardation have resulted in conceptual changes regarding what constitutes retardation. Once seen as more or less permanent, retardation is now viewed as a classification which may be used at one period of a person's life, but not at another. The decision as to whether a person is retarded will now be made, "in relation to behavioral standards and norms and in comparison to the individual's own chronological age group."[1]

Further clarification of what constitutes retardation is provided by the American Association on Mental Deficiency's (AAMD) current definition:

Mental retardation refers to significantly subaverage general intellectual functioning existing concurrently with deficits in adaptive behavior and manifested during the developmental period.[2]

The key words in this revised definition are: ". . . significantly subaverage"; "existing concurrently with deficits in adaptive behavior"; and "developmental period."

1

In respect to the first set of key words, retardation is no longer used to label borderline cases. Instead, the term *mild retardation* is used to indicate the beginning of "significant subaverage intellectual functioning" and must be two standard deviations below the mean for the I.Q. test being used. For example, the standard deviation in the Stanford-Binet I.Q. test is sixteen. Therefore, two standard deviations, or thirty-two points below the mean of one hundred, would place the upper limit for the mild classification at sixty-eight and the lower limit at fifty-two, or forty-eight points below the mean.

The second set of key words, "Existing concurrently with deficits in adaptive behavior," makes it imperative to classify a person as retarded only when both adaptive behavior and intellectual deficits of at least two standard deviations exist concurrently. Persons exhibiting acceptable adaptive behavior or social behavior cannot, therefore, be arbitrarily labeled mentally retarded.

The third set of key words relates to the fact that the above mentioned subaverage intellectual functioning and deficits in adaptive behavior must be manifested during the developmental period, which is now considered to extend through eighteen years of age.

The determination of mental ability or intelligence has traditionally, in the United States, rested upon the administration of one or more intelligence tests with resulting I.Q. scores. Other countries have not relied as heavily on I.Q. scores as we have. Although some experimentation is taking place with Piagetian developmental approaches, professionals in the United States are still basically committed to the use of standardized intelligence tests for the determination of mental ability.

The determination of social or adaptive behavior is the second component in the classification of retardation and is one of the most difficult areas to properly assess. The social behavior of individuals refers to their ability to understand, cope with, or adapt to various social situations and demands. Since these differ markedly, depending upon a person's cultural background, values, and norms, the determination of retardation due to inappropriate social behavior becomes extremely difficult to measure with precision. In a later chapter we will deal with the area of adaptive behavior in more detail.

---

[1] H. J. Grossman, ed., *Manual on Terminology and Classification in Mental Retardation,* 1973 revision (Washington, D.C.: American Association on Mental Deficiency, 1973), p. 14.

[2] Ibid., p. 11.

The step-by-step procedure used in the United States to determine whether mental retardation exists in the clinical sense is: first, to administer a battery of known intelligence tests considered to be reliable indicators; second, to examine the developmental anomalies due to toxic, genetic, infectious, traumatic, or other physiologic causes; and third, to examine the adaptive behavior, i.e., the ability to cope with societal needs and demands as they relate to self-help skills, getting along with others, ability to work in some job capacity, and functioning with some degree of independence in the community.

In general, the following examples indicate some of the *adaptive* behavior deficiencies which need examination:

1. In infancy and early childhood, before the age of three, one must observe the child's development in respect to such items as sitting up, standing, walking, holding the head up, and other responses to environmental stimuli (eye movements would be one example). Children whose response patterns fall outside the norms for these developmental states need examination in terms of impairment in adaptive behavior.
2. In preschool children, impairment of self-help skills, such as walking, talking, dressing, or eating, are the primary determinants upon which judgment of impaired adaptive behavior is made.
3. For school-aged children, impairment of self-help skills along with the inability to communicate normal needs and desires, plus inability to cope with basic academic skills needed in daily life situations, would indicate adaptive behavior deficiences.
4. With adults, impairment in adaptive behavior is indicated by an inability to function independently in the community or maintain adequacy in job performance.[3]

In concluding this introductory chapter we would like to call attention to the fact that the terminology used in the field of retardation varies. A major attempt was made in 1954 by the World Health Organization to divide the subject into two areas: *mental deficiency*, where causative factors were organic, and *mental retardation*, for subnormality resulting from some learning disability. In the United States this approach to terminology was never accepted by the field of retardation. Therefore, the terms mental retardation and mental deficiency are used interchangeably.

---

[3] For further examination of adaptive behavior see Lesson Four of this book; see also, H. J. Grossman, previously cited.

QUESTIONS

Please answer each of the following questions carefully. After each possible answer, you will be referred to a frame in the answer section (A-1, A-2, and so on) where you will be told whether or not your choice is correct. If the alternative you have selected is correct, you will be told in the answer frame which frame in the "Questions" section to turn to next. If your choice is incorrect, your answer will tell you to return to the question frame you have just answered to review and to try again. Please note that you will always be given your instructions according to frame number. Frames designated with "Q" indicate a frame in the "Questions" section (e.g., "Q-1, Q-2"). Frames designated with an "A" indicate answers. Only occasionally will you be given a page number to which to turn. It is most important that you follow the instructions for *each individual question or answer frame* most carefully.

WHAT IS MENTAL RETARDATION?

Q-1   In the latest AAMD revision, mental retardation has been defined in the following manner: "mental retardation refers to significantly sub-average general intellectual functioning existing concurrently with deficits in adaptive behavior and manifested during the development period".[4] Let's break this definition into its constituent parts.

First, mental retardation refers to significantly subaverage intellectual functioning. The mentally retarded are those individuals whose normal intellectual growth has been arrested to a significant degree of at least two standard deviations below the mean for the intelligence test being employed.

One major characteristic of a person considered mentally retarded is that he or she has a significant degree of mental impairment.

a. This is a true statement.   Turn to A-4.
b. This is a false statement.   Turn to A-18.

Q-2   The second important aspect of mental retardation is that the adaptive behavior of the retarded individual is also impaired and that this impairment and significantly impaired intellectual func-

---

[4] Grossman, *Manual on Terminology*, p. 14.

tioning must both be present if an individual is to be considered retarded.

Adaptive behavior impairment may include skills associated with:

1. Self-help.
2. Motor.
3. Communication.
4. Occupation.
5. Self-direction (goal direction).
6. Socialization.

An individual who has subaverage intellectual functioning and demonstrates no adaptive behavior impairment would be considered mentally retarded.

a. This is a true statement.   Turn to A-21.
b. This is a false statement.   Turn to A-1.

Which of the skills listed below is/are associated with adaptive   Q-3
behavior?

a. Motor skills.   Turn to A-12.
b. Skills associated with an occupation.   Turn to A-22.
c. Socialization skills.   Turn to A-15.
d. Self-help skills (i.e., eating, dressing, etc.).   Turn to A-19.
e. Goal-directed skills.   Turn to A-8.
f. Communication skills.   Turn to A-13.
g. All of the above.   Turn to A-3.

Now please list six skills associated with adaptive behavior. When   Q-4
you have completed your list turn to A-20.

a. _____

b. _____

c. _____

d. _____

e. _____

f. _____

Q-5   The third and final aspect of the definition of mental retardation is that to be considered retarded an individual must have suffered arrested intellectual growth or development and evidence adaptive behavior impairment *during the developmental period.*

The developmental period includes all of the following stages:

1. The prenatal period.
2. The birth process.
3. The period from birth through eighteen years of age.

When must a retarded individual have suffered arrested intellectual and adaptive behavioral growth or development?

a. During the developmental period.   Turn to A-11.
b. After the developmental period.   Turn to A-7.
c. Both of the above.   Turn to A-2.

Q-6   The developmental period includes:

a. The prenatal period.   Turn to A-14.
b. The birth process.   Turn to A-9.
c. The period from birth through eighteen
     years of age.   Turn to A-5.
d. All of the above.   Turn to A-16.

Q-7   Mental retardation, we now realize, refers to which of the following?

1. Significantly subaverage intellectual functioning.
2. A condition that may originate during adult life.
3. Adaptive behavior impairments of all kinds.
4. A condition that is associated with only gross impairment in adaptive behavior.
5. A condition that originates during the developmental period.

Choose the only answer from those given below which corresponds to the three elements of mental retardation.

a. 1, 2, 3.   Turn to A-17.
b. 1, 3, 5.   Turn to A-10.
c. 1, 2, 4.   Turn to A-6.

Please follow the same instructions as those you were given on page 4 in working with this section. It is most important that you remember to follow the individual instructions in each answer frame.

Right you are! Mentally retarded individuals evidence varying de- A-1
grees of impairment in adaptive behavior along with a significant
impairment in mental development.

Continue now with Q-3.

You have responded that a mentally retarded individual may have A-2
suffered arrested intellectual growth and adaptive behavioral growth
or development during or after the developmental period. You are
correct in part. A mentally retarded individual may have suffered
arrested intellectual growth or development during the developmental period but *not* during his adult life (after the developmental period). Return now to Q-5 and select the correct answer.

Yes, adaptive behavior does include all six types of skills. A-3

Continue now with Q-4.

Right you are. Mental retardation refers to significantly subaverage A-4
intellectual functioning.

Continue now with Q-2.

A-5   Yes, the period from birth through eighteen years of age is part of the developmental period but not all of it.

Return to Q-5 for a review before selecting another answer to Q-6.

A-6   You have selected as the three elements of mental retardation the following:

1. Significantly subaverage intellectual functioning. This is correct.
2. A condition that can originate during the adult years. This is incorrect.
3. A condition that is associated with only gross impairment in adaptive behavior. This is also incorrect.

It is recommended that you return to Q-1 and briefly review the lesson from that point on. Then select the correct answer for Q-7.

A-7   You have answered that a mentally retarded individual must suffer arrested intellectual growth or development *after* the developmental period. However, an individual who suffers some form of brain defect after the developmental period is *not* considered mentally retarded since his mental processes were fully developed by the time of his injury.

Return to Q-5 and select the correct answer.

A-8   This is only a partial answer.

Return to Q-3 and make another selection.

Yes, the developmental period includes the birth process, but this is only a part of the developmental period.

A-9

Return to Q-6 and select another answer.

Excellent! Putting three elements together, you have realized that mental retardation refers to significantly subaverage intellectual functioning which originates during the developmental period and includes adaptive behavior impairment.

A-10

Turn now to the conclusion found at the end of this lesson after A-22.

You said that a mentally retarded individual must have suffered arrested intellectual and adaptive behavioral growth or development during the developmental period and you are absolutely correct.

A-11

Continue now with Q-6.

You have said that adaptive behavior includes only motor skills; however, it also includes other skills.

A-12

Return to Q-3 and select another answer.

This is only a partial answer.

A-13

Return to Q-3 and make another selection.

A-14   Yes, the prenatal period is a part of the developmental period but only a part.

Return to Q-6 and select another answer

A-15   This is only a partial answer.

Return to Q-3 and make another selection.

A-16   Right! The developmental period includes the prenatal period, the birth process, and the period from birth through eighteen years of age.

Continue now with Q-7.

A-17   You have said that mental retardation refers to significantly sub-average intellectual functioning which originates during the adult years and includes adaptive behavior impairment. You are two-thirds correct. Mental retardation does *not* originate during adult life.

Return to Q-7 and select the correct answer.

A-18   You have said that mental retardation does not refer to a significant degree of subaverage intellectual functioning, when, in actuality, a mentally retarded individual is always hampered by intellectual functioning which is significantly below average.

Return to Q-1 and select the correct answer.

This is only a partial answer.

Return to Q-3 and make another selection.

Although there are a great many skills associated with adaptive behavior, six extremely important skills are:

a. Motor skills.
b. Occupational skills.
c. Socialization skills.
d. Self-help skills.
e. Goal-directed skills.
f. Communication skills.

Continue with Q-5 after you have reviewed and corrected any errors you may have made in Q-4.

You have said that the mentally retarded do not have to exhibit evidence of impairment in adaptive behavior. However, a mentally retarded individual does evidence such behavior along with a significant impairment in mental development. Both impairments must be evidenced concurrently if an individual is to be considered retarded.

Return to Q-2 and select the correct answer.

It is true that adaptive behavior includes skills associated with an occupation, but you have neglected to include other skills.

Return to Q-3 and select another answer.

CONCLUSION

You have now completed this lesson. Please turn to the Review Questions for Lesson One and take the examination covering this lesson before going on to Lesson Two. After completing the review questions, please be sure to check your answers against the ones provided. Then, in order to reinforce the correct answer, go back and review every case where you did not give the correct answer. Do this immediately so that you will retain only the correct answers. When you have completed the review questions and have reviewed your answers proceed to Lesson Two.

Questions

This review covers the programmed Lesson One. Circle the *letter* corresponding to the answer of your choice.

1. Which of the following are included in the latest definition of mental retardation?

   a. Significant impairment in intellectual functioning along with impairment in adaptive behavior.
   b. Originates only before birth or during the birth process.
   c. Involves impairment in intellectual functioning only.
   d. a and b above.
   e. b and c above.

2. Mental retardation originates:

   a. Only during the period of gestation or pregnancy.
   b. During pregnancy, during the birth process, or during the developmental period.
   c. Anytime during the life span.
   d. Only before birth or during the birth process.

3. Adaptive behavior may be impaired by which of the following?

   a. Motor and self-help skills.
   b. Communication and socialization skills.
   c. Occupational skills.
   d. All of the above.
   e. None of the above.

Answers

The answers to the preceding questions are:

1. a.
2. b.
3. d.

SELECTED READINGS

Blatt, B. "Towards a More Acceptable Terminology in Mental Retardation." *Training School Bulletin* 58 (1961): 47-51.

Committee on Nomenclature and Statistics of the American Psychiatric Association. *Diagnostic and Statistical Manual for Mental Disorders.* Washington, D.C.: The American Psychiatric Association, 1968.

Grossman, H. J., ed. *Manual on Terminology and Classification in Mental Retardation,* 1973 revision. American Association on Mental Deficiency, Special Publication Series No. 2, 1973, p. 14.

Heber, R. F. "A Manual on Terminology and Classification in Mental Retardation." *American Journal of Mental Deficiency* 64 (1959). Monograph Supplement.

_____. "Modification in the Manual of Terminology and Classification in Mental Retardation." *American Journal of Mental Deficiency* 65 (1961): 499.

Kauffman, J. M. and Payne, J. S., eds. *Mental Retardation: Introduction and Personal Perspectives.* Columbus, Ohio: Charles E. Merrill, 1975.

Kidd, J. W. "Toward a More Precise Definition of Mental Retardation." *Mental Retardation* 2 (1964): 209-12.

Perry, S. E. "Some Theoretical Problems of Mental Deficiency and Their Action Implications." *Psychiatry* 17 (1954): 45-73.

President's Committee on Mental Retardation. *Mental Retardation 67: A First Report to the President on the Nation's Progress and Remaining Great Needs in the Campaign to Combat Mental Retardation.* Washington, D.C.: U. S. Department of Health, Education and Welfare, 1967.

_____. *Mental Retardation 68: The Edge of Change.* Washington, D.C.: U.S. Department of Health, Education and Welfare, 1968.

_____. *Mental Retardation 69: Toward Progress—The Story of a Decade.* Washington, D.C.: U.S. Department of Health, Education and Welfare, 1969.

_____. *Mental Retardation 70: The Decisive Decade.* Washington, D.C.: U.S. Department of Health, Education and Welfare, 1970.

_____. *Mental Retardation 71: Entering the Era of Human Ecology.* Washington, D.C.: U.S. Department of Health, Education and Welfare, 1971.

_____. *Mental Retardation 73: The Goal is Freedom.* Washington, D.C.: U.S. Department of Health, Education and Welfare, 1973.

_____. *Mental Retardation 74: A Friend in Washington.* Washington, D.C.: U.S. Department of Health, Education and Welfare, 1974.

_____. *The Mentally Retarded . . . Their New Hope.* Washington, D.C.: U.S. Department of Health, Education and Welfare, 1966.

President's Panel on Mental Retardation. *A Proposed Program for National Action to Combat Mental Retardation.* Washington, D.C.: Government Printing Office, 1962.

Secretary's Committee on Mental Retardation. *The Problem of Mental Retardation.* Washington, D.C.: U.S. Department of Health, Education and Welfare, 1966.

Tredgold, R. F. and Soddy, K. *Tredgold's Mental Retardation,* 11th ed. Baltimore: The Williams and Wilkins Company, 1970.

LESSON TWO
A Brief History of
Mental Retardation

Historical records reveal that mentally retarded individuals have been recognized throughout all centuries of recorded history. Legends still persist from ancient times of "differences" that were noticed by many observers. There are references in history and literature to the fact that the Spartans in ancient Greece made a practice of eliminating defective children by deliberately exposing them to the elements. In Roman times, those who were retarded were sometimes kept in wealthy homes for purposes of amusement. The Romans were more tolerant of those whose mental deficiencies were less noticeable than of physical disorders, and treatment of the mentally retarded was perhaps better than that provided for those suffering from obvious physical disabilities, such as blindness, deafness, or lameness. It was believed that it was better to eliminate weaklings; physical and mental fitness were considered to be important and to the "glory of the state."

With the advent of the Christian doctrine, a more humanitarian and charitable approach developed toward the retarded. There was some hope for those who had previously been outcasts or who were labeled as fools. During the period of the rise of Christianity, a change of attitude toward all persons as individuals came to be illustrated in the more compassionate attitude toward the retarded. In the fourth century, the first protector of those who were considered retarded arose in the person of the Bishop of Myra, who was also known as "St. Nicholas the Wonder Worker" and who became the prototype for the modern Santa Claus. The Bishop of Myra indicated a particularly strong compassion for those who were retarded and urged that they be given tender care.

During the Middle Ages, society's attitude toward those who were different became somewhat more sympathetic. It was during the medieval period that the first asylums were built as places of refuge and haven for the retarded and others who were in need of protection or safety. Sponsored, for the most part, by the Christian churches, they offered the residents "protection under God." During this period too, the mentally deficient in certain areas of Europe were provided free license to roam where they pleased because they were considered to be "the infants of a good God."

But society changes slowly in its attitudes, and some of the mentally retarded during the Middle Ages were laughed at and became the playthings of royalty. Under the reign of Charles the Fifth of France, the province Champagne held exclusive rights to provide fools for his court. Tycho Brahe, the renowned astronomer, is known to have kept a retardate as a close companion and listened to his statements for their hidden wisdom. The religious leader Martin Luther showed his low regard for the retarded when he described a twelve-year-old mentally retarded person as being Godless: "He did nothing but gorge himself as much as four peasants or threshers. He ate, defecated, and drooled."[1] Phillip the Fourth of Spain gathered almost every kind of retardate in his court, as did the early Aztec emperor Montezuma. It is known from available records that Montezuma kept a human menagerie of those with mental defects and associated physical anomalies. Despite their lack of understanding, both of these regal rulers did permit the mentally retarded the freedom of the royal court and the opportunity to eat all they could as well as to dress in the finest of clothes. But royalty in Europe often treated the retarded as court jesters or fools and made them scapegoats. Nonetheless, some of these mentally deficient individuals seemed to survive relatively well within the royal court and before long "fool societies" arose in which people wore the bell-capped garments of

---

[1] Martin Luther; *Colloquia Mensalia* (London: William Du-Gard, 1952), p. 387.

the court fool so that they would not be held responsible for any of their words or deeds. In twelfth-century France, a "feast of fools" developed in which minor clergymen assumed the roles of their superiors. This feast permitted free reign to those who wished to act out their most base desires—to drink and to otherwise behave in a fashion not usually regarded as appropriate or acceptable. The "feast of fools" reached such proportions that by the sixteenth century, Victor Hugo incorporated some of the tradition of the holiday in an incident in the *Hunchback of Notre Dame* in which the grotesque and mentally deficient Quasimodo was enthroned for a day as the "Lord of Misrule."

Attitudes were in flux again at the time of the Renaissance. The literature of the period indicates that the derogatory terms "Simple Simon," "village idiot," "fools," "bumpkins," "gulls," "dolts," and "asses" were used to refer to the mentally retarded. In contrast, it was also during the Renaissance that learning and education began to assume a more important place in society. Each individual's personality was deemed sacred, but each individual was also held responsible for his own actions. This attitude placed an increased burden and a great deal of pressure upon those who were mentally retarded and resulted in harsh and often cruel treatment for those with limited intellectual endowment. These individuals were placed in dungeons for punishment and were given a "keeper" rather than a "protector" as had been the case in the asylums. Through most of this period, there was no attempt made to deal with retardation in a reasonable manner.

The first person to show some slight desire to treat the subject of mental deficiency scientifically was Sir Anthony Fitz-Herbert who attempted to define (in the terminology of the times) an "idiot." Sir Anthony's attempt in 1534 was not followed by any other efforts at definition until John Locke in 1690 specifically attempted to distinguish between those who were idiots and those who were insane.

The history of education for the retarded had its beginnings approximately sixty-five years prior to Locke's attempt to distinguish idiocy from insanity when Juan Pablo Bonet created a program of education for the deaf. In the middle of the eighteenth century, two men, Jacob-Rodrigues Pereire and the Abbé de L'Epee, developed sensory-motor training in the education of those who were deaf.

The first attempt to teach a severely retarded child started with a naked boy who had been seen running through the French woods of Aveyron in the period from 1794-1798. Called the "Wild Boy of Aveyron," he was finally caught and brought to Paris in 1798 as a specimen of a feral man—one who is wild or savage. The child was incredibly dirty, approximately eleven years of age, and, according to descriptions of the time, had a constant tendency to trot or gallop. He ate refuse; his movements were spasmodic; he swayed back and forth in monkeylike fashion; he paid attention to practically nothing; and he had eyes which were relatively expressionless. The only sounds he would make were guttural and made no sense in terms of communication.

This wild boy was placed under the care of Dr. Jean Itard who was chief medical officer of the National Institution for the Deaf and Dumb in France. Itard believed that the boy's mental faculties had been arrested because of his environment and thought that his condition was curable. He discovered that the boy, whom he named Victor, did not have the intelligence to climb a chair to obtain food placed out of his reach, had no sensitivity to heat or cold, and could squat half-naked in a pouring rain for hours on end without visible ill effects. After two years of instruction, the "Wild Boy of Aveyron" appeared relatively normal except that he still could not speak. He was affectionate and clean and was able to read and understand several words, but that was the extent of his reading and speaking skills. At the end of five years of training, it was obvious to Itard that he had made only slight progress and was not going to be able to train the boy to have more than very limited speech, limited use of sense skills, and no reliable skill in handling his emotions. It was at this point then that Itard reluctantly ceased his work with Victor. We, therefore, can fix the beginning of the 1800s as the date when an interest in the problem of educating the mentally retarded began.

Meanwhile, other physician-educators were also becoming interested in mental deficiency. Dr. Edouard Seguin, a young doctor in France who had become associated with Dr. Itard, felt that much had been accomplished with the "Wild Boy of Aveyron" even though Itard had become quite discouraged. On the basis of the work done by Itard with Victor, Seguin had come to feel that the education of the mentally deficient could be enhanced by emphasizing the development of the sense organs. Aware of the previous work of Pereire and de L'Epee, he developed a systematic program of sensory-motor training which he felt would make possible the education of the retarded if only they could be subjected to enough physiological stimuli. In 1848, Seguin emigrated to the United States where he played a major role in helping to increase the educational programs for the mentally retarded in this country.

In 1846, Dr. Samuel Howe, another leader in the field of mental deficiency, led an investigation making inquiry into what could be done on behalf of a number of retarded persons living in the state of Massachusetts. Using as a model an earlier institution which had been started for cretins in Switzerland by Dr. Johann Jakob Guggenbuhl, Dr. Howe became the first to initiate institutional care for the retarded in the United States.

In 1860, the first compulsory school laws were passed in the United States, but they were not enforced in any way during the Civil War. During the Depression of the 1890s, these laws did help to solve financial problems by sending children to schools so that more adults could be employed. With many more children attending school, attention came to be focused on various kinds of mental retardation present in the school population. Although there was renewed interest in the retarded being generated in both America and Europe, France led the way professionally in 1899 when the first laboratory for training teachers for the mentally retarded was established at the Sorbonne in Paris.

The late nineteenth century also saw the rise of professional organizations for those who worked with the retarded. After living and working in the United States for almost thirty years, Dr. Seguin helped to develop and served as the first president of one of the oldest professional organizations concerned with the problems of mental retardation. This organization, now known as the American Association on Mental Deficiency, was organized in 1876. In 1922, another professional organization developed to serve "special children." The organization, which is now known as the Council for Exceptional Children, sought to provide opportunities for special educators to share experiences and information through publications and meetings. In 1950, the National Association for Retarded Children held its first meeting.[2] At its beginning, this organization was composed principally of parents of retarded children, but over the years it has broadened its membership to include many professional workers.

At the turn of the century, Dr. Maria Montessori, an Italian physician, concluded that mental deficiency was an educational rather than a medical problem. She became a pioneer in the field of education for retarded children using many of the sensory training methods devised by Seguin. Her program was a refinement of ideas of earlier physician-educators for she felt that children learned not

---

[2]Now known as the National Association for Retarded Citizens.

only from their teacher and their environment but also from other children. She tried to make use of natural settings to help in providing sensory-motor training.

It was around the beginning of the twentieth century that French physicians began to attack the problem of how to select retarded children for education. In 1904 the French government organized a commission and set aside money to study the problem and determine which of the retarded should attend day classes. The government authorized two men to head the commission and develop screening tests. They were Dr. Theodore Simon, a physician, and Dr. Alfred Binet, a psychologist. Dr. Binet, through these studies, became the first to develop the concept of "mental age." He worked arduously to develop individual performance tests for each age level. Before his untimely death in 1911, he had laid a foundation upon which others could build.

The accomplishments and setbacks of the past are a matter of historical record. In October 1961 the late John F. Kennedy, because of his strong interest, named a panel of eminent professionals to recommend a national plan of action to combat the problem of mental retardation. In 1962 this panel reported to President Kennedy listing many suggested actions to improve programs and services for the retarded.

Since the time of the President's panel, the field of retardation has received increasingly more attention from both lay as well as professional people. Such factors as the relationship between poverty and retardation have been scrutinized and differences have been expressed as to the effect of poverty in producing mental retardation. Many of the problems of improper institutional care and dehumanizing treatment that retarded persons once received have also been exposed, and this has led to considerable improvement in services. In addition, there has been a serious movement toward the establishment of adequate standards of operation for both residential and community program facilities. These standards, in large measure, were promoted by the Joint Commission on Accreditation of Hospitals through their publications, "Standards of Residential Facilities for the Mentally Retarded" and "Standards for Community Agencies Serving Persons with Mental Retardation and other Developmental Disabilities."

Recently, the term *normalization* has become an important concept for the retarded. This concept originated in the Scandinavian countries (Denmark's "Act of 1959" and Sweden's "1968 Normalization Law") and was introduced into the United States in a publication of the President's Committee on Mental Retardation.[3] Normalization essentially emphasizes the importance of helping retarded persons, to the extent that is possible, to live just like everyone else. Although the principle of normalization was first primarily concerned with the care and treatment of the retarded in residential facilities, only a short time elapsed before the idea was expanded to include community services. As a result, many retarded persons who previously had been committed to institutions, often without proper legal procedures, and then left to sit and stare at bare walls for the rest of their lives, now no longer suffer from this type of treatment. Presently there is far greater acceptance of the importance of family living for these individuals. This emphasis has shifted treatment for the retarded away from institutions and into community placement. Living in the more normalized surroundings of small foster home and boarding care facilities and, when possible, in their own homes with their parents, is recognized as being one way to achieve a more normal life for retarded persons in contrast to living in large institutional facilities.

This extremely brief historical background is intended only to acquaint you with a few of the many names of people who have been important in the field of mental retardation. Of necessity, many more names were left out than could possibly be dealt with adequately in this short space. Therefore, you are referred to any of the texts listed at the end of this chapter for a background of greater depth.

---

[3]See Robert B. Kugel and Wolf Wolfensberger, eds., *Changing Patterns in Residential Services for the Mentally Retarded.* President's Committee on Mental Retardation, Washington, D.C. 20201, January 10, 1969. See especially the article by Bengt Nirje, "The Normalization Principle and Its Human Management Implications," pp. 179-95. Also see chapter fifteen of this text regarding recent legislation affecting the civil rights of the retarded.

OBJECTIVES

This lesson presents a brief history of mental retardation and some of the significant changes that have occurred in attitudes and treatment. When you have completed this lesson, you should be able to accomplish the following tasks:

1. Given the name of an historical period, make or identify a statement concerning the prevailing attitudes and/or treatment of the retarded during this period.
2. Given the name of an individual who played a prominent role in the history of mental retardation, make or identify a statement concerning the role played by that individual.
3. Given a statement concerning a mental retardation organization, identify the organization.
4. Define, in your own words, the term *normalization*.

Please answer each of the following questions carefully. After each possible answer, you will be referred to a frame in the section beginning on p. 29 where you will be told whether or not your choice is correct. If the alternative you have selected is correct, you will be told in the answer frame which frame in the "Questions" section to turn to next. If your choice is incorrect, your answer will tell you to return to the question frame you have just answered to review and to try again. Please note that you will always be given your instructions according to frame number. Frames designated with "Q" indicate a frame in the "Questions" section (e.g., "Q-1, Q-2"). Frames designated with an "A" indicate answers. Only occasionally will you be given a page number to which to turn. It is most important that you follow the instructions for *each individual question or answer frame* most carefully.

ATTITUDES TOWARD AND TREATMENT OF THE RETARDED THROUGH THE AGES

The Spartans of ancient Greece, believing in the philosophy of the survival of the fittest, viewed the retarded as unfit to live and exposed them to the elements so that they would die as infants. Wealthy Romans often used the retarded for purposes of amusement, although they, too, were concerned with preserving only those who were mentally and physically fit.

Q-1

Christian Era—Medieval Period

The rise of Christianity and its accompanying humanitarian approach to human beings helped change the attitudes of some persons toward the retarded when churches for the first time began granting protection in special asylums. However, the retarded were still treated cruelly and laughed at by many.

During the Medieval Period, the retarded were:

a. Treated cruelly.   Turn to A-3.
b. Given protection in asylums
     for the first time.   Turn to A-16.
c. Both of the above.   Turn to A-8.

Renaissance Period

During the Renaissance, learning and education began to assume greater importance. Each individual, therefore, was to be held accountable for his actions. The retarded, unable to meet the standards imposed, were harshly treated because of their behavior and were often placed in dungeons with "keepers" instead of "protectors."

1800 to the Present—The Modern Era

Although the history of education and scientific interest in the retarded began before 1800, it was not until the Modern Era that the most profound improvements began to occur in knowledge, attitudes, and treatment of the retarded. Despite such efforts, there are still many persons, even at present, who treat the retarded in an inhumane manner.

Circle those periods listed below during which many so-called "normal" people treated the retarded in an inhumane manner. Then turn to A-1 for the answer.

a. B. C.
b. Medieval Period.
c. Renaissance Period.
d. Modern Period.

INDIVIDUALS WHO HAVE CONTRIBUTED GREATLY TO AN INCREASED UNDERSTANDING AND ACCEPTANCE OF THE RETARDED

Just prior to the development of protective asylum given to the retarded by Christian churches, the Bishop of Myra, who was also known as St. Nicholas the Wonder Worker, became the first person to offer protection to those considered to be retarded.

The first person to attempt to define an "idiot" was Sir Anthony Fitz-Herbert in 1534. It was not until 1690 that the next definitive effort was made by John Locke, who attempted to distinguish between those who were idiots and those who were insane.

The first person to offer protection to the retarded was:

a. Sir Anthony Fitz-Herbert.   Turn to A-6.
b. The Bishop of Myra.   Turn to A-10.

Explain below the roles played by Sir Anthony Fitz-Herbert and   Q-4
John Locke and then turn to A-2 to check your answer.

_____

_____

_____

EDUCATION

The history of education for the retarded began in approximately   Q-5
1625 when Juan Pablo Bonet created an education program for
the deaf. In the eighteenth century two men, Jacob-Rodrigues
Pereire and the Abbé de L'Epee, further developed sensory-motor
training for the deaf.

A famous experiment in education for the retarded was conducted
by Dr. Jean Itard. He became the first to attempt to teach a
severely retarded child in 1798. The child was the "Wild Boy of
Aveyron" who was found to have been living alone in the forests
of Aveyron until he was approximately eleven years of age. Itard
believed that the boy's mental faculties had been retarded mainly
because of his environment. Although Itard taught the boy many
social amenities as well as how to live in his new environment, he
was unable to teach him to read or to speak more than a few words.

In the middle of the nineteenth century, Dr. Edouard Seguin used
some of the work of these men to develop a program of education
which he believed could be used to teach the retarded. Seguin
proclaimed in his early writing that the retarded could be taught
but that they learned at a slower rate than other people.

13707/

Match the names below with the contributions each made to the education of the mentally retarded. Choose your answer from those given in the paragraph which follows.

A. Juan Pablo Bonet.
B. Dr. Jean Itard.
C. Dr. Edouard Seguin.
D. Wild Boy of Aveyron.

1. Concluded that retardation was an educational rather than a medical problem.
2. First severely retarded person to be taught.
3. Created an educational program for the deaf which influenced the development of a system of education for the retarded.
4. Developed an educational system for the retarded; proclaimed that the retarded could be taught but that they learned slower than others.
5. The first to teach a severely retarded person.

Choose your answer from below:

a. A4; B5; C3; D2.   Turn to A-9.
b. A3; B5; C4; D2.   Turn to A-19.
c. A5; B1; C4; D2.   Turn to A-14.

Q-6   In 1846, Dr. Samuel Howe was the first to initiate institutional care for the retarded in the United States.

Around 1900, Dr. Maria Montessori, an Italian physician, proclaimed her belief that mental deficiency was an educational rather than a medical problem. She developed a program that made use of natural settings to help provide sensory-motor training for the retarded. With this program, the retarded could learn not only from their teacher and environment but also from other children.

With the advent of compulsory school attendance in the United States, more attention was focused on the retarded child in the school population. However, it was France that led the way professionally in developing school programs for the retarded. The French government established the first laboratory for training teachers for the retarded and subsidized the work of Dr. Alfred Binet who, along with Theodore Simon, developed the concept of "mental age" and, in 1908, published the first tests for each age group. In this country the name of Lewis M. Terman is well known for his revision of the IQ tests which came to be known as the Revised Stanford-Binet Test.

Again, match the following individuals with their contributions.

A. Dr. Samuel Howe.
B. Dr. Alfred Binet.
C. Dr. Jean Itard.
D. Dr. Maria Montessori

1. Was the first to teach a severely retarded child.
2. Was the first to initiate institutional care for the retarded in the United States.
3. Developed a program to teach sensory-motor skills to the retarded. Believed that children learned from other children as well as from teachers and the environment.
4. Developed the concept of "mental age" as well as performance tests for retarded persons in each age level.

Choose your answer from among those presented below:

a. A2; B4; C1; D3.   Turn to A-12.
b. A3; B4; C1; D2.   Turn to A-4.
c. A1; B3; C2; D4.   Turn to A-18.

Mental Retardation Organizations

There are three major national organizations concerned with the   Q-7
retarded in the United States. These include:

1. The American Association on Mental Deficiency (AAMD).
2. The Council for Exceptional Children (CEC).
3. The National Association for Retarded Citizens (NARC).

One of the oldest professional organizations dealing with the scientific and terminological problems of mental retardation is the American Association on Mental Deficiency organized in 1876. Dr. Seguin was its first president.

The Council for Exceptional Children was organized in 1922 to provide opportunities for special educators to share experiences and information through publications and meetings.

The National Association for Retarded Children[4] was organized in 1950. Originally, it was composed mainly of parents of retarded children, but its membership now includes many professional workers. Its major goals include helping parents adjust to the problems inherent in having a retarded child and fighting for favorable societal changes for the retarded.

Test yourself with the following question.

The organization that was established to provide opportunities for special educators to share their experiences is the:

a. National Association for Retarded
   Children (NARC).   Turn to A-17.
b. Council for Exceptional Children (CEC).   Turn to A-13.
c. American Association on Mental
   Deficiency (AAMD).   Turn to A-7.

Q-8   Circle below the organization that was established to provide parents of retarded children with opportunities to share their experiences and work toward positive changes in society concerning the retarded individual.

        a. NARC.   Turn to A-15.
        b. CEC.   Turn to A-11.
        c. AAMD.   Turn to A-5.

Q-9   State in your own words what is meant by "normalization." Turn to A-20 to check your answer.

---

[4]Now known as the National Association for Retarded Citizens.

ANSWERS

Please follow the same instructions as those you were given on page 23 in working with this section. It is most important that you remember to follow the individual instructions in each answer frame.

You should have circled all four periods listed in Q-2. Although inhumane treatment of the retarded as well as other handicapped individuals has been reduced greatly from ancient times to the present, there are still those who mistreat these individuals.

A-1

Continue now with Q-3.

Sir Anthony Fitz-Herbert and John Locke both attempted to describe the mentally retarded. Locke also attempted to distinguish between the retarded and the insane.

A-2

Continue now with Q-5.

Yes, during the Medieval Period the retarded were treated cruelly by many—public attitudes change slowly. However, this was only one aspect of the treatment afforded the retarded during this period.

A-3

Return to page 18 for a review before answering Q-1 correctly.

A-4   Since you have confused the contributions of Dr. Howe and Dr. Montessori, it is recommended that you return to Q-6 and review the material presented there before selecting the correct answer to the question.

A-5   You are incorrect. The AAMD is one of the oldest organizations dealing with the problem of mental retardation.

Return to Q-8 and choose another answer.

A-6   Sir Anthony Fitz-Herbert was the first to attempt to describe the mentally retarded in any definitive manner.

Return to page 19 for a review before answering Q-3 correctly.

A-7   No, the American Association on Mental Deficiency was organized by leaders in the field of mental retardation to deal with the problems of retardation, especially scientific questions, definitive problems, etc.

Return to page 27 for a review of the different national organizations concerned with the mentally retarded before selecting the correct answer for Q-7.

A-8   This is correct. As is true in most eras, public attitudes were diverse. During the Middle Ages, some persons treated the retarded humanely while others treated them cruelly. However, it was during this period that the retarded were first afforded protection. Before this period, the retarded were treated, for the most part, in an inhumane manner.

Continue now with Q-2.

This is incorrect. You have confused the contribution of Bonet and Seguin.   A-9

Return to page 25 for a brief review before answering Q-5 correctly.

This is correct. The Bishop of Myra urged that the retarded be given tender care and he was the first known person to offer these individuals protection.   A-10

Continue now with Q-4.

You are incorrect. CEC was organized for special educators.   A-11

Return to Q-7 for a review and then choose the correct answer to Q-8.

Exactly—you have correctly matched the individuals with their contributions to the education of the retarded.   A-12

Continue now with Q-7.

A-13 Right—CEC was established to provide special educators with an opportunity to share their experiences and to help improve their teaching skills.

Continue now with Q-8.

A-14 There are only two correct responses included in this answer—C4 and D2.

Since you had trouble with this question, it is recommended that you return to page 25 for a review and then answer Q-5 correctly.

A-15 You have circled the letter "a" or NARC—National Association for Retarded Children—and you are correct.

Continue now with Q-9.

A-16 During the Medieval Period, the Christian principle of humane treatment for all individuals was upheld by some, especially Christians, and churches began protecting the retarded and other less fortunate individuals. However, this was only one aspect of the treatment of the retarded during this period in history.

Return to page 18 for a brief review before answering Q-1 correctly.

This is incorrect. NARC was established to allow for shared experiences of parents of retarded children rather than for special educators.

Return to page 28 for a review and then select the correct answer for Q-7.

A-17

You have confused the contribution of all four of these individuals. This choice indicates the need to review the material starting on page 17 before you attempt to answer Q-6 again.

A-18

This is correct—well done.

Continue now with Q-6.

A-19

If your definition included the following ideas give yourself a pat on the back and then turn to the next page to read the conclusion for this lesson.

A-20

A.   Helping the retarded to live like others.
B.   Live in the community rather than in institutions.

CONCLUSION

You have now completed the programmed material in Lesson Two. You probably have a pretty good idea of how you are doing, but just to check your progress, answer the review questions that follow; then check the answers provided.

Questions

Circle the *letter* corresponding to the answer of your choice.

1. Through the ages the retarded have been:

    a. Badly mistreated.
    b. Considered Godlike.
    c. Thought to be possessed by devils.
    d. All of the above.

2. The Greeks were generally _____ toward the retarded and handicapped:

    a. Tolerant.
    b. Harsh.
    c. Ambivalent.
    d. Apathetic.

3. The first record of a religious leader who attempted to protect those considered to be retarded was:

    a. John Calvin.
    b. Martin Luther.
    c. Bishop of Myra.
    d. Pope Liberius.

4. The advent of Christianity brought about changes in the treatment for the retarded which can best be described as:

    a. Charitable.
    b. Compassionate.
    c. Humanitarian.
    d. All of the above.

5. The first asylums that were developed during the Medieval Period for those who were retarded as well as others:

    a. Were places of help and refuge.
    b. Were so bad that admission tickets were sold to see asylum people as though they were animals in a zoo.
    c. Were generally under religious sponsorship.
    d. a and c above.

6. The period of the Renaissance brought with it the responsibility of the individual for his own actions. This concept led to the following type of treatment for the retarded:

   a. Humane care and treatment.
   b. Apathy and little concern.
   c. Cruel and harsh treatment.
   d. Institutionalization and sterilization.

7. The first person who attempted to distinguish between mental retardation and mental illness was:

   a. John Calvin.
   b. John Locke.
   c. John Brown.
   d. John Wesley.

8. The first person who tried to teach a wild retarded boy by using a system which had been developed for teaching the deaf was:

   a. Jean Itard.
   b. Edouard Seguin.
   c. Maria Montessori.
   d. Samuel Howe.

9. An Italian physician-educator who emphasized learning by use of sensory-motor training was:

   a. Maria Montessori.
   b. Edouard Seguin.
   c. Samuel Howe.
   d. Johann Juggenbahl.

10. An associate of Dr. Jean Itard who furthered Dr. Itard's first efforts with the retarded was:

    a. Alfred Binet.
    b. Edouard Seguin.
    c. Simon-Binet.
    d. None of the above.

11. The country which in the late eighteenth and early nineteenth centuries led the way professionally for determining how best to educate the retarded was:

    a. Russia.
    b. England.
    c. United States.
    d. France.

12. In 1876, Dr. Seguin helped to organize and became the first president of what is now known as the:

    a. National Association for Retarded Children.
    b. American Association on Mental Deficiency.
    c. Council for Exceptional Children.
    d. International League for the Handicapped.

Answers

The answers to the questions on pages 35 and 36 are:

1. d.
2. b.
3. c.
4. d.
5. d.
6. c.
7. b.
8. a.
9. a.
10. b.
11. d.
12. b.

SELECTED READINGS

Barr, M. W. *Mental Defectives: Their History, Treatment and Training.* Philadelphia: Blakiston, 1913.

Buck, Pearl S. and Zarfoss, Gweneth. *The Gifts They Bring.* New York: John Day, 1965.

Davies, S. P. and Ecob, Katherine G. *The Mentally Retarded in Society.* New York: Columbia University Press, 1959.

Doll, E. A. "Trends and Problems in the Education of the Mentally Retarded: 1800-1940." *American Journal of Mental Deficiency* 72 (1967): 175-83.

_____. "Yesterday, Today, and Tomorrow." *Mental Retardation* 2 (1964): 203-8.

Fernald, W. E. "The History of the Treatment of the Feebleminded." In *Proceedings of the National Conference on Charities and Correction, Twentieth Annual Session,* edited by I. C. Burrows, pp. 203-21. Boston: George H. Ellis, 1893.

Goddard, H. H. *The Kalikak Family.* New York: Macmillan, 1912.

Haskell, R. H. "Mental Deficiency over a Hundred Years: A Brief Historical Sketch of Trends in This Field." *American Journal of Psychiatry* 100 (1944): 107-18.

Itard, J. M. G. *The Wild Boy of Aveyron,* translated by George and Muriel Humphrey. New York: Meredith Publishing Co., 1962.

Kanner, L. *A History of the Care and Study of the Mentally Retarded.* Springfield, Illinois: Charles Thomas, 1964.

_____. "Medicine in the History of Mental Retardation: 1800-1965." *American Journal of Mental Deficiency* 72 (1967): 165-70.

Kugel, R. B. and Wolfensberger, W., eds. *Changing Patterns in Residential Services for the Mentally Retarded.* President's Committee on Mental Retardation, Washington, D. C. 20201, January 10, 1969.

Nirje, B. "The Normalization Principle and Its Human Management," in Kugel, R. and Wolfensberger, W., eds., *Changing Patterns in Residential Services for the Mentally Retarded,* pp. 179-95.

Sarason, S. B. and Doris, J. *Psychological Problems in Mental Deficiency,* 4th ed. New York: Harper and Row, 1969.

Seguin, E. *Idiocy: And Its Treatment by the Psysiological Method.* New York: Wood, 1866.

_____. "Origin of the Treatment and Training of Idiots." *Barnard's American Journal of Education* 2 (1856): 145-52.

Talbot, M. E. "Edouard Seguin." *American Journal of Mental Deficiency* 72 (1967): 184-89.

_____. *Edward Seguin: A Study of an Educational Approach to the Treatment of Mentally Defective Children.* New York: Teachers College, Columbia University, 1964.

Wallin, J. E. W. "Training of the Severely Retarded Viewed in Historical Perspective." *Journal of General Psychology* 74 (1966): 107-27.

Whitney, E. A. "Mental Deficiency in the 1880s and 1940s." *American Journal of Mental Deficiency* 54 (1949): 151-54.

Wolfson, I. N. "History of Training and Treatment of Retarded Adolescents." *International Record of Medicine and Practice* 172 (1961): 139-49.

Wylie, A. R. T. "Fifty Years in Retrospect." *Journal of Psycho-Asthenics* 21 (1925-1926): 219-33.

UNIT 1

LESSON THREE
Classifying Individuals with Subaverage Intellectual Functioning by the Measurement of Intelligence

As indicated in Lesson One, the customary procedure in the United States has been to measure intelligence by means of standardized intelligence tests. Four types of tests have been in general use: The Stanford-Binet (also known as the Terman-Merrill); the Wechsler Intelligence Scale for Children (WISC); the Wechsler Adult Intelligence Scale (WAIS); and the Wechsler Preschool and Primary Scale of Intelligence (WPPSI). Both the Binet and Wechsler scales are currently being revised. Other scales, such as the Cattell and the Kuhlmann-Binet, have proven useful for infants or severely retarded children unable to respond verbally to questioning.

With the elimination of the borderline category, which was one standard deviation below the mean, the new practice is to start the mild classification at two standard deviations below the mean for the particular test employed. In the Wechsler scales which indicate one standard deviation (s.d.) as being fifteen points, two standard deviations below the mean of 100 would be 70 on the normal curve. The mild classification in this example would be 69-55. The Stanford-Binet and Cattell scales have a standard deviation of 16, which slightly alters the figures for each category.[1] In this text, however, we have chosen the Wechsler scales for our programmed material.

The specific IQ values for the most frequently used scales are:

Levels	Obtained Intelligence Quotient	
	Stanford-Binet and Cattell (s.d. 16)	Wechsler scales (s.d. 15)
Mild	68-52	69-55
Moderate	51-36	54-40
Severe	35-20	39-25 (extrapolated)
Profound	19 and below	24 and below (extrapolated)

THE INTELLIGENCE TESTING CONTROVERSY

It appears that the measurement of mental ability will continue to be based on the results of IQ tests for some time to come. However, the storms of controversy are loud and there are indications that additional or other means will be used in the future.[2] Cultural differences need to be considered. Jane Mercer has worked on this problem and developed a System of Multicultural Pluralistic Assessment (SOMPA) to evaluate a child as a multidimensional person being socialized within a particular setting.[3] Presently, the use of the developmental schemas resulting from Piaget's work with children appear to hold some promise for newer methods to re-

---

[1] H. J. Grossman, ed. *Manual on Terminology and Classification in Mental Retardation,* 1973 revision. American Association on Mental Deficiency. Special Publication Series No. 2, 1973, p. 18.

[2] John W. Filler, Jr., et al., "Mental Retardation," in Nicholas Hobbs, ed., *Issues in the Classification of Children,* vol. I. (San Francisco: Jossey-Bass Publishers, 1975), pp. 215-31. Further discussion may also be found in John L. Phillipps, Jr., *The Origins of Intellect, Piaget's Theory,* 2nd ed. (San Francisco: W. H. Freeman, 1975), pp. 162-78, in which Phillipps discusses the complexities of the Piagetian system as researched by Monique Laurendeau and Adrien Pinard at the University of Montreal.

[3] Jane R. Mercer, "Sociocultural Factors in Educational Labeling," in M. J. Begab and S. A. Richardson, eds., *The Mentally Retarded and Society* (Proceedings of the Conference supported by the National Institute of Child Health and Human Development April 1974) (Baltimore: University Park Press, 1975), pp. 141-57.

place traditional IQ tests. The difficulties of standardization and the need for extensive training of those administering the tests has, however, slowed down the ready utilization of Piaget's developmental methods. For the time being, therefore, although experimentation will continue, we will continue to see the use of IQ testing as an important element in the classification of retarded persons. Even J. W. Filler, Jr., who, along with his cowriters is critical of IQ tests, does indicate their potential as "legitimate instruments for use in the scientific study of individual differences, ... for convenient operational definition, and ... valid predictors of large-scale differences in academic achievement."[4]

PURPOSE OF CLASSIFICATION

The main purpose in having and using any classification system in retardation is to help in planning appropriate programs and services for individuals whose range of intelligence falls within the different levels of mental retardation. Therefore, it is important to keep in mind that individuals vary in their abilities and skills. Just because an individual generally falls within a particular level of retardation does not mean that he may not function better or worse on specific tasks than would be indicated by his general classification. Because of these variations in individual competencies, no person should be classified rigidly within one category, nor should he be considered to remain within a particular category for an indefinite period of time. Rather, the retarded person must be viewed as an individual who possesses varying degrees of ability in different areas which may change as the individual matures and is offered training and assistance.

---

[4]Filler, "Mental Retardation," p. 227.

OBJECTIVES

The following lesson concerns the classification of individuals based on the results of intelligence quotient or IQ scores.

When you have successfully completed this lesson, you will be able to accomplish the following tasks:

1. Identify the IQ score of an individual with average intelligence and the IQ score of an individual with significantly subaverage intelligence.
2. Name the four classifications of individuals with significantly subaverage intelligence.
3. Rank the four classifications from lowest to highest intelligence.
4. Identify the classification of a given range of IQ scores or of an individual with a given IQ score.

QUESTIONS

Please answer each of the following questions carefully. After each possible answer, you will be referred to a frame in the section beginning on p. 48 where you will be told whether or not your choice is correct. If the alternative you have selected is correct, you will be told in the answer frame which frame in the "Questions" section to turn to next. If your choice is incorrect, your answer will tell you to return to the question frame you have just answered to review and to try again. Please note that you will always be given your instructions according to frame number. Frames designated with "Q" indicate a frame in the "Questions" section (e.g., "Q-1, Q-2"). Frames designated with an "A" indicate answers. Only occasionally will you be given a page number to which to turn. It is most important that you follow the instructions for *each individual question or answer frame* most carefully.

AVERAGE AND SIGNIFICANTLY
SUBAVERAGE INTELLIGENCE

Q-1   Intelligence tests, though imperfect, attempt to measure the amount of intelligence possessed by an individual. Due to differing statistical methods, the "cut-off point" for "normal" will vary a few points from test to test. According to one of the widely used mental ability tests, an individual is considered to possess "normal" intelligence if he scores 70 or above and significantly subaverage in intelligence if he scores 69 or below.

It must be remembered, that if the IQ score is the only information that we possess about an individual, we are *unable* to say for sure that he is mentally retarded. We can only say that he appears to be significantly subaverage in intellectual functioning.

If an individual has an IQ score of 65, he would be considered significantly subaverage in intelligence and, therefore, mentally retarded.
The above statement is:

a. True.   Turn to A-3.
b. False.   Turn to A-7.

Here is a question which will help you to review the material you   Q-2
have previously studied and which is important for understanding
the present lesson.

Name below the two types of functioning that must be taken into
consideration when attempting to diagnose whether or not an
individual is mentally retarded; write your answers and then turn
to A-5.

a. _____

b. _____

In this lesson we will deal with the classification of individuals   Q-3
with significant subaverage intellectual functioning only. In the
next lesson, we will deal with the evaluation of adaptive behavior.

There are four generally accepted classifications of individuals with
subaverage intelligence. These classifications are: *mild, moderate,
severe, profound.*

Individuals in the *profound* classification have the *lowest* intelligence, while those in the *mild* classification have the *highest* intelligence.

In the space below, arrange the four mental retardation classifications in order from highest to lowest intelligence. Individuals in
the first classification will have the highest intelligence, while
individuals in the fourth classification will have the lowest intelligence.

a. _____

b. _____

c. _____

d. _____

Now turn to A-2 to check your answers.

Q-4   Each of the four classifications has a corresponding range of IQ scores. The following chart (Wechsler Scale) shows the classifications and corresponding IQ scores ranging from *highest to lowest* intelligence.

Classification	IQ Scores
Mild	55 to 69
Moderate	40 to 54
Severe	25 to 39
Profound	24 and below

To aid your memory, you may wish to remember that, *except* in the case of the profound classification, this text uses a *range of fifteen points* within each classification.

Test yourself with the following question.

Individuals with the highest classification (mild) will have the following range of IQ scores: _____ .

Individuals classified as profoundly retarded (the lowest classification of intelligence) will have the following IQ scores: _____ .

Fill in the blanks and then turn to A-8 to check your answers.

Match the following IQ scores with the proper classifications, placing them *in the correct order*, from highest to lowest intelligence.

a. Severe

b. Profound

c. Mild

d. Moderate

1. 24 or less

2. 40 to 54

3. 25 to 39

4. 55 to 69

Choose your answer from among the following:

a. C1; B2; D3; A4   Turn to A-10.

b. B1; A3; C2; D4   Turn to A-4.

c. C4; D2; A3; B1   Turn to A-1.

Fill in the blanks below and then turn to A-6 to check your answer.

Classification	IQ Score
Severe	___ to ___
_____	___ to ___
Moderate	40 to 54
_____	24 or less

Individuals with the IQ scores shown below are in which classifications? Fill in the proper classifications and then turn to A-9 for the answers.

IQ Score	Classification
20	_____
68	_____
34	_____
42	_____

ANSWERS

Please follow the same instructions as those you were given on page 44 in working with this section. It is most important that you remember to follow the individual instructions in each answer frame.

A-1   You said that mild equals 55 to 69; moderate, 40 to 54; severe, 25 to 39; and profound, 24 or less; in order from highest to lowest intelligence, and this is absolutely correct.

Continue now with Q-6.

A-2   The five classifications from highest to lowest intelligence are:

    a. Mild.
    b. Moderate.
    c. Severe.
    d. Profound.

Continue now with Q-4.

A-3   You have said that an individual with an IQ of 65 is of subaverage intelligence and, therefore, mentally retarded. Although an individual with an IQ *below* 65 may be considered as possessing significantly subaverage intelligence, we are *not* able to assume on this information alone that he is mentally retarded.

Return to Q-1 and reread the information presented there before again answering this question.

If you selected this answer, you have correctly matched the   A-4
approximate IQ scores with the proper classifications, but you
have the order from highest to lowest intelligence reversed. The
correct order from highest to lowest intelligence is: mild, moderate,
severe, and profound.

Return to Q-5 and select the correct answer.

The two types of functioning that are taken into consideration   A-5
when diagnosing an individual for mental retardation include
intellectual functioning and adaptive behavior functioning.

Did you get this right? We hope so. Continue now with Q-3.

Classification	*IQ Scores*	A-6
Severe	25 to 39	
Mild	55 to 69	
Moderate	40 to 54	
Profound	24 or less	

If you failed to answer any of the above items correctly, return to
Q-4 to review the material, and when you feel you are ready, go
back to the problem in Q-6.

If you have learned the proper classifications and their corresponding IQ scores, turn to Q-7 for a final review of the material.

A-7   Correct! An individual with an IQ score of 65 would be significantly *subaverage* in intelligence, but unless his social adaptation was also inadequate, he might not necessarily be considered retarded.

Continue now with Q-2.

A-8   Individuals in the *profound* classification have the lowest intelligence (IQ scores less than 25); those in the mild classification range from 55-69.

Continue now with Q-5.

A-9   The proper classifications follow:

IQ Scores	Classification
20	Profound
68	Mild
34	Severe
42	Moderate

If you made a mistake on any of the above, restudy the text in Q-4. You will not have completed this lesson successfully until you are able to correctly classify individuals with different IQ scores.

If you made a perfect score, you are ready to take the Review Questions on page 52 for a final check on yourself.

Mild retardation refers to IQ scores of less than 25. Profound retardation refers to IQ scores between 40 and 54. Severe retardation refers to IQ scores between 55 and 69. Moderate retardation refers to IQ scores between 70 and 84.

You are incorrect in each case. Please return to Q-4 and restudy the classifications before attempting to answer Q-5 again.

REVIEW QUESTIONS—LESSON THREE

Questions

Circle the *letter* corresponding to the answer of your choice.

1. An individual is not considered to be of significantly subaverage intelligence if his IQ score is:

   a. 75 or above.
   b. 65 or above.
   c. 55 or above.
   d. 45 or above.

2. Individuals with IQ scores between 40 and 54 are in which classification of retardation?

   a. Mild.
   b. Moderate.
   c. Severe.
   d. Profound.

3. If an individual has an IQ of 32, his intellectual classification is:

   a. Moderate.
   b. Mild.
   c. Severe.
   d. Average or normal.

4. Which of the following lists of classifications of individuals with subaverage intelligence is in correct order from *lowest* to *highest* intelligence?

   a. Profound, severe, mild, moderate.
   b. Severe, profound, moderate, mild.
   c. Profound, severe, moderate, mild.
   d. Mild, moderate, severe, profound.

5. An individual with an IQ of 21 is in which intellectual classification?

   a. Profound.
   b. Severe.
   c. Moderate.
   d. Mild.

The answers to the questions on page 52 are:

1. a.
2. b.
3. c.
4. c.
5. a.

How did you do?

SELECTED READINGS

American Psychiatric Association. *Diagnostic and Statistical Manual of Mental Disorders*, 2nd ed. Washington, D.C.: The American Psychiatric Association, 1968.

Bazelon, D. L. "Mental Disorders: The Need for a Unified Approach." *American Journal of Orthopsychiatry* 34 (1964): 39-44.

Benton, A. L. "Some Aspects of Mental Retardation." *American Journal of Orthopsychiatry* 35 (1965): 830-37.

Doll, E. A. "Annotated Bibliography on the Vineland Social Maturity Scale." *Journal of Consulting Psychology* 4 (1940): 123-32.

———. "A Genetic Scale of Social Maturity." *American Journal of Orthopsychiatry* 5 (1935): 180-88.

———. Measurement of Social Competence. Minneapolis: Educational Publishers, 1953.

———. Social Age as a Basis for Classification and Training." *American Journal of Mental Deficiency* 46 (1942): 214-19.

———. "The Vineland Social Maturity Scale." In *Mental Retardation: Readings and Resources*, edited by J. H. Rothstein. New York: Holt, 1961.

Engel, M. "Dilemmas of Classification and Diagnosis." *Journal of Special Education* 3 (1969): 231-39.

Filler, J. W., Jr. et al. "Mental Retardation." In Hobbs, N., *Issues in the Classification of Children*, vol. 1, 1975, pp. 194-238.

Gelof, M. "Comparison of Systems of Classification Relating Degree of Retardation to Measured Intelligence." *American Journal of Mental Deficiency* 68 (1963): 297-317.

Grossman, H., ed. *Manual on Terminology and Classification in Mental Retardation*. Washington, D.C.: American Association on Mental Deficiency, 1973.

Heber, R. "A Manual on Terminology and Classification in Mental Retardation." *Monograph Supplement to the American Journal of Mental Deficiency* 64 (1959). Monograph supplement, rev. ed., 1961.

———. "Modifications in the Manual on Terminology and Classification in Mental Retardation." *American Journal of Mental Deficiency* 69 (1961): 499.

Hobbs, N., ed. *Issues in the Classification of Children*, vol. 1. San Francisco: Jossey-Bass Publishers, 1975.

Mental Retardation: Improving the Classification Through Research. Columbus, Ohio. Work conference sponsored by the American Association on Mental Deficiency, 1965, pp. 1-68.

Phillips, J. L., Jr. *The Origins of Intellect: Piaget's Theory*, 2nd ed. San Francisco: W. H. Freeman and Company, 1975, pp. 162-78.

Polloway, E. A. and Payne, J. S. "Comparison of the AAMD Heber and Grossman Manuals on Terminology and Classification in Mental Retardation." *Mental Retardation* 13 (1975): 12-14.

Robinson, N. M. and Robinson, H. *The Mentally Retarded Child, A Psychological Approach*, 2nd ed. New York: McGraw-Hill Book Co., 1976.

Wechsler, D. *The Measurement and Appraisal of Adult Intelligence*, 4th ed. Baltimore: Williams & Wilkins Company, 1958.

World Health Organization. "Classification of Mental Retardation." *Supplement to the American Journal of Psychiatry* 128 (1972): 1-45.

UNIT 1

LESSON FOUR
Adaptive Behavior

In Lesson One we introduced the latest revision of the AAMD definition of mental retardation (Grossman 1973), which defines retardation as: "significantly subaverage general intellectual functioning existing concurrently with deficits in adaptive behavior and manifested during the developmental period."

From this definition, it can be seen that there are two major factors which determine a judgment regarding mental retardation: significant subaverage intellectual functioning and the existence concurrently of deficits in adaptive behavior. The Grossman definition and statement of the problem makes it quite clear that no one is to be labeled "retarded" on the basis of intellectual assessment alone. The previous definition (Heber 1961) also called attention to this fact but the use of the phrase by Grossman of "existing concurrently" adds greater emphasis to the consideration of the adaptive behavior of the individual being assessed. This adaptive behavior is assumed to have two aspects which need to be examined: the ability to function independently and the ability to meet social and cultural demands. Examples of items assessed in the AAMD

Adaptive Behavior Scale include Part I: independent functioning; physical development; economic activity; language development; number and time concept; occupation-domestic; occupation-general; self-direction; responsibilities; and socialization. Part II includes violent and destructive behavior; antisocial behavior; rebellious behavior; untrustworthy behavior; withdrawal; stereotyped behavior; inappropriate vocal habits; unacceptable habits; self-abusive behavior; hyperactive tendencies; sexually aberrant behavior; psychological disturbances; and use of medications.[1]

Various scales have been devised to assess the adaptive behavior of the retarded: the Vineland Social Maturity Scale; the AAMD Adaptive Behavior Scales; the Cain-Levine Social Competency Scale; the Central Wisconsin Colony Scale; and the TMR Performance Scale. In addition there are others that are either modifications of the above or experimental. There does not appear to be any agreement at this time that one scale is better than another. However, there are experiments going on to obtain deviation social quotients (DSQ) using the Vineland scale, which may result in making this scale quite useful. Other experiments are going on with the development of the revised AAMD Adaptive Behavior Scales. From the above experiments it is expected that a more objective method of assessing adaptive behavior will be developed. In the meantime attention is directed to the AAMD sixth revision by Grossman dealing with adaptive behavior and the tables given for each of the four levels.[2]

The impairment of adaptive behavior shows itself in three different basic and interrelated ways—maturation, learning, and social adjustment. Adaptation capabilities vary in part as a function of age. For example, during the preschool years development of motor skills, such as walking, balancing, running, and of verbal skills, such as talking, are of considerable importance in aiding the child's adaptation to the environment. During the school years, the child's ability to learn, especially in the school setting, becomes increasingly important. In the postschool period and in adult life, social adaptation is determined mainly by the individual's ability to maintain himself independently in the community. This independence results usually only when he is able to be gainfully employed and to conform to the demands, both personal and social, which society establishes as constituting acceptable behavior.

---

[1] *Adaptive Behavior Scales Manual*, rev. (Washington, D.C.: American Association on Mental Deficiency, 1970), p. 13.

[2] See Grossman, "Tables of Illustrations of Adaptive Behavior Levels by Age," in *Manual on Terminology and Classification in Mental Retardation*, pp. 23-33.

There are some important reasons why adaptive behavior should be considered concurrently when evaluating the degree of subnormal intellectual functioning. First of all, there is neither a generally agreed upon definition of intelligence nor agreement regarding what factors intelligence tests actually measure. The tests are fallible in that they are not culture-free. That is, persons from cultures different from those on whom the test was standardized will usually do less well than persons of equal intelligence who came from a group on whom the test was standardized. Also, intelligence tests are subject to unintentional errors of measurement. The extent of induced error depends upon the persons doing the testing, the attitudes and physical well-being of the person being tested, and the nature of the surroundings. Still another difficulty inherent in the scoring of intelligence tests is the fact that these tests measure the average of a range of abilities. For those who are retarded, the results of intelligence tests can be misinterpreted easily, especially if an individual scores high in certain portions of the test and low in others. The average score under these circumstances may have very little meaning in understanding the individual's varying intellectual capabilities.

Thus, because of some rather basic problems with intelligence testing, it appears unwise to use an IQ score alone in determining retardation. However, coupling an IQ score with the criteria of social adaptability results in a much more meaningful assessment of the individual's level of functioning.

The AAMD adaptive behavior scales use four classifications: mild, moderate, severe, and profound. It is important to note that adaptive behavior scales classify individuals through *descriptive* data regarding a particular category based on factors of maturation, learning, and social adjustment. Measured intelligence, as we indicated previously, develops IQ scores from which classifications of retardation are derived. The latest AAMD revision (Grossman 1973) continues to use the four levels of adaptive behavior but adds a specified age for each of the given levels.[3]

The adaptive behavior classifications are the following:

1. *Mild.* Some individuals in this category are also referred to as being *educable*, since they are able to profit from educational programs. Even though they develop slowly, they will grow up to be in large part economically and socially

---

[3] Ibid., p. 23. The reader is advised to carefully study the "Tables of Illustrations of Adaptive Behavior Levels by Age," as presented in the Grossman edition. They must be studied as a complete set, covering all phases and ages, in order to be properly understood.

independent. Although they need educational programs directed toward adjustment to accepted social patterns and realistic occupational goals, they also need skilled guidance in selecting and holding suitable jobs. Most of the individuals in this classification are capable of managing their own affairs under favorable circumstances. On occasion, they may need special counseling and guidance to meet major life crises, but most are able to work in competitive positions and are able to live independent lives.

2. *Moderate.* Although retarded in their development, many of these individuals are called *trainable* and can be taught to care for themselves. Even though they will need supervision and support all their lives, they eventually can be taught to do useful tasks at home and can be prepared for working at simple jobs (e.g., in sheltered workshops maintained by agencies for special work training). Some of these individuals may need to be placed in residential care centers, but only when there are no responsible relatives or friends will it be necessary for society to assume a protective role for them.

3. *Severe.* In these cases, language, motor capabilities, and speech are limited. This level of retardation often has associated physical handicaps. Usually, such individuals have impaired judgment and are unable to make important life decisions for themselves. They are capable of learning certain self-care skills and can develop some facility for self-protection. Although some may need to be placed in residential centers for various reasons, many can live happily at home with their parents.

4. *Profound.* These persons need total care or supervision. They manifest major impairment in physical coordination and sensory-motor development and most often require complete custodial care. Usually, they have concomitant physically handicapping conditions and need supervision hour by hour, either at home or in a specially designed residential facility. These individuals may achieve very minimal basic self-help skills and some modest speech development, but they remain childlike in their need for affection and care.

Thus, to summarize, adaptive behavior is always determined by the degree to which a person meets the standards of personal independence and social responsibility normally expected for his chronological age.

OBJECTIVES

In a previous lesson, you learned that the mentally retarded are identified by both significant subaverage intelligence and concurrent adaptive behavior impairments. In another lesson you learned the classification of individuals with significant subaverage intelligence using intelligence quotients or IQ scores. In this lesson, you will learn the adaptive behavior capabilities of those individuals diagnosed as mentally retarded in each of the four adaptive behavior classifications.

When you have successfully completed this lesson, you will be able to:

1. Identify the capabilities of individuals in the four adaptive behavior classifications.
2. Describe the adaptive capabilities of individuals in the four adaptive behavior classifications.

Please answer each of the following questions carefully. After each possible answer, you will be referred to a frame in the section beginning on p. 65 where you will be told whether or not your choice is correct. If the alternative you have selected is correct, you will be told in the answer frame which frame in the "Questions" section to turn to next. If your choice is incorrect, your answer will tell you to return to the question frame you have just answered to review and to try again. Please note that you will always be given your instructions according to frame number. Frames designated with "Q" indicate a frame in the "Questions" section (e.g., "Q-1, Q-2"). Frames designated with an "A" indicate answers. Only occasionally will you be given a page number to which to turn. It is most important that you follow the instructions for *each individual question or answer frame* most carefully.

ADAPTIVE CAPABILITIES OF THE MENTALLY RETARDED

As far as we can ascertain at the present time, the adaptive capabilities of the mentally retarded refer to the potential that an individual within each classification is capable of attaining as an adult.

The Profoundly Retarded

The profoundly retarded are characterized by *gross impairment* in physical coordination and sensory development. In addition, they usually suffer from a physical handicap, and, therefore, are capable of only very minimal motor and speech development. Some of these individuals can profit to some extent from special types of *training*, yet they can *achieve* only very limited *self-care* and they will need nursing *care* and supervision *throughout* their lives.

Q-1

Gross impairment in physical coordination and sensory development and the need for nursing care and supervision throughout their lives are characteristics of the profoundly retarded.

a. This is a true statement.   Turn to A-6.
b. This is a false statement.   Turn to A-14.

The Severely Retarded

Q-2   The severely retarded are often physically handicapped. They may contribute partially to self-maintenance but only under conditions of complete supervision. They *profit* from systematic habit *training* and can develop self-protection skills to a minimal but useful level. They are, therefore, not as dependent as are the profoundly retarded, but, like the profoundly retarded, they must live in a controlled environment *throughout* their lives.

Which of the following individuals must live in a controlled environment throughout their lives?

a. Severely retarded.   Turn to A-8.
b. Profoundly retarded.   Turn to A-1.
c. Both of the above.   Turn to A-12.

Q-3   Since profoundly and severely retarded individuals have so little potential for development, they are unable to benefit from training.

a. This is a true statement.   Turn to A-10.
b. This is a false statement.   Turn to A-7.

The moderately retarded are backward in their development. **Q-4**
Some of them are capable of progressing to a *second-grade* level
and most are capable of being trained to *care for themselves*, given
sufficient training. With appropriate training, they may also
achieve self-maintenance in *unskilled or semiskilled work under
sheltered conditions*. Sheltered conditions are important since
these individuals need supervision and guidance, especially when
subjected to modest social or economic stress.

Although they are backward in their development, some of the

moderately retarded are capable of progressing to the _____

_____ level in academic subjects.

Fill in the blanks and then see A-2 for the answer.

Given sufficient training, the moderately retarded are able to work   **Q-5**
at _____ or _____ jobs under sheltered conditions.

Fill in blanks and then see A-4 for the answer.

The Mildly Retarded

Q-6   Although the development of the mildly retarded is slow, these persons are capable of being educated to approximately the *sixth-grade* level. They usually can achieve social and vocational skills adequate to allow minimal self-support. They are able to work at *unskilled*, *semiskilled*, and even *skilled jobs* in competitive employment and to live independent lives. However, they often need guidance and assistance when under unusual social or economic stress.

The _____ retarded individual is capable of working at an unskilled or semiskilled job with supervision, while the _____ retarded individual is capable of working at a skilled job without close supervision.

a. Moderately, mildly.   Turn to A-3.
b. Mildly, moderately.   Turn to A-11.

Q-7   The mildly retarded individual is often capable of progressing to the _____ grade in academic subjects, while the moderately retarded individual is usually capable of progressing to the _____ grade.

Choose your answer from those below.

a. Second; sixth.   Turn to A-9.
b. Eighth; third.   Turn to A-13.
c. Sixth; second.   Turn to A-5.

ANSWERS

Please follow the same instructions as those you were given on page 61 in working with this section. It is most important that you remember to follow the individual instructions in each answer frame.

You're only half right on this one. The profoundly retarded do indeed need constant care and supervision throughout their lives but so do the severely retarded. Both must live in a controlled environment throughout their lives.

Return to Q-2 and try to answer the question again.

A-1

Some of the moderately retarded are capable of progressing to the *second-grade* level in academic subjects.

Continue now with Q-5.

A-2

Absolutely correct. The *moderately* retarded individual is usually capable of working at an unskilled or semiskilled job with supervision, while the *mildly* retarded individual is most often capable of working at a skilled job without close supervision. Of course, the mildly retarded individual is also able to work at unskilled or semiskilled jobs with or without close supervision.

Continue now with Q-7.

A-3

A-4   The moderately retarded are able to work at *unskilled* or *semi-skilled* jobs under sheltered conditions.

Continue now with Q-6.

A-5   Right you are! At present, the mildly retarded are usually capable of progressing to the *sixth-grade* level, and the moderately retarded are capable of progressing to the *second-grade* level. However, it is hoped that with new methods of teaching and other improvements, these individuals will be able to progress much further academically.

Turn now to page 69 for a concluding statement.

A-6   Right; the profoundly retarded are characterized by gross impairment in physical coordination and sensory development and need nursing care and supervision throughout their lives.

Continue now with Q-2.

A-7   Your answer is correct.

Information now available indicates that all human beings, no matter what their level of intelligence, are able to benefit in varying degrees from interaction with other human beings. Since training involves interaction with another human being, even the profoundly and severely retarded may be helped.

Continue now with Q-4.

A-8   Yes, the severely retarded do need constant supervision and must live in a controlled environment throughout their lives, but they are not alone. The profoundly retarded also must live in such an environment.

Return to Q-2 and answer the question again.

A-9   If you chose this answer, you have confused the capabilities of the moderately and mildly retarded. Your answer states that the mildly retarded person is capable of progressing to the second-grade level in academic subjects and that the moderately retarded individual is capable of progressing to the sixth-grade level. However, just the reverse of this situation is true.

Return to page 64 and review the lesson from there on before trying to answer Q-7 again.

A-10   You have answered *true*, saying that the profoundly and severely retarded are unable to benefit from training. Current knowledge, however, would suggest that most individuals in these groups can benefit, especially from the interactive aspect of training.

Return to Q-3 and answer it correctly.

A-11   As our understanding of the mentally retarded increases and our training methods improve, both moderately and mildly retarded individuals may be able to work at more difficult and responsible jobs, but, at present, the moderately retarded individual generally is not capable of working at a skilled job.

Return to pages 63 and 64 and reread the material on the moderately and mildly retarded before answering Q-6 again.

A-12   That's right. *Both* the profoundly and the severely retarded must live in a controlled environment throughout their lives.

     The profoundly and severely retarded are sometimes referred to as custodial cases by the mental retardation hospitals or other institutions that provide care for them.

Continue now with Q-3.

A-13   It is hoped that this answer will be correct within the not too distant future, but, at present, most mildly retarded individuals are capable of progressing to the *sixth-grade* and not the eighth-grade level, and most moderately retarded are able to progress to the *second-grade* but generally not the third-grade level.

Return to page 64 and review the material in Q-6 before trying to answer Q-7 again.

A-14   You have said that the profoundly retarded are *not* characterized by gross impairment in physical coordination and sensory development and do not need nursing care and supervision throughout their lives. This is, we are sorry to say, entirely wrong. The exact opposite is true.

Return to Q-1 and reread the material presented there.

CONCLUSION

We would like to close this lesson with two well-established and very important facts that you should know if you are to be successful in working with the retarded.

First, approximately 89 percent or nine out of every ten mentally retarded individuals have only a mild degree of retardation.

Second, all retarded individuals can, with help, improve their adaptive capabilities. The less the retardation, the greater are their chances of becoming independent human beings.

If one combines these two facts, remembering that about 89 percent of all the retarded are in the mild categories, it is easy to realize that most of the mentally retarded can, indeed, become independent adults with the help and support of society.

Continue now with the Review Questions that begin on the following page.

REVIEW QUESTIONS—LESSON FOUR

Questions

Circle the *letter* corresponding to the answer of your choice.

1. As far as we are able to surmise at the present time, an individual who is profoundly retarded is capable of:

   a. Working at a skilled job with supervision.
   b. Working at an unskilled job with supervision.
   c. Working at a semiskilled job with supervision.
   d. None of the above.

2. A child diagnosed as severely retarded could be expected to:

   a. Develop self-protection skills.
   b. Progress to the sixth-grade level in academic subjects.
   c. Work in a sheltered workshop at a semiskilled job.
   d. Develop no skills no matter what training he received.

3. Which of the following are characterized by *gross* impairment in physical coordination and sensory development?

   a. Severely retarded.
   b. Mildly retarded.
   c. Profoundly retarded.
   d. Both a and c above.
   e. a, b, and c above.

4. Individuals in which of the following classifications are able to benefit from training?

   a. Severely retarded.
   b. Moderately retarded.
   c. Profoundly retarded.
   d. Both a and b above.
   e. a, b, and c above.

5. Most mildly retarded persons are:

   a. Able to progress to the sixth-grade level in academic subjects.
   b. Capable of self-support.
   c. Capable of working at skilled jobs.
   d. Both a and b above.
   e. a, b, and c above.

6. Most moderately retarded individuals are capable of:

   a. Caring for themselves (i.e. eating, dressing, etc.).
   b. Progressing to the fifth-grade level in academic subjects.
   c. Working at a semiskilled job under sheltered conditions.
   d. Both a and c above.
   e. a, b, and c above.

Answers

The answers to the review questions are:

1. d.
2. a.
3. c.
4. e.
5. e.
6. d.

SELECTED READINGS

Balthazar, E. E., and English, G. E. "A System for Classifying the Social Behaviors of the Severely Retarded." *Central Wisconsin Colony and Training School Research Findings.* Monograph Supplement No. 4, 1969.

———. "A System for the Social Classification of the More Severely Mentally Retarded." *American Journal of Mental Deficiency* 74 (1969): 361-68.

Doll, E. A. "Annotated Bibliography on the Vineland Social Maturity Scale." *Journal of Consulting Psychology* 4 (1940): 123-32.

———. "The Vineland Social Maturity Scale." In *Mental Retardation: Readings and Resources,* edited by J. H. Rothstein. New York: Holt, 1961.

Engel, M. "Dilemmas of Classification and Diagnosis." *Journal of Special Education* 3 (1969): 231-39.

Foster, R., and Nihira, K. "Adaptive Behavior as a Measure of Psychiatric Impairment." *American Journal of Mental Deficiency* 74 (1969): 401-04.

Grossman, H. J., ed. *Manual on Terminology and Classification in Mental Retardation,* 1973 revision. Washington, D.C.: American Association on Mental Deficiency, 1973.

Hartman, H. *Ego Psychology and the Problem of Adaptation.* New York: International University Press, 1958.

Hebb, D. O. *The Organization of Behavior.* New York: John Wiley & Sons, 1949.

Heber, R. "A Manual on Terminology and Classification in Mental Retardation." *Monograph Supplement to the American Journal of Mental Deficiency,* rev. ed. (1961).

Horrocks, J. E. *Assessment of Behavior.* Columbus, Ohio: Charles E. Merrill Publishing Co., 1964.

Leland, H.; Shellhaas, M.; Nihira, K.; and Foster, R. "Adaptive Behavior: A New Dimension in the Classification of the Mentally Retarded." *Mental Retardation Abstracts* 4 (1967): 359-87.

Leland, H.; Nihira, K.; Foster, R.; and Shellhaas, M. "The Demonstration and Measurement of Adaptive Behavior." In *Proceedings of the First Congress of the International Association for the Scientific Study of Mental Deficiency,* edited by B. W. Richards, pp. 74-80. Surrey, England: Michael Jackson Publishing Co., Ltd., 1968.

Nihira, K.; Foster, R.; Shellhaas, M.; and Leland, H. *Adaptive Behavior Scales,* rev. ed. Washington, D.C.: American Association on Mental Deficiency, 1970.

Nihira, K.; Foster, R.; and Spencer, L. "Measurement of Adaptive Behavior: A Descriptive System for Mental Retardation." *American Journal of Orthopsychiatry* 38 (1968): 622-34.

Porter, R. B. "Needed: A More Realistic Classification of Mentally Retarded Children." *Training School Bulletin* 67 (1970): 30-32.

Robinson, Halbert, and Robinson, Nancy M. *The Mentally Retarded Child, A Psychological Approach.* New York: McGraw Hill Book Company, 1965.

LESSON FIVE
Distinguishing between Mental Retardation and Mental Illness

Any discussion regarding the differences between mental retardation and mental illness must take into consideration that it is often difficult to separate one condition from the other when making a diagnosis for a person affected with both conditions. In spite of the difficulty, there are certain specifics which can be described and which will help to point up the difference between these two mentally handicapping conditions.

Mental retardation is characterized as a condition of faulty intellectual development which limits an individual's ability to learn and to adapt to the demands of society. Mental retardation exists when developmental abnormalities impair an individual's functioning, thereby adversely affecting his ability to learn or put learning to use. Mental retardation develops during the formative years, usually before nineteen years of age.

Mental illness, on the other hand, includes problems of personality and behavioral disorders. This condition is one in which an individual with so-called normal intelligence cannot function because his thinking has become disorganized or inefficient.

Mental illness, of course, may occur at any age from childhood through adulthood. In contrast, mental retardation may develop only in utero or during the developmental years prior to the nineteenth birthday; although functionally retardation may occur at any time due to brain injury.

Many types of mental illnesses can be traced directly to the tensions and strains of an individual's life experiences. This is not the case with mental retardation, which generally occurs because of some type of developmental defect.

Mental illness can be present in a retarded person; for example, severe early emotional deprivation can create mental illness in a retarded individual. The reverse is also true, in that a child afflicted with mental illness may have a defect in intellectual functioning because his mind cannot work properly due to excessive anxieties and conflicts.

In many cases, mental illness responds to therapy, often with a reduction of symptoms leading to recovery. Mental retardation, however, cannot be cured once it occurs. In some instances, retardation can be prevented, but treatment for the retarded will not produce a remission or recovery from the condition itself. Nonetheless, treatment can help the retarded individual to use programs and services which will help him to attain an optimum level of functioning within the limitations of his own intellect. The reader is reminded that persons may be labeled retarded at certain periods in life (e.g., during the school years), but at a later period may well be regarded as "normal" and not labeled as retarded.

OBJECTIVES

The purpose of this lesson is to introduce you to mental illness and to distinguish this condition from mental retardation. When you have completed this lesson, you will be able to:

1. Identify or describe the similarities between mental retardation and mental illness.
2. Explain the difference between mental retardation and mental illness regarding intellectual functioning.
3. Explain or identify when, during the life span of an individual, he may be labeled mentally retarded and when mentally ill.
4. Identify or state the conditions from which mental retardation and mental illness result.
5. Explain or identify reasons why specific individuals could be considered mentally retarded or mentally ill or both mentally retarded and mentally ill.
6. Assess the condition of an individual and identify or state his classification if he is assessed as mentally retarded.

QUESTIONS

Please answer each of the following questions carefully. After each possible answer, you will be referred to a frame in the section beginning on p. 79 where you will be told whether or not your choice is correct. If the alternative you have selected is correct, you will be told in the answer frame which frame in the "Questions" section to turn to next. If your choice is incorrect, your answer will tell you to return to the question frame you have just answered to review and to try again. Please note that you will always be given your instructions according to frame number. Frames designated with "Q" indicate a frame in the "Questions" section (e.g., "Q-1, Q-2"). Frames designated with an "A" indicate answers. Only occasionally will you be given a page number to which to turn. It is most important that you follow the instructions for *each individual question or answer frame* most carefully.

Q-1   In all but a few instances, mental illness and mental retardation are *separate problems*. There are only two instances in which they are similar. *First*, they *both* may be present in the same person; second, *no one* is *immune* to either of these conditions. They strike without regard to race, creed, or color.

Would you say that mental illness and mental retardation are similar conditions in most respects?

a. Yes.   A-4.
b. No.   A-13.

In considering the similar aspects of mental illness and mental retardation, which of the following statements would you now say is correct?

a. Certain people are immune to
   mental illness and/or mental retardation.   Turn to A-9.
b. No one is immune to mental illness
   or mental retardation, but the same person cannot be
   afflicted with both conditions.   Turn to A-3.
c. Mental illness and mental retardation can
   strike anyone, and the same individual
   can be afflicted with both conditions.   Turn to A-11.

Can you recall the three components of the definition of mental retardation that you learned earlier? In order to test yourself, fill in the following sentences.

a. Mental retardation refers to _____ _____ _____ intellectual functioning.

b. Existing concurrently with deficits in _____ _____ .

c. And manifested during the _____ _____ .

After filling in the answers above, turn to A-5.

Which of the following statements is true?

a. Mental retardation may or may not
   involve a deficit in intellectual functioning.   Turn to A-10.
b. Mental illness may or may not involve
   a deficit in intellectual functioning.   Turn to A-1.
c. Mental illness always involves a deficit
   in intellectual functioning.   Turn to A-6.

Q-5 Mental retardation always involves a deficit in intellectual functioning while mental illness may or may not involve such a deficit.

How about the second component of mental retardation? When does it originate? Write your answer below and then turn to A-8.

_____

_____

_____

Q-6 We now turn to the third component of mental retardation. State in the space provided below the type of behavior with which mental retardation is associated and then turn to A-2.

_____

_____

_____

Q-7 Impairments in both intellectual functioning and adaptive behavior are results of developmental abnormalities in which condition?

a. Mental retardation.   Turn to A-12.
b. Mental illness.   Turn to A-7.

Please follow the same instructions as those you were given on page 76 in working with this section. It is most important that you remember to follow the individual instructions in each answer frame.

True. Mental illness may or may not involve a deficit in intel-   A-1
lectual functioning.

Continue now with Q-5.

Mental retardation is associated with *deficits in adaptive be-*   A-2
havior. Mental retardation, therefore, includes impairment in both intellectual functioning and adaptive behavior. Both of these kinds of impairment are *direct results of developmental abnor-malities of the brain or injuries to the brain suffered during the developmental period.*

Mental illness, on the other hand, includes *problems of personality resulting from intra-psychic and emotional disturbances* which may or may not affect intellectual functioning and/or adaptive behavior.

Go on to Q-7.

The first part of this answer is correct—no one is immune to mental   A-3
illness or mental retardation. However, the second part says that the same person cannot be afflicted with both conditions, and this is definitely incorrect.

Please return to Q-2 and select another answer.

A-4   Mental illness and mental retardation are really *not* similar in most respects.

Please go back to page 73 and reread the material presented there before going on to try the other answers in Q-1.

A-5   Let's take the three components one at a time. First, you remember that mental retardation refers to *significant subaverage intellectual* functioning. There is *always* a deficit in intellectual functioning in mental retardation. Second, mental retardation originates *before, during, or after the birth process and up through the end of the developmental period* (around eighteen years of age). Third, mental retardation is associated with *deficits in adaptive behavior.*

Did you get all three items correct? If not, take time to review material covered so far before going on to Q-4. If you knew all three items, move right on to Q-4.

A-6   You have said that mental illness always involves a deficit in intellectual functioning. This answer is false.

Return to Q-4 and select another answer.

A-7   Although there may or may not be impairment in intellectual and/or adaptive behavior in the mentally ill, the impairment is never caused by developmental abnormalities; rather, it is caused by intra-psychic and emotional disturbances.

See the correct answer in A-12.

Mental retardation originates during the developmental period,   A-8
which includes the period of gestation or pregnancy, the birth
process, and the first eighteen years of life.

Mental illness usually manifests itself after a period of relatively
normal development. Of course, there are many children who are
mentally ill, but the majority of persons who are mentally ill are
adults.

To repeat, mental retardation always originates before age eighteen,
while mental illness most often occurs or manifests itself after that
age.

Continue now with Q-6.

No, no one is immune to either mental retardation or mental   A-9
illness.

Return to item Q-2 and select another answer.

You said that mental retardation may or may not involve a deficit   A-10
in intellectual functioning. Sorry, but this is an incorrect answer.
Mental retardation always involves a deficit in intellectual functioning.

Please return to Q-4 and select another answer.

True. You said that mental illness and mental retardation are   A-11
similar in that they can strike anyone and you also said that the
same individual can be afflicted with both conditions at the same
time. Very good.

Continue now with Q-3.

A-12   You're absolutely correct when you say that a mentally retarded individual suffers impairment in both intellectual and adaptive behavior functioning as a result of developmental abnormalities of the brain.

In most instances, then, mental retardation and mental illness are separate problems.

Turn now to the following page for a listing of the similarities and differences between the two conditions.

A-13   The answer is *no* and, therefore, you are correct. Mental illness and mental retardation are separate conditions, dissimilar in most respects.

Please turn back to Q-2 and continue with the lesson.

A SUMMARY OF THE SIMILARITIES AND DIFFERENCES BETWEEN MENTAL RETARDATION AND MENTAL ILLNESS

Similarities

1. Both may be present in the same person at the same time as primary conditions or one may be secondary to the other.
2. No one is immune to either of these conditions.

Differences

Characteristic	Mental Retardation	Mental Illness
1. Originates before birth.	Often	Rarely
2. Originates during the birth process.	Often	Rarely
3. Originates during the first eighteen years of life.	Always	Occasionally
4. Manifests itself for the first time during adulthood.	Rarely	Often
5. Results from developmental abnormalities of the brain.	Usually	Rarely
6. Results from emotional or intra-psychic disturbances.	Rarely	Usually
7. Deficit in intellectual functioning.	Always	May or may not
8. Deficit in adaptive functioning.	Always	May or may not
9. Consists mainly of personality problems.	Rarely	Usually

You have now completed this lesson. As a way of evaluating yourself, answer the review questions which begin on the following page; then review the answers which follow the questions.

REVIEW QUESTIONS—LESSON FIVE

Questions

Circle the *letter* corresponding to the answer of your choice.

1. During the years from conception through age eighteen, an individual may be immune to which of the following?

   a. Mental retardation.
   b. Mental illness.
   c. Both a and b above.
   d. Neither a nor b above.

2. Persons suffering from which of the following conditions always demonstrate a deficit in intellectual functioning?

   a. Mental illness.
   b. Mental retardation.
   c. Both a and b above.
   d. Neither a nor b above.

3. Mental illness usually originates during:

   a. Pregnancy.
   b. The birth process.
   c. The first eighteen years of life.
   d. Adulthood or the period beyond the age of eighteen.

4. Mental illness usually results from:

   a. Emotional disturbances.
   b. Developmental abnormalities of the brain.
   c. Nutritional deficiency.
   d. None of the above.

5. Bill A's case history: Bill is eight years old and is unable to perform in academic studies beyond the first-grade level. He needs help dressing, eating, etc.

   Bill is probably retarded since he evidences:

   a. Emotional problems.
   b. A deficit in intellectual functioning.
   c. A deficit in adaptive behavioral functioning.
   d. b and c above.
   e. a, b, and c above.

Refer to the following case history when answering Questions 6, 7 and 8.

Sally is seven years old. Her IQ is 46. She has six brothers and sisters. Her parents are poor. She has been unable to perform well in second grade. She finds it difficult to perform self-help skills and often throws tantrums when attempting to eat or dress by herself. She has a morbid and unrealistic fear of walking up and down stairs.

6. Sally is probably:

   a. Mentally retarded.
   b. Mentally ill.
   c. a and b above
   d. Neither a nor b above.

7. Sally's intellectual functioning would place her in which classification of mental retardation?

   a. Severe.
   b. Mild.
   c. Profound.
   d. Moderate.

8. Which of the following pieces of evidence points to the possibility that Sally is mentally retarded?

   a. She has temper tantrums.
   b. She has a morbid fear of stairs.
   c. She has an impairment in intellectual functioning.
   d. All of the above.

Refer to the following case history when answering Questions 9, 10, and 11.

Phil is fourteen years old. His IQ is 65. His brain was injured during birth. He has progressed through the fifth grade in school but can progress no further. He is able to dress and feed himself as well as to communicate with his parents and friends.

9. Phil is probably:

   a. Mentally retarded.
   b. Mentally ill.
   c. Normal.
   d. a and b above.

10. Phil's IQ would place him in which intellectual functioning classification?

    a. Moderate retardation.
    b. Mild retardation.
    c. Severe retardation.
    d. Normal.

11. Which of the following statements is evidence of the possibility that Phil is mentally ill?

    a. He is fourteen years old and is unable to progress beyond the fifth-grade level.
    b. He was brain damaged during birth.
    c. He has an impairment in adaptive behavior.
    d. a and b above.
    e. None of the above.

Answers

1. d.
2. b.
3. d.
4. a.
5. d.
6. c.
7. d.
8. c.
9. a.
10. b.
11. e.

Balthazar, E. E. and Stevens, H. A. *The Emotionally Disturbed Mentally Retarded.* Englewood Cliffs, N. J.: Prentice-Hall, 1975.

Benda, C. E.; Farrell, M. J.; and Chipman, Catherine, E. "The Inadequacy of Present Day Concepts of Mental Deficiency and Mental Illness in Child Psychiatry." *American Journal of Psychiatry* 107 (1951): 721-29.

Bender, L. "Autism in Children with Mental Deficiency." *American Journal of Mental Deficiency* 64 (1959): 81-86.

Bialer, I. "Relationship of Mental Retardation to Emotional Disturbance and Physical Disability," in Haywood, H. C., ed., *Social-Cultural Aspects of Mental Retardation.* New York: Appleton-Century-Crofts, 1970.

Chapman, L. J., and Pathman, J. H. "Errors in the Diagnosis of Mental Deficiency in Schizophrenia." *Journal of Consulting Psychology* 23 (1959): 432-34.

Craft, M. "Mental Disorder in a Series of English Out-Patient Defectives." *American Journal of Mental Deficiency* 64 (1960): 718-24.

Cutts, R. A. "Differentiation between Pseudomental Defective with Emotional Disorders and Mental Defectives with Emotional Disturbances." *American Journal of Mental Deficiency* 61 (1957): 761-72.

Eisenberg, L. "Emotional Determinants of Mental Deficiency." *American Medical Association Archives of Neurology and Psychiatry* 80 (1958): 114-24.

Garfield, S. L.; Wilcott, Johanna B.; and Milgram, N. "Emotional Disturbance and Suspected Mental Deficiency." *American Journal of Mental Deficiency* 66 (1961): 23-29.

Glassman, L. "Is Dull Normal Intelligence a Contraindication for Psychotherapy? *Smith College Studies in Social Work* 13 (1942): 275-98.

Heber, R. "Promising Areas for Psychological Research in Mental Retardation." *American Journal of Mental Deficiency* 63 (1959): 975-80.

Masland, R. L.; Sarason, S. B.; and Gladwin, T. *Mental Subnormality.* New York: Basic Books, Inc., 1958.

Menolascino, F. J. "Emotional Disturbances in Mentally Retarded Children." *American Journal of Psychiatry* 126 (1969): 168-76.

Menolascino, F. J.; editor. *Psychiatric Approaches to Mental Retardation.* New York: Basic Books, Inc., 1970.

_____. editor. *Psychiatric Aspects of the Diagnosis and Treatment of Mental Retardation.* Seattle: Special Child Publications, 1971.

O'Connor, N. "Neuroticism and Emotional Instability in High-Grade Male Defectives." *Journal of Neurological and Neurosurgical Psychiatry* 14 (1951): 226-30.

O'Gorman, G. "Psychosis as a Cause of Mental Defect." *Journal of Mental Science* 100 (1954): 934-43.

Pollack, H. M. "Mental Disease among Mental Defectives." *American Journal of Mental Deficiency* 49 (1945): 477-80.

Pollack, M. "Brain Damage, Mental Retardation and Childhood Schizophrenia." *American Journal of Psychiatry* 115 (1958): 422-28.

Potter, H. W. "Mental Deficiency and the Psychiatrist." *American Journal of Psychiatry* 6 (1927): 691-700.

Raub, E. S.; Mercer, M.; and Hecker, A. O. "A Study of Psychotic Patients Assumed to Be Mentally Deficient on the Basis of School Progress and Social Adjustment." *American Journal of Mental Deficiency* 57 (1952): 82-88.

Robinson, R. C., and Paseward, R. "Behavior in Intellectual Deficit: A Critical Review of the Literature." *American Journal of Mental Deficiency* 55 (1951): 598-607.

Sarason, S. B., and Gladwin, T. "Psychological and Cultural Problems in Mental Subnormality: A Review of Research." *Genetic Psychology Monograph* 57 (1958): 3-289.

Sarason, S. B., and Sarason, D. J. *Psychological Problems in Mental Deficiency*, 4th ed. New York: Harper and Row, 1969.

Schacter, F. F.; Meyer, L. R.; and Loomis, E. A. "Childhood Schizophrenia and Mental Retardation: Differential Diagnosis before and after One Year of Psychotherapy." *American Journal of Orthopsychiatry* 32 (1962): 584-95.

Shepherd, M., and Davies, D. L., editors. *Studies in Psychiatry*. London: Oxford University Press, 1968.

Szurek, S. A., and Berlin, I. N., editors. *Psychosomatic Disorders and Mental Retardation in Children*. Palo Alto, California: Science and Behavior Books, 1968.

Thorne, F. C. "Counseling and Psychotherapy with Mental Defectives." *American Journal of Mental Deficiency* 52 (1948): 263-71.

Weaver, R. T. "The Incident of Maladjustment among Mental Defectives in Military Environment." *American Journal of Mental Deficiency* 51 (1946): 238-46.

Wolfensberger, W. Schizophrenia in Mental Retardates: Three Hypotheses." *American Journal of Mental Deficiency* 64 (1960): 704-06.

UNIT 2

LESSON SIX
The Scope of the Problem of Mental Retardation

In discussing the scope of the problem of mental retardation, it should be kept clearly in mind that no survey has yet been conducted which meets the criteria for an accurate census of the mentally retarded. These criteria consist essentially of four basic and interrelated concepts:

1. *Interpretation.* What is mental retardation? How retarded does an individual have to be in order to be considered retarded for census purposes?

2. *Differentiation.* How is it to be determined whether or not a person actually fits the accepted interpretation of what mental retardation is considered to be?

3. *Detection.* How can the retarded be located? Can they be located through individuals or agencies?

4. *Measurement.* How will the retarded be counted and on the basis of what classifications?

Prevalence rate studies show that the numbers of mentally retarded range from a low of 3.4 to as high as 77.0 per thousand. These inconsistent findings have resulted from differing IQ cut-off points for mental retardation, differing sources of information, and differing populations from which the survey data have been obtained. The results are so inconsistent that little can be concluded about the prevalence of mental retardation from existing studies.

For the United States, however, the present accepted prevalence rate of mental retardation is 3 percent of the total population. This figure is accepted by national organizations, such as the National Association for Retarded Citizens, the American Association on Mental Deficiency, and the US Department of Health, Education, and Welfare. Using the 3 percent figure as the prevalence rate and a total US population of approximately 200 million, officials estimate that a total number of six million individuals in this country fall into the retarded ranges. This figure, of course, will increase as the population of our country increases.

Because each retarded person comes from a family of approximately three or four other individuals, including parents and siblings, it is estimated that the problem of mental retardation directly affects approximately twenty million people in the US who are immediate family members of a retarded child or adult.

The overall classification of mental retardation usually lists the five levels of retardation which have been described previously—borderline, mild, moderate, severe, and profound. However, since the borderline group often is not mentioned when dealing with the scope of the problem, this lesson will deal with the other four classifications only.

By far the greatest majority of the retarded are to be found in the level of mild retardation. This group represents, in round numbers, about 5,340,000 persons, or about 89 percent of the total of all retarded persons in this country.

Of the total number of retarded people, approximately 6 percent, or 360,000, are in the level of moderate retardation. About 3 1/2 percent, or 210,000 individuals, are found in the severe level.

It is estimated that approximately 1 1/2 percent of the total of six million retarded individuals fall into the profound level. This means that there are about 90,000 persons who are considered to be profoundly retarded.

Thus far in this lesson, we have been discussing the prevalence of mental retardation. "Prevalence" as a term should be understood, and it is important to know how the term relates to the concept of "incidence." "Prevalence" is defined as the number of cases of mental retardation present in the whole population for any given period of time. In order to arrive at prevalence, the size and characteristics of the population have to be specified and the time interval has to be stipulated. "Incidence," on the other hand, represents the number of new cases of mental retardation which are added to the population within some specified interval of time. Prevalence and incidence are related concepts, but prevalence differs from incidence in that all of the known cases of mental retardation in the population during some specified period of time are included. Incidence, on the other hand, includes only the new cases.

The prevalence of mental retardation has been stated to be approximately 3 percent of the total population, or six million people. The incidence of children who are born retarded or are destined to become so is based on an estimate made from the total annual birth rate for the country of 4,000,000 births. It is estimated that approximately 120,000 children are born annually who are or will become retarded.

The rate of retardation varies in relation to age groupings. Most studies show a substantial increase in the number of retarded children from birth to five and from five to nine years of age. After nine, the rate rises increasingly until between ten and fifteen years of age when the rate reaches its highest percentage. After fifteen years of age, the rate sharply declines until seventeen years of age to about half of those found from ten to fifteen years of age. After seventeen years of age, the rate continues to reduce until about thirty years of age where it evens off until the age of sixty plus. The sharp rise in rates is largely attributable to the child's entrance into school where a better reporting system exists and where he finds increasing demands for both intellectual and social achievement. The decline at ages seventeen and older most likely reflects the child's leaving school, becoming integrated into the work force, and thus losing his "label" as a retarded individual.

So, although an overall 3 percent figure is used, one can readily see the differences which exist by age as well as the differences which occur because of sampling methods, IQ cut-off points, sources of information, and the reliability of the instruments used.

With the exception of mental illness, mental retardation is one of the most prevalent handicapping conditions in the US today. For example, epilepsy is considered to be a fairly common problem, and yet for every 1,000 people in the general population, there are only five epileptics as compared to thirty retardates. Rheumatic heart disease, which is considered to be even more prevalent than epilepsy, only afflicts seven individuals out of every 1,000, while thirty retarded individuals are found in each 1,000 of the population. Even prior to the development of the Salk vaccine, polio only afflicted two out of every 1,000 of our population. Thus, the problem of mental retardation is a sizable one because it affects so many people in our country today.

OBJECTIVES

This lesson is designed to teach you about the prevalence of mental retardation in the United States. More specifically, when you have completed this lesson, you will be able to:

1. Identify the approximate percentage of the total population of the United States who are mentally retarded, considering the retarded population as a whole and in each category of retardation.
2. Identify the approximate number of individuals presently in the United States who are considered to be mentally retarded as well as the approximate number of profoundly retarded, severely retarded, moderately retarded, and mildly retarded individuals in the United States.
3. Identify the approximate number of individuals born each year who will be born or become mentally retarded.
4. Identify the approximate percentage of the population of the United States, as well as the number of people this figure presently represents, who are personally touched by this condition (i.e., the mentally retarded and their families).

Please answer each of the following questions carefully. After each possible answer, you will be referred to a frame in the section beginning on p. 97 where you will be told whether or not your choice is correct. If the alternative you have selected is correct, you will be told in the answer frame which frame in the "Questions" section to turn to next. If your choice is incorrect, your answer will tell you to return to the question frame you have just answered to review and to try again. Please note that you will always be given your instructions according to frame number. Frames designated with "Q" indicate a frame in the "Questions" section (e.g., "Q-1, Q-2"). Frames designated with an "A" indicate answers. Only occasionally will you be given a page number to which to turn. It is most important that you follow the instructions for *each individual question or answer frame* most carefully.

Q-1

In terms of numbers of persons affected, mental retardation is a very large problem. In order to better comprehend its dimensions, let us first consider how many individuals in the United States are estimated to be mentally retarded. All figures presented throughout this lesson will be approximations.

In round numbers, there are 200 million people in the United States at present. Of this total, 3 percent, or six million individuals, are considered mentally retarded.

Of those with an IQ in the retarded ranges, the breakdown of the six million mentally retarded persons falls into the following four classifications:

Classification	Number of Persons in Each Classification	Percentages of the Retarded in Each Classification
Profound	90,000	1.5
Severe	210,000	3.5
Moderate	360,000	6.0
Mild	5,340,000	89.0
Total	6,000,000	100.0

There are approximately 200 million persons in the United States at present.

Of the 200 million persons in the United States _____ percent or _____ persons are mentally retarded.

Fill in blanks and then turn to A-5.

Q-2   In the blanks provided below, fill in the estimated number of persons in the United States who fall in each classification of retardation.

Severely Retarded _____

Mildly Retarded _____

Moderately Retarded _____

Profoundly Retarded _____

Fill in the blanks and then turn to A-3.

The important thing to remember about these figures is that those individuals who are least retarded, the mildly retarded, comprise the overwhelming majority of the four classifications of the retarded population to be discussed here.

Q-3

The estimated percentage for this group is _____ .

Fill in the blank and then turn to A-1.

The mentally retarded are not the only persons affected by their condition. Their immediate families are also deeply affected. It is estimated that the mentally retarded and their families comprise about 10 *percent* of the population of the United States or *twenty million* people.

Q-4

Another figure you need to know is the number of individuals born each year who are or will become retarded. Since there are approximately four million births per year in the United States,

there are approximately _____ babies born who are or will become mentally retarded before the end of the developmental period.

Fill in the blank and then turn to A-4.

Just to be sure that you have all the figures correct, test yourself by filling in the blanks below. Review the material for any items that you miss.

Q-5

Total population of the US   _____

Percent of the population who
are mentally retarded   _____

(Continued on next page.)

Number of mentally retarded
persons in the US   ———————

Number of profoundly
retarded persons   ———————

Number of severely
retarded persons   ———————

Number of moderately
retarded persons   ———————

Number of mildly
retarded persons   ———————

Number of babies born
every year who are
or will become retarded   ———————

Number of persons who are
directly affected by
the condition of retardation   ———————

Turn to A-2 for the answers.

Please follow the same instructions as those you were given on page 93 in working with this section. It is most important that you remember to follow the individual instructions in each answer frame.

The percentage estimated for this group is 89 percent of the total   A-1
of some six million retarded persons.

Continue now with Q-4.

Population of the US	200,000,000.	A-2
Percent of retarded	3 percent.	
Number of retarded	6,000,000.	
Number of profoundly retarded	90,000.	
Number of severely retarded	210,000.	
Number of moderately retarded	360,000.	
Number of mildly retarded	5,340,000.	
Number of retarded babies born each year	120,000.	
The retarded and their families	20,000,000.	

Turn now to the conclusion on page 99.

There are approximately 210,000 severely retarded individuals in   A-3
the US; 5,340,000 mildly retarded persons; 360,000 moderately
retarded persons; and 90,000 profoundly retarded persons.

Continue now with Q-3.

A-4   You should have inserted the figure of 120,000 babies born each year who are or will become mentally retarded. This is based on the 3 percent figure used earlier (.03 × 4,000,000 = 120,000).

Continue now with Q-5.

A-5   Three percent of the population of the US is mentally retarded. This figure includes 6,000,000 individuals.

Continue now with Q-2.

CONCLUSION

By now you should have a good idea of the extent of the condition called mental retardation. It is one of the biggest and most challenging problems in our country today.

Please go on to the review questions on the next page. After you finish, either go back over this lesson or go on to the next lesson.

REVIEW QUESTIONS—LESSON SIX

Questions

Circle the *letter* corresponding to the answer of your choice.

1. What is the approximate population of the United States at the present time?

   a. 100,000,000.
   b. 200,000,000.
   c. 300,000,000.
   d. 400,000,000.

2. Based on expert opinion, the figure most commonly cited for the percentage of the total population of the United States who are mentally retarded is approximately:

   a. 5 percent.
   b. 4 percent.
   c. 3 percent.
   d. 2 percent.

3. Approximately how many retarded individuals are there in the United States at the present time?

   a. 2,000,000.
   b. 4,000,000.
   c. 6,000,000.
   d. 8,000,000.

4. The number of profoundly retarded individuals in the United States at the present time is approximately:

   a. 90,000.
   b. 150,000.
   c. 210,000.
   d. 270,000.

5. Approximately how many moderately retarded persons are there in the United States at the present time?

   a. 400,000.
   b. 360,000.
   c. 310,000.
   d. 250,000.

6. What is the approximate number of mildly retarded persons in the United States at the present time?

   a. 3,340,000.
   b. 4,340,000.
   c. 5,340,000.
   d. 6,340,000.

7. Approximately what percent of the total population of the United States are directly involved with the retarded (i.e. the families of the retarded)?

   a. 5 percent.
   b. 10 percent.
   c. 15 percent.
   d. 20 percent.

8. The mentally retarded and their families comprise approximately how many persons?

   a. 10,000,000.
   b. 20,000,000.
   c. 30,000,000.
   d. 40,000,000.

9. Approximately how many infants are born every year who are or will become mentally retarded?

   a. 50,000.
   b. 75,000.
   c. 100,000.
   d. 120,000.

To check your answers, see the following section.

Answers

The answers to the preceding questions are:

1. b.
2. c.
3. c.
4. a.
5. b.
6. c.
7. b.
8. b.
9. d.

SELECTED READINGS

Bateman, Barbara D., and Kirk, S. A. *Ten Years of Research at the Institute for Research on Exceptional Children.* Memeographed. Urbana: University of Illinois, 1952-1962.

Dingman, H. F., and Tarjan, G. "Mental Retardations and the Normal Curve." *American Journal of Mental Deficiency* 64 (1960): 991-94.

Farber, B. *Prevalence of Exceptional Children in Illinois in 1958,* Cicular Census IA. Springfield: Illinois Superintendent of Public Instruction, 1959.

Ferguson, R. G. "A Study of the Problem of Mental Retardation in a Large Urban Community." *American Journal of Orthopsychiatry* 27 (1957): 490-501.

Goodman, M. B.; Gruenberg, E.; Downing, J.; and Rogot, E. "A Prevalence Study of Mental Retardation in a Metropolitan Area." *American Journal of Public Health* 46 (1956): 702-07.

Goodman N., and Tizard, J. "Prevalence of Imbecility and Idiocy among Children." *British Medical Journal* 5273 (1962): 216-19.

Gruenberg, E. M. "Epidemiology." In *Mental Retardation,* edited by H. A. Stevens and R. Heber. Chicago: University of Chicago Press, 1964.

Jastak, J. R.; McPhee, H. M.; and Whiteman, M. *Mental Retardation: Its Nature and Incidence,* Newark: University of Delaware Press, 1963.

———. *Mental Retardation, Its Nature and Incidence: A Population Survey of the State of Delaware.* Newark: University of Delaware Press, 1963.

Lapouse, R., and Weitzner, M. "Epidemiology." In *Mental Retardation: An Annual Review,* edited by J. Wortis. New York: Grune & Stratton, 1970.

Lemkau, P.; Tietze, C.; and Cooper, M. "Mental Hygiene Problems in an Urban District." *Mental Hygiene* 26 (1942): 275-88.

Levinson, Elizabeth J. *Retarded Children in Maine, A Survey and Analysis.* Orono: University of Maine Press, 1962.

Lewis, E. O. *Report on an Investigation into the Incidence of Mental Deficiency in Six Areas,* 1925-1927 (Part 15 of *Report of the Mental Deficiency Committee Being a Joining Committee of the Board of Education and Board of Control).* London, H. M. Stationery Office, 1929.

Malzberg, B. "Sex Differences in the Prevalence of Mental Deficiency." *American Journal of Mental Deficiency* 58 (1953): 301-05.

New York State Department of Mental Hygiene, Mental Health Research Unit 1955. "A Special Census of Suspected Referred Mental Retardation, Onondaga County, New York." *Technical Report of the Mental Health Research Unit.* Syracuse, New York: Syracuse University Press, 1955.

Richardson, W. P., and Higgins, A. C. "The Handicapped Children of Alamance County, North Carolina." *A Medical and Sociological Study.* Wilmington, Delaware: Nemours Foundation, 1965.

Roselle, E. N. "New Horizons for the Mentally Retarded when a School Looks at the Problem as a Whole." *American Journal of Mental Deficiency* 59 (1955): 359-73.

Scheerenberger, R. C. "Mental Retardation: Definition, Classification and Prevalence." *Mental Retardation Abstracts,* pp. 432-40. Washington, D.C.: National Institutes of Health, 1964.

Wallin, J. E. W. "Prevalence of Mental Retardates." *School and Society* 86 (1958): 55-56.

Wirtz, M. A., and Guenther, R. "The Incidence of Trainable Mentally Handicapped Children." *Exceptional Children* 23 (1957): 171-72; 175.

Wishik, S. H. "Georgia Study of Handicapped Children: Report on a Study of Prevalence, Disability, Needs, Resources, and Contributing Factors." *Publications for Program Administration and Community Organization.* Atlanta: Georgia Department of Public Health, 1964.

_____. "Handicapped Children in Georgia: A Study of Prevalence, Needs, and Resources." *American Journal of Public Health* 46 (1956): 195-203.

UNIT 2

LESSON SEVEN
Etiology of Mental Retardation

The mentally retarded can be divided broadly into two major groupings. The first and largest group is composed of individuals who are retarded, but the causes are not understood. About 75 percent of all retarded persons fall into this category. Usually, individuals who are in this group show no brain damage, are only mildly retarded, and are capable of functioning—albeit in limited ways. Broadly speaking, those who are in this group are retarded because of presumed psychological, social, and/or genetic factors. Retardation, for most of these individuals, occurs as a result of one or a combination of any of the three following factors. First, retardation may be caused by a complex hereditary condition which is not fully understood at present. In this case, whole families tend to be retarded. Second, retardation may be caused by poor environmental factors where the individual has not had proper intellectual stimulation or adequate social relationships to help him develop properly. Third, certain health problems or illnesses may produce brain damage that is so minimal as to be unobservable upon examination. Poor nutrition and inadequate prenatal care are often regarded as examples of this third factor.

The second major grouping consists of those individuals whose brains have not developed properly or have been injured or damaged by some condition or disease. About 25 percent of the diagnosed cases show some demonstrable brain damage where a specific condition or disease can be recognized as having been the cause.

The Grossman revision[1] of the previously accepted AAMD categories for this group retained the major classifications, but subdivides them differently and adds "chromosomal abnormality" and "gestational disorders" as follows:

1. *Infections and Intoxications* which include: prenatal infection, postnatal infection, and intoxication. Examples would include mothers who contract Rubella (German measles) within the first three months of pregnancy (also called the first trimester of the pregnancy). Other prenatal infections include syphilis and toxoplasmosis. Postnatal cerebral infections include viral and bacterial infections. The toxic subdivision includes toxemia of pregnancy, maternal PKU, Hyperbilirubinemia (too much bile in the blood), lead poisoning, and other toxic conditions.

2. *Trauma or Physical Agent.* This area has five subdivisions: prenatal injury; mechanical injury at birth; prenatal hypoxia; postnatal hypoxia; and postnatal injury. Examples include: prenatal irradiation; prenatal hypoxia (lack of oxygen); complications and difficulties of labor; prenatal placenta separation; massive hemorrhage, and such other severe trauma as may occur from a fractured skull, contusions of the brain, or other injuries.

3. *Metabolism or Nutrition.* This area includes all disorders resulting from metabolic, nutritional, endocrine, or growth dysfunction. Examples include, but are not limited to: Tay-Sachs disease and other lipoid (fat or fatlike substances) diseases such as galactosemia; hypoglycemia; phenylketurnuria (PKU); and cretinism.

4. *Gross Brain Disease* (postnatal). This area includes many disorders in which the etiology is unknown or uncertain. Examples include, but are not limited to: neurofibromatosis (multiple tumors of the skin, nerves, bones, or brain); tuberous sclerosis; new growths (tumors); Huntington's chorea (characterized by progressive demetia and death).

---

[1] H. J. Grossman, ed., *Manual on Terminology and Classification in Mental Retardation*, 1973 revision (Washington, D.C.: American Association on Mental Deficiency, 1973).

5. *Unknown Prenatal Influence.*   This area covers conditions presumed to exist at or prior to birth for which no known etiology has been established. Included in this category are: cerebral malformation; anencephaly (partial or complete absence of the cerebrum, cerebellum, and flat bones of the skull); Cornelia de Lange syndrome; microcephaly (abnormally small head) and macrocephaly (excessively large head); hydrocephalus (head enlarged with cerebral spinal fluid) and hydraencephaly, among other disorders of this unknown prenatal influence.

6. *Chromosomal Abnormality.*   Examples of this area include, but are not limited to, all types of gene mutations, drug and other chemical effects on the chromosomes, and viruses: Cri-du-chat or cat cry syndrome, characterized by a weak, high pitched cry and various physical anomalies, such as hypertelorism (widespread eyes), epicanthal (fold of skin at the side of the eye) folds, downward palpebral (eyelid) slant, and low-set ears; the various trisomies, including the Down's Syndrome (trisomy 21); Klinefelter's Syndrome; and Turner's Syndrome.

7. *Gestational Disorders.*   A significant number of cases seem to fit into this category, which includes all atypical gestational disorders. Examples include: prematurity (live infants delivered before thirty-seven weeks from the first day of the last menstrual period); low birth weight; postmaturity (infant exceeds normal gestation period by seven or more days); and other gestational disorders.

In addition to the above seven classifications, the Grossman revision specifies three other areas: (1) Following Psychiatric Disorder, in which there is no evidence of cerebral pathology; (2) Environmental Influences, which includes psycho-social disadvantages and sensory deprivation; and (3) "other conditions," which may be specific (blindness or deafness) or unspecified disorders.

The above medical descriptions, which are covered in more detail in the 1973 AAMD manual, should be carefully studied by all persons interested in the area of retardation. However, it should be noted that the manual covers many causes of retardation and that, although over 100 causes have been described, these only account for approximately 25 percent of all identified cases of retardation. No one knows what the total number of causes might be, although research is going on constantly not only to identify causes but also to find preventive measures.

In order to further understand the condition of mental retardation, it is helpful to learn its etiology, or primary causes. At the conclusion of this lesson you should be able to:

1. Name the two major causal groupings which are known to lead to varying degrees of mental retardation.
2. Describe or identify the three factors which are presumed to be the causal factors in those cases where the causal condition is not yet completely understood.
3. Describe or identify the seven major medical classifications and name at least one example in each classification.

QUESTIONS

Please answer each of the following questions carefully. After each possible answer, you will be referred to a frame in the section beginning on p. 117 where you will be told whether or not your choice is correct. If the alternative you have selected is correct, you will be told in the answer frame which frame in the "Questions" section to turn to next. If your choice is incorrect, your answer will tell you to return to the question frame you have just answered to review and to try again. Please note that you will always be given your instructions according to frame number. Frames designated with "Q" indicate a frame in the "Questions" section (e.g., "Q-1, Q-2"). Frames designated with an "A" indicate answers. Only occasionally will you be given a page number to which to turn. It is most important that you follow the instructions for *each individual question or answer frame* most carefully.

CONDITIONS WHICH MAY LEAD TO VARYING DEGREES OF MENTAL RETARDATION

Q-1   Any condition which effects an individual's intellectual growth may lead to retardation. Since mental processes develop throughout the developmental period, any condition which has an adverse effect on mental development during this period can cause retardation. There are two broad groupings of these causal conditions:

1. The causal condition is not understood but probably stems from any one or a combination of psychological, social, and/or genetic factors. There is usually no brain damage evidenced by individuals in this grouping.
2. The causal condition is identifiable and there is some demonstrable brain damage.

There are two causal groupings of conditions which may lead to mental retardation. These conditions include:

a. Those cases where the causal condition is not _____ but stems from any one or a combination of _____, _____, and/or _____ factors.

b. Those cases where the causal condition is _____ and the individual is _____ _____ .

Fill in the blanks above and then turn to A-11.

In approximately 75 percent of all cases of persons diagnosed as being mentally retarded, the specific causes of the condition are not yet clearly understood.

Q-2

In only about 25 per cent of the cases can a specific entity be held directly responsible for the condition.

In approximately _____ percent of all cases of persons diagnosed as being retarded, there is no one clearly identifiable cause for the condition. The cause is not understood.

Fill in the blank above and then see A-13.

Therefore, in only _____ percent of all cases of mental retardation is there a specific known cause of the condition.

Q-3

Please see A-9 after you fill in the blank above.

FACTORS PLAYING A CONTRIBUTORY ROLE IN CAUSATION OF MOST CASES OF MILD MENTAL RETARDATION

We shall now identify the three major factors believed to play a causal role in the cases which comprise 75 percent of all those who are retarded.

Q-4

Although we do not know specifically how or why these individuals are retarded, it is believed that the condition is caused by one or more of the following:

1. Heredity and related chromosomal factors.
2. Adverse psychological, social or environmental conditions.
3. Inadequate prenatal and/or postnatal health care, and other pre- and postnatal factors.

It appears that the *first* factor, *heredity*, is significant because there are some individuals who may carry a complex, but as yet unknown, genetic condition which may be passed on to their offspring. Members of these families will often be retarded to some degree, usually only mildly. Whether the condition is caused solely by heredity or by a combination of heredity with environmental factors is debatable—as you will see in Lesson Nine. Nevertheless it is assumed by many experts that heredity does play a part in cases of mental retardation even though the degree to which this is true is unknown.

The *second* factor which is believed to contribute to the causation of retardation but as yet is not fully understood includes *adverse psychological and/or social conditions* in the environment of the growing child. Although it is not as yet possible to pinpoint any one element that may contribute to this condition, it is believed that in an environment where the child is given very little, if any, emotional and/or intellectual stimulation, his mind will not develop properly even though there is no apparent brain damage.

The *last* factor believed to play a contributory role where the causation of retardation is not fully understood is *inadequate health care*. This cause may include:

1. Inadequate pre- and postnatal care.
2. Inadequate medical care for the growing child during the developmental period.
3. Inadequate nutrition for the mother or child.

Three factors which are believed to play contributory roles where the causation of mental retardation is not fully understood include:

1. _____

2. _____

3. _____

First fill in the blanks above and then see A-16.

As you learned earlier, ＿＿＿＿＿ percent of all cases of retardation have a known etiology.

Q-5

This second major causal grouping consists of those individuals whose brains have been demonstrably damaged by some identifiable condition or disease.

Turn to A-1 after filling in the blank.

There are *seven major categories* of factors which have been identified as *specific causes of brain damage and resultant mental retardation.*

Q-6

The *first* category contains two subcategories: *infections and intoxications affecting the mother during pregnancy or the infant after birth.* Examples of infections contracted by the mother during pregnancy include:

1. *German measles*, especially if contracted during the first three months of pregnancy.
2. *Syphilis.*

Examples of infections in the infant leading to retardation include:

1. *Meningitis.*
2. *Encephalitis.*
3. *Measles.*

Examples of intoxications include: (1) drugs taken by the mother, (2) industrial chemicals, (3) lead poisoning, etc.

Two types of infectious diseases which often lead to retardation in the fetus when contracted or carried by the mother during pregnancy are ＿＿＿＿＿ and ＿＿＿＿＿ .

Fill in the blanks above and then see A-18.

Q-7   In the space below name two of three types of infections which often lead to mental retardation.

1. _____

2. _____

Name a third type below if you are able and then see A-8.

3. _____

Q-8   A *second* category of factors includes *poisonous or toxic agents* affecting the mother and child. *Carbon monoxide, lead, and arsenic* poisoning are prime examples of toxic agents which, if inhaled or ingested by the mother during pregnancy or by the child after birth, can lead to mental retardation.

Carbon monoxide, lead, and arsenic are examples of _____ or

_____ _____ which can, if inhaled or ingested by mother or child, lead to retardation.

Fill in the blanks above and then see A-15.

Q-9   In the space below, write the two categories presented so far along with two examples of each.

Category	*Examples*
1. _____	1. _____
	2. _____
2. _____	1. _____
	2. _____

Turn to A-3 to check your answers.

Injuries to the brain of the growing child are included in the *second* category of factors leading to retardation. This category is called *physical or traumatic agents* and includes such things as *lack of oxygen at the time of birth, brain injuries occurring prior to or during delivery,* and *brain injury during childhood resulting from accidents.*

Q-10

Lack of oxygen and brain injuries occurring during the developmental period are examples of _____ or _____ agents.

When you have filled in the blanks turn to A-5.

The *third* category of factors which can lead to retardation includes *metabolic and nutritional disorders* affecting the child. A few of these disorders are *phenylketonuria* or PKU, *galactosemia, hypoglycemia, and cretinism.*

Q-11

Phenylketonuria results from a metabolic protein disorder. Galactosemia results from a metabolic carbohydrate disorder. Hypoglycemia results from low blood sugar. Cretinism refers to a congenital lack of the thyroid hormone thyroxin; this lack occurs due to the absence or malfunctioning of the thyroid gland or to a metabolic error in its secretion.

Phenylketonuria and galactosemia are examples of _____ _____ which lead to mental retardation.

Fill in the blanks above and then go on to A-7 to check your answer.

Q-12   The *fourth* category of factors known to cause mental retardation includes *abnormal growths.* There are some cases where *tumors, nodules,* or *other growths* within the brain can lead to retardation.

Tumors and nodules in the brain are examples of the fourth category of factors causing mental retardation. Retardation then can be caused by _____ in the brain. Fill in the blank space, then turn to A-17 to check your answer.

Q-13   The *fifth* category of factors leading to mental retardation includes innumerable *unknown prenatal factors* which cause inadequate development of the brain. The brain may be damaged at birth or just prior to birth. Examples of this category include: microcephaly, macrocephaly, and hydrocephaly.

Microcephalics have very small heads; macrocephalics have enlarged heads; and hydrocephalics (a condition caused by an increase in cerebrospinal fluid) may or may not have enlarged heads.

One example of an unknown prenatal factor which causes inadequate development of the brain and may exist at or prior to birth is:

a. Encephalitis.   Turn to A-2.
b. Microcephalus.   Turn to A-12.
c. Jaundice.   Turn to A-21.

Q-14   The mentally retarded condition in which a person may have an enlarged head caused by an increase in cerebrospinal fluid is called:

a. Hydrocephaly.   Turn to A-4.
b. Microcephaly.   Turn to A-10.

The *sixth* category—*Chromosomal Abnormalities*—includes damage   Q-15
to the brain presumed due to various gene abnormalities. Down's
syndrome (mongolism), previously classified under "unknown prenatal influence," is in this sixth category due to the finding that
mongoloids have an extra chromosome presumed to be a causal
factor in the retardation of these individuals.

In the space below, identify at least two chromosomal abnormalities, other than the Down's syndrome. Check your answer by turning to A-14.

1. _____
2. _____

The *seventh* category—*Gestational Disorders*—includes the most   Q-16
obvious disorder of *prematurity*. What are the other two most
obvious gestational disorders? Turn to A-19 to check your
answers.

1. _____
2. _____

The last three classifications in the Grossman revision of the   Q-17
Manual on Terminology and Classification include: "Following
Psychiatric Disorder," "Environmental Influences," and "other
conditions," such as blindness and deafness. Which of these three
classifications includes the psycho-social factor and sensory deprivation? Write your answer below then turn to A-20.

_____

Q-18   List below the seven major classifications identified by the American Association on Mental Deficiency and cite at least one example of each before going on to A-6 to check your answers.

Category   *Examples*

1. _____   1. _____

   _____   _____

   _____   _____

2. _____   2. _____

   _____   _____

   _____   _____

3. _____   3. _____

   _____   _____

   _____   _____

4. _____   4. _____

   _____   _____

   _____   _____

5. _____   5. _____

   _____   _____

   _____   _____

6. _____   6. _____

   _____   _____

   _____   _____

7. _____   7. _____

   _____   _____

   _____   _____

Please follow the same instructions as those you were given on page 108 in working with this section. It is most important that you remember to follow the individual instructions in each answer frame.

The answer is, of course, 25 percent.   A-1

Move on now to Q-6.

No, this is not an example of an unknown prenatal factor which   A-2
causes inadequate development of the brain. Encephalitis is an
infection which causes damage to the brain resulting in mental
retardation.

Return to page 114 and review the material in Q-13 before making
a correct response to the question presented in Q-13.

Category	*Examples*	A-3
1. Infections in the mother during pregnancy or Infectious childhood diseases	German measles; Syphilis Meningitis; Encephalitis; Measles	
2. Toxic agents affecting mother or child	Carbon monoxide; Lead poisoning; Arsenic	

Once you are able to name the two categories and examples of each go on to Q-10.

A-4   This is correct. Hydrocephaly is a condition causing retardation which is of unknown prenatal origin and in which the child's head often becomes enlarged due to an increase in cerebrospinal fluid.

Continue with Q-15.

A-5   Lack of oxygen and brain injuries occurring during the developmental period are examples of *physical* or *traumatic* agents.

Continue with Q-11.

A-6

Category	Examples
1. Infections and intoxications.	1. *Infections:* German measles, syphilis, encephalitis. *Intoxications* (toxic conditions): drugs, lead, arsenic poisoning, carbon monoxide.
2. Physical or traumatic agents.	2. Lack of oxygen, childhood brain injury, labor complications, prenatal irradiation.
3. Metabolic or nutritional disorders.	3. Phenylketonuria (PKU), galactocemia, hypoglycemia, Tay-Sach's disease, cretinism.
4. Gross brain disease.	4. Tumors, nodules, and other growths.
5. Unknown prenatal factors.	5. Microcephaly, hydrocephaly, macrocephaly, cerebral malformation, Cornelia de Lange syndrome.
6. Chromosomal abnormalities.	6. Down's syndrome, Cri-du-chat, Klinefelter's syndrome, Turner's syndrome.
7. Gestational disorders.	7. Prematurity, small for date of birth (low birth weight), postmaturity.

If you identified the seven major categories and at least one example of each, you have successfully completed this lesson. Remember that the *Manual on Terminology and Classification in Mental Retardation* (Grossman 1973) lists *ten* categories and that, although we have selected the first seven of the classifications as the major ones, you should know all ten. If you need to review this lesson turn to page 104. If you are ready to go to the review questions, turn to page 124.

If you said that phenylketonuria and galactosemia are examples of metabolic disorders leading to mental retardation, you are quite correct. Other examples of metabolic disorders leading to retardation are hypoglycemia and cretinism.

A-7

Continue on to Q-12.

Two prenatal infections are: German measles (Rubella) and syphilis. The postnatal infections include encephalitis and other syndromes resulting from infection by viruses, bacteria, and so forth.

A-8

Continue now with Q-8.

In only *25* percent of all cases of retardation is there a specific known cause of the condition.

A-9

Go on to Q-4.

A-10   Microcephaly is a condition of mental retardation in which a person has a very small head rather than an enlarged head.

Return to page 106 for a review before answering Q-14 correctly.

A-11   The causal groupings include:

1. Those cases where the causal condition is not *understood* but probably stems from any one or a combination of *psychological*, *social*, and/or *genetic* factors.
2. Those cases where the causal condition is *identifiable*, and the individual is demonstrably *brain damaged*.

Continue now with Q-2.

A-12   You have said that microcephaly is one example of an unknown prenatal factor which causes inadequate development of the brain. This is correct.

Continue now with Q-14.

In approximately 75 percent of all cases of retardation, there is no   A-13
one specific cause known. Did you get this correct?

Go on now to Q-3.

Other chromosomal abnormalities would include: A-14

1. Cri-du-chat.
2. Klinefelter's syndrome.
3. Turner's syndrome.

Continue with Q-16.

Carbon monoxide, lead, and arsenic poisoning are examples of   A-15
poisonous or toxic agents which can lead to mental retardation if
inhaled or ingested by the mother or child.

Continue now with Q-9.

The three factors playing contributory roles in causation include: A-16

1. Heredity.
2. Adverse psychological and/or social conditions.
3. Inadequate prenatal and/or postnatal health care.

Once you clearly understand these answers, go on to Q-5.

A-17   Retardation can also be caused by *abnormal growths* in the brain, such as nodules, tumors, and other growths.

Continue with Q-13.

A-18   *German measles* and *syphilis* when contracted or carried by the mother during pregnancy often result in a mentally retarded child.

To continue, turn to Q-7.

A-19   Did you identify the following as *gestational disorders*?

1. Low birth weight i.e., weighing 5 pounds, 8 ounces, or less, at birth).
2. Postmaturity (exceeding normal time period by seven days or more).

If you identified the above correctly, you are ready to continue with Q-17.

A-20   If you answered the *environmental influences,* you are entirely correct. This area is most often a factor in cases of mild retardation.

Continue with Q-18.

No. Jaundice is an example of an excess of bile pigment in the A-21 system which may cause damage to the brain. It is not an example of an unknown prenatal factor causing inadequate development of the brain.

Return to pages 105 - 106 and review the seven categories before answering Q-13 correctly.

REVIEW QUESTIONS

Questions

Circle the *letter* corresponding to the answer of your choice.

1. In approximately what percent of all cases of persons diagnosed as mentally retarded can a specific entity be held directly responsible for the condition?

   a. 5 percent.
   b. 25 percent.
   c. 35 percent.
   d. 50 percent.

2. Which condition leads to varying degrees of retardation?

   a. Any condition which interferes with the prenatal development of the brain.
   b. Unfavorable conditions within a child's environment.
   c. Any condition which injures the structure of the brain during birth or during the early years of life.
   d. a and c above.
   e. a, b, and c above.

3. Which of the following have been identified as specific causes of mental retardation?

   a. Toxic agents affecting the mother during pregnancy or the child during the early years of life.
   b. Accidental brain injury after the developmental period.
   c. Infectious childhood diseases.
   d. a and c above.
   e. a, b, and c above.

4. A faulty metabolic process causes:

   a. Hydrocephaly.
   b. Downs Syndrome.
   c. Cretinism.
   d. Microcephaly.

5. An individual with which of the following conditions has an enlarged head which may be caused by an increase in cerebrospinal fluid?

   a. Microcephaly.
   b. Downs Syndrome.
   c. Hydrocephaly.
   d. Cretinism.

6. One condition which causes mental retardation results from abnormal chromosomal groupings. This condition is called:

   a. Down's Syndrome.
   b. Lead poisoning.
   c. Encephalitis.
   d. Jaundice.

7. One or more of the following examples of social conditions that are believed to play contributory roles in the causation of mental retardation include:

   a. Inadequate prenatal care.
   b. Heredity.
   c. Adverse social conditions.
   d. a and b above.
   e. a, b, and c above.

8. It is estimated that over _____ causes of mental retardation have been identified:

   a. 25.
   b. 100.
   c. 400.
   d. 1,000.

9. Which one of the following causes of retardation is considered to be a toxic agent?

   a. Tumors.
   b. Carbon monoxide.
   c. Asphyxiation.
   d. Cerebrospinal fluid.

Answers

The answers to the preceding questions are:

1. b.
2. e.
3. d.
4. c.
5. c.
6. a.
7. e.
8. b.
9. b.

SELECTED READINGS

Apgar, V. "Neonatal Anoxia: I. A Study of the Relation of Oxygenation at Birth to Intellectual Development." *Pediatrics* 15 (1955): 652-62.

Benda, C. E. "Congenital Syphilis in Mental Deficiency." *American Journal of Mental Deficiency* 47 (1942): 40-48.

—— "Mongolism: A Comprehensive Review." *Archives of Pediatrics* 73 (1956): 391-407.

Bourne, H. "Does Virus Encephalitis Cause Mental Defect?" *American Journal of Mental Deficiency* 61 (1956): 198-203.

Bowman, P. W., and Mautner, H. V. *Proceedings of the First International Medical Conference on Mental Retardation.* New York: Grune and Stratton, 1960.

Chisholm, J. J., Jr., and Kaplan, E. "Lead Poisoning in Childhood— Comprehensive Management and Prevention." *Journal of Pediatrics* 73 (1968): 942-50.

Centerwell, W., and Centerwell, S. A. "Phenylketonuria, The Story of Its Discovery." *Journal of Historical Medicine* 16 (1961): 292-96.

Cohen, G. J., and Ahrens, W. E. "Chronic Lead Poisoning." *Journal of Pediatrics* 54 (1959): 271-84.

Dekaban, A.; O'Rourke, J.; and Cornman, T. "Abnormalities in Offspring Related to Maternal Rubella during Pregnancy." *Neurology* 8 (1958): 387-95.

Eichenlaub, J. E. "Meningitis." *Today's Health* 52 (1955): 40-42.

Etiologic Factors in Mental Retardation. Report of the twenty-third Ross Pediatric Research Conference. Columbus, Ohio: Ross Laboratories, 1957, pp. 4-93.

Glasser, F. B.; Jacobs, M.; and Schain, R. "The Relation of Rh to Mental Deficiency." *Psychiatric Quarterly* 25 (1951): 282-87.

Greenberg, M., and Pelleteri, O. "Frequency of Defects in Infants Whose Mothers Had Rubella during Pregnancy." *Journal of the American Medical Association* 165 (1957): 675-77.

Jordan, T. E. *The Mentally Retarded*, 3rd ed. Columbus, Ohio: Charles E. Merrill Publishing Co., 1972.

Kratter, F. E. "Mental Deficiency and Its Causations." *Diseases of the Nervous System* 21 (1960): 163-64.

Lejeune, J., and Turpin, R. "Chromosomal Aberrations in Man." *American Journal of Human Genetics* 13 (1961): 175-84.

Lennox, B. "Chromosomes for Beginners." *Lancet* 1 (1961): 1046-051.

Levinson, A. "Medical Aspects of Mental Deficiency." *American Journal of Mental Deficiency* 54 (1950): 476-83.

Masland, R. L. "Methodological Approaches to Research in Etiology." *American Journal of Mental Deficiency* 64 (1960): 305-10.

Mautner, H. *Mental Retardation: Its Care, Treatment, and Physiological Base.* New York: Pergamon Press, 1959.

Robinson, H. B., and Robinson, N. M. *The Mentally Retarded Child.* New York: McGraw-Hill Book Co., 1965.

Rundle, A. T. "Etiological Factors in Mental Retardation: I. Biochemical, II. Endocrinological." *American Journal of Mental Deficiency* 67 (1962): 61-78.

Smith, A. J., and Field, A. M. "A Study of the Effect of Nutrition on Mental Growth." *Journal of Home Economics* 18 (1926): 686-90.

Tarjan, G. "Research in Mental Deficiency with Emphasis on Etiology." *Bulletin of the Menninger Clinic* 24 (1960): 57-69.

Tredgold, R. F. and Soddy, K. *Tredgold's Mental Retardation*, 11th ed. Baltimore: The Williams and Wilkins Co., 1970.

Wright, S. W.; Tarjan, G.; Lippman, R. W.; and Perry, T. L. "Etiologic Factors in Mental Deficiency." *American Journal of Diseases of Children* 95 (1958): 541-62.

Yannet, H. "Classification and Etiological Factors in Mental Retardation." *Journal of Pediatrics* 50 (1957): 226-30.

UNIT 2

LESSON EIGHT
Poverty, Retardation, and the Disadvantaged Child

The total population of the United States now has passed the 210 million mark. Of this total, it is estimated that at least fifteen million families and as many as sixty million individuals are economically and socially disadvantaged because of inadequate educational programs, lack of financial resources, and limited employment opportunities. These individuals come from both the slum areas of the central city and the deprived rural areas of the country. While 3 percent of the population is considered to be mentally retarded, conservative estimates indicate that 75 percent of those known to be retarded are to be found in the depressed and impoverished urban and rural poverty areas of the country.

Children from the lower socioeconomic groups tend to enter school at a disadvantage. Because of their lack of preschool training, most such children do not learn at the same rate as other children. Although they show no observable brain damage they continue to fall farther and farther behind in their school work as they grow older. Their initial lack of readiness and continuing inadequate development appear to result from a deprivation of intellectual stimulation in a home and family life which reflect both insecurity and instability. They are born and raised in a defeatist atmosphere; their future appears bleak.

Disadvantaged children from poverty areas usually have inferior feelings about themselves which frequently are caused by unsatisfactory school experiences that continuously point up to the children their own inadequacies.

In addition, the disadvantaged frequently do not receive adequate physical care and protection. Their parents are often unable to provide housing that is reasonably safe, clean, and comfortable. Substandard living conditions are often associated with and compounded by the family's inability to provide food on a regular basis that is nourishing and well prepared. There is also inconsistent and inadequate supervision and discipline in these homes. The parents usually are so beset by their own problems that they have difficulty in accepting the responsibility for their children's development.

Children from socially deprived or culturally disadvantaged families do not receive sufficient stimulation to motivate them to achieve in school. They do not learn how to get along with others, how to wait their turn, or how to apply themselves to the development of new skills. In addition, their opportunities for acquiring a normal vocabulary are restricted for books in their homes frequently are scarce and parental interest in learning is limited; exposure to intellectual matters is light. The disadvantaged child, despite his normal potential, is destined to be the "child who will never catch up." School experiences are usually discouraging and disillusioning for him; an anti-intellectual response toward learning and a negative attitude toward school in general frequently develops in him.

Families of children from slum areas may be unable to provide protection from degrading conditions for their children. Poverty-stricken parents must live in areas where children are often exposed to many dangers; overcrowded households may force children into the streets and into places where they may come into conflict with the law. Many of these children come from broken homes or from situations in which the family as a unit is disorganized or demoralized. The child in these conditions learns to see only the reality of today; he can not see the possibility for something different in the future.

In essence, the disadvantaged child is one who often cannot postpone gratification of a desire. Tomorrow is too far off; his standards dictate that he must live for today. The desire to work toward any goal, unless it can be immediately achieved, is often nonexistent.

Thus, the disadvantaged child lives in quite a different world from that of the middle-class child. While, in general, the middle-class child learns to achieve and tends to place a high value on achievement, the disadvantaged child frequently lacks motivation and can see no real purpose in striving to make progress. While the middle-class child develops language skills which lead toward fluent use of the standard English language, the culturally disadvantaged child is linguistically impoverished. While the middle-class child frequently realizes the advantages of schooling and understands that future living standards will be influenced to a great extent by the degree of his educational achievements, the child from the poverty area views school as one more frustrating experience, which becomes increasingly more unpleasant as the years pass. While, for the most part, the middle-class child has a positive self-image, the disadvantaged child tends to place a low value on his worth as a person. Although the stability of marriage in the middle-class family appears to be on the decline, there is still generally sufficient cohesiveness to provide an adequate nurturing for the middle-class child. For this reason, the middle-class family is usually able to cope with or ward off traumatic problems. The disadvantaged retarded child, on the other hand, more often than not lives in a disrupted and disorganized family unit where the father may not be present, where social position is at its lowest, and where the family is continuously encountering stressful situations.

Yet not everything within the cultural milieu of the disadvantaged child is negative. His society does not force upon him the highly competitive struggle to outdo and surpass his peers that is frequently found in middle-class children. Though there is some degree of competition, strongly competitive rivalry is considerably less than that which is found in the middle-class group. Though there is frequently inadequate supervision for the disadvantaged child, there is also a lesser degree of family overprotection; consequently, he is sometimes freer to develop in surroundings which do not place undue demands on him.

Thus, the child from the slums or poverty-stricken sections of our country is usually a poorer performer for three major reasons. First, a lack of motivation toward achievement and toward standards of high performance hinders him. Second, the home environment fails to develop the kind of thinking and perceiving that is common in the more favored middle-class child. Third, the family structure may be unstable and, in fact, emotionally crippling to the child.

It is heartening to know that teachers are beginning to discover that pupils from disadvantaged homes do have a great capacity for learning, just as other pupils do; however, teachers and others need to realize that these children have their own ways of learning and that these often differ from the ways pupils from middle-class families learn. For example, the disadvantaged are often the children who have difficulty understanding concepts unless they do something physically. Therefore, they may need to use their hands or their bodies in trying to understand a concept. These children tend to be what might be termed "experiential learners" who learn best by doing. In other words, the disadvantaged child is typically a physical learner, and the physical learner tends to be the slow learner. If his rate of learning appears to be slower, this is probably a result of the fact that he is not at ease in the school environment. For example, he has more language ability than he is frequently given credit for having. Such linguistic skills can often be observed by permitting him to speak on subjects that are of interest to him using his own idioms. In addition, many disadvantaged children have considerable creative potential which can be aroused when properly motivated. These, then, are the children who, unlike truly mentally retarded children, need to be brought into the academic mainstream by skilled teachers and by use of a curriculum that is in keeping with the child's needs and interests.

OBJECTIVES

The adverse effects of poverty are the subject of this lesson. Upon completion you should be able to accomplish the following tasks:

1. State or identify the approximate percentage of the mentally retarded who are from the poverty areas of America.
2. Explain or identify the cause of retarded intellectual development of the majority of retarded poor.
3. State or identify the three major reasons why children from poverty areas enter school at a disadvantage.
4. Given different conditions, distinguish between those that prevail in the homes and lives of children from poverty areas and those that prevail in the homes and lives of children from middle-class America.
5. Given a description of a child from a poverty area, cite or identify methods that can be used to help the child improve his learning ability.

Please answer each of the following questions carefully. After each possible answer, you will be referred to a frame in the section beginning on p. 139 where you will be told whether or not your choice is correct. If the alternative you have selected is correct, you will be told in the answer frame which frame in the "Questions" section to turn to next. If your choice is incorrect, your answer will tell you to return to the question frame you have just answered to review and to try again. Please note that you will always be given your instructions according to frame number. Frames designated with "Q" indicate a frame in the "Questions" section (e.g., "Q-1, Q-2"). Frames designated with an "A" indicate answers. Only occasionally will you be given a page number to which to turn. It is most important that you follow the instructions for *each individual question or answer frame* most carefully.

What is Poverty?

The culturally and economically deprived comprise approximately 30 percent of the total population of America. This is a staggering figure in a country of such wealth and one with implications the more fortunate American often does not understand, for the poor are not just economically poor. Their condition is more than just a lack of money. Rather, for those who are born into it, poverty also means inadequate medical care, inadequate educational programs, and inadequate employment opportunities. It also means a culture which is different from and often regarded as being inferior by the mainstream of middle America. In sum, poverty refers to a combination of social, economic, and cultural factors. Most of the societal advantages that are taken for granted by the rest of the population are lacking in the lives of the poor.

Q-1

Poverty refers to:

a. A lack of money. Turn to A-10.
b. Adverse social, economic, and cultural conditions. Turn to A-5.

The Percentage of the Retarded
Who Come From Poverty-Stricken Homes

Q-2   It is no coincidence that an overwhelming majority of the retarded—75 percent is the estimate made by most experts in the field—come from poverty-stricken homes. This fact often offers prejudiced or ignorant people a substantiation for their erroneous claim that the poor, as a class, are poor and will always be poor because when compared to other classes in society, they have inferior intellectual endowment. It is important to note that most practitioners in the field of mental retardation regard this notion as a myth and as a way of stereotyping the poor.

The remainder of this lesson will focus on some factual data showing why an individual from a non-retarded poverty-stricken environment is at a tremendous disadvantage when entering school and in society in general.

Of all the mentally retarded individuals in the United States, _____ come from poverty-stricken homes.

a. 25 percent   Turn to A-2.
b. 75 percent   Turn to A-13.

Mental Retardation among the Poor

Q-3   There are indications that mental retardation among the poor is not necessarily related to any identifiable lack of intellectual endowment. Although a disproportionate number of the retarded are from deprived areas, a high percentage of this group is functionally retarded even though not necessarily lacking in native intelligence. In other words, it most often appears that the adverse *environmental conditions* present in the child's life retard the normal healthy development of the intellectual processes rather than the "bad" genes he has inherited from his parents.

Test yourself with this question:

From currently available information, it would appear that the major cause of mental retardation among the poor is:

a. Retarded intellectual functioning
    due to environment.   Turn to A-8.
b. Poor intellectual endowment.   Turn to A-15.

Although in most cases it is difficult to pinpoint those specific   Q-4
environmental factors leading directly to mental retardation among
the poor, it has been shown that the *cumulative effect* of *many
adverse conditions* may and often does lead to retarded development.

Which answer appears more nearly correct?

a. It is easy to pinpoint a
   specific environmental condition
   leading to mental retardation.   Turn to A-4.
b. It is the cumulative effect of
   many adverse environmental
   conditions that may lead to retardation.   Turn to A-11.

Can Children From Disadvantaged Homes Learn?

More and more teachers and other professionals are becoming   Q-5
aware of the fact that children from disadvantaged homes do have
a greater capacity to learn. At one time it was assumed that

since they could not learn at the same pace as other children, the poor were slow and, therefore, unable to learn beyond a certain level. However, as knowledge of the conditions of poverty has increased and the reasons for the poor performance of these children has become known, this notion has come to be regarded as obsolete. It has been found that these individuals probably have their own ways of learning, ways which often differ from the methods of individuals in other socioeconomic classes. New teaching methods have emerged which take these learning differences into consideration.

Most individuals from the lower socio-economic classes are:

a. Able to learn as quickly as those
   of other classes.   Turn to A-14.
b. Unable to learn beyond a certain level.   Turn to A-1.
c. Endowed with similar capacities as those
   of other classes but learn differently and
   more slowly.   Turn to A-6.

Major Reasons for Poorer
Performance by Disadvantaged Children

Q-6   There are three major reasons that can be cited to explain why most children of poverty are poorer performers in school than other children. These reasons include:

1. A *lack of motivation* toward achievement and standards of high performance. An anti-school, anti-intellectual attitude often prevails among these children. In addition, language skills are not developed early.
2. A tendency on the part of those in the child's immediate environment to foster in him *a feeling of inferiority*. The ability to work toward goals that cannot be achieved immediately is almost nonexistent among these children if they perceive failure as inevitable. Too often, this defeatist attitude prevails.
3. An *unstable family structure* where the father may not be present, where social position is low, and where the family is constantly encountering unmanageable, stressful situations.

RETARDATION AND THE DISADVANTAGED CHILD

Children from middle- or upper-class homes usually have the following major advantages which lead to greater achievement in society:

1. A *high degree of motivation and intellectual stimulation* is usually present, and achievement is given a high priority in the environment. Because education is viewed as very important, the necessary books and other materials are usually present in the home or immediate environment. Therefore, skills are developed early.
2. A *positive self-image* is fostered in the child by those in the immediate environment. Success is often assured in early life and fear of failure minimized.
3. Although a tendency toward a lack of stability in some middle- and upper-class homes is emerging, there is usually *sufficient cohesiveness* to provide an adequate nurturing for the child. These families are generally able to ward off traumatic problems themselves or to get outside help when it is needed.

Distinguish between those factors listed below that help to explain the poor performances of many children from low socioeconomic classes and those that help to explain the higher performances of those from the middle class by placing a *P* in the space beside the reasons for poor performances and an *H* beside the reasons for higher performances. Turn to A-12 to check your answers.

_____ Lack of motivation.

_____ Defeatist attitude fostered in early life.

_____ Feeling of self-worth fostered in early life.

_____ Inferiority feelings fostered in early life.

_____ Family cohesiveness.

_____ Achievement motivated.

_____ Presence of books and magazines in the home.

_____ Unstable home.

Q-7   Briefly state the three major reasons why the socioeconomically deprived child is often a poor performer in school. Then turn to A-9.

1. _____

2. _____

3. _____

How the Disadvantaged Child Learns Best

Q-8   Children from poverty are oriented more toward the physical than toward abstract processes. Therefore, they tend to learn best by doing something physical. Such activity helps them in trying to learn concepts. They tend to be experiential learners.

These children have better and more extensive linguistic abilities than may be apparent to the inexperienced or untrained teacher. If permitted, they will speak on subjects of interest to them using their own idioms (and they have a firm grasp of a rich idiomatic vocabulary). With the freedom to express themselves in their own way, they usually will make their abilities readily apparent.

Try the following question.

The disadvantaged child learns best by:

a. Conceptualizing.   Turn to A-7.
b. Doing.   Turn to A-3.

Please follow the same instructions as those you were given on page 133 in working with this section. It is most important that you remember to follow the individual instructions in each answer frame.

This statement is entirely untrue for the majority of the children from lower socioeconomic groups. It appears that the relatively small percentage of individuals who are intellectually limited at birth is the same in all socioeconomic groups. The rest of the members of these groups probably have normal potential even if they have learning disabilities.

A-1

Return to Q-5 and select another answer.

No, 25 percent of the retarded come from the more affluent homes in America. Mental retardation, like many other handicaps, is not a problem of the poor alone. It cuts across all socioeconomic classes.

A-2

Please return to Q-2 and select the other answer.

Most disadvantaged children whose disabilities are caused by adverse environmental factors do not conceptualize easily or readily. They tend to be experiential learners who learn best by doing something physical.

A-3

Please turn now to the review questions on page 143.

A-4   At the present time, it is generally difficult to pinpoint those specific adverse environmental conditions that may lead to mental retardation.

Return to Q-4 and select the other answer.

A-5   Exactly! Poverty refers to a lack of most of the social, economic, and cultural advantages that are often taken for granted by the majority of individuals in America.

Continue now with Q-2.

A-6   Yes, apparently this statement is true. The learning capacity of the majority of children from the low socioeconomic classes is not unlike that of children from the other classes in our society. Their methods of learning, however, are different, and they tend to learn more slowly.

Continue now with Q-6.

A-7   The more fortunate child appears to change more easily from a physical type of learning to a conceptual type of learning than the disadvantaged child, mainly because of the stimulating opportunities which surround him. The child of poverty has few, if any, of these opportunities and often remains at the physical learning stage for a longer period of time than his more affluent peer.

Please return to Q-8 and select the other answer.

Yes, a very large percentage of the retarded from poverty areas   A-8
appear to be so because of their environment rather than because
of faulty genes.

Continue now with Q-4.

The three major reasons for the poor performances of children   A-9
from low socioeconomic groups include:

1. A lack of motivation to achieve.
2. A low self-concept and feelings of inferiority.
3. An unstable home environment.

Did you get the correct answers? If you did, then turn to Q-8 to
continue this program.

Yes, a lack of money is at the root of poverty. However, lack of   A-10
money alone does not explain the meaning of poverty for those
living under its conditions.

Return to Q-1 and select the other answer.

Right. It appears to be the cumulative effect of many adverse   A-11
environmental conditions that may lead to retardation even
though the retarded person has no observable brain damage.

Continue now with Q-5.

A-12   You should have answered:

P—Lack of motivation.
P—Defeatist attitudes fostered.
H—Feeling of self-worth fostered.
P—Feelings of inferiority fostered.
H—Family cohesiveness.
H—Achievement motivated.
H—Presence of books and other learning materials in the home.
P—Unstable home.

How well did you do? Review any answers you missed and then turn to Q-7.

A-13   Yes, approximately 75 percent of the retarded come from poverty-stricken homes. However, mental retardation is not, as many people originally believed, a problem of the poor alone. It cuts across all socioeconomic classes.

Continue now with Q-3.

A-14   This is not the case for the majority of children from the lower class, mainly because adverse environmental conditions tend to slow down the learning capabilities of these children.

Return to Q-5 and select another answer.

A-15   Although this is a cause of mental retardation for individuals in all socioeconomic classes, it does not appear to be the *major* cause of retardation among the poor.

Please return to Q-3 and select the other answer.

Circle the *letter* corresponding to the answer of your choice.

1. The percentage of people in this country who come from economically and socially disadvantaged areas is estimated to be between:

    a. 25-30 percent.
    b. 10-20 percent.
    c. 5-10 percent.
    d. 1-3 percent.

2. The percentage of those known to be retarded who come from depressed and impoverished areas of the country is estimated to be approximately:

    a. 75 percent.
    b. 60 percent.
    c. 45 percent.
    d. 25 percent.

3. Children from poverty areas generally:

    a. Enter school at a disadvantage.
    b. Do not learn at the same rate as other children.
    c. Show no observable brain damage.
    d. All of the above.

4. Retardation in children from poverty areas appears to be caused primarily by:

    a. Faulty housing.
    b. Inadequate intellectual stimulation.
    c. Inadequate financial resources.
    d. Reading too many comic books rather than educational texts.

5. Most disadvantaged children see themselves as being:

    a. Superior.
    b. Totally adequate.
    c. Inferior.
    d. They could care less because they have no concept of themselves.

6. Most disadvantaged children from slum areas are not particularly concerned about their education because:

   a. They never seem to be able to catch up with the other children.
   b. They have an anti-intellectual attitude which comes from the home.
   c. They have poor vocabularies which make learning difficult.
   d. All of the above.

7. A lack of strenuous competition together with a lesser degree of family overprotection appears on the positive side of the ledger for the child who is from:

   a. A rich family,
   b. An average-income family.
   c. A poor family.
   d. None of the above because such conditions do not exist in any type of family.

8. Although everyone learns by physically doing something, those who seem to learn best and easiest by this method are the:

   a. Intellectually gifted children.
   b. Average children from wealthy homes.
   c. Culturally and socially deprived children.
   d. Profoundly retarded children.

9. Which of the following is not a reason for poor performance by children from slum areas?

   a. They lack native intelligence.
   b. They lack motivation to achieve.
   c. They lack an adequate home environment that supports educational achievement.
   d. They lack a stable family structure and this lack may adversely effect their emotional make-up.

Answers

The answers to the preceding questions are:

1. a.	4. b.	7. c.
2. a.	5. c.	8. c.
3. d.	6. d.	9. a.

Briggs, R. F. "The Language of Culturally Deprived Children." *Forward Trends* 10 (1966): 61-69.

Burchinal, L. G., and Siff, Hilda. "Rural Poverty." *Journal of Marriage and the Family* 26 (1964): 399-405.

Calia, V. F. "The Culturally Deprived Client: A Reformulation of the Counselor's Role." *"Journal of Counseling Psychology* 13 (1966): 100-05.

Chilman, Catherine S. *Growing Up Poor.* Washington, D.C.: U.S. Department of Health, Education, and Welfare, Welfare Administration, 1966.

Conant, J. B. *Slums and Suburbs.* New York: McGraw-Hill, 1961.

Della-Dora, D. "The Culturally Disadvantaged: Further Observations." *Exceptional Children* 29 (1963): 226-36.

Deutsch, M. "The Disadvantaged Child and the Learning Process." *Education in Depressed Areas*, edited by A. H. Possow, pp. 163-80. New York: Teachers College, Columbia University, 1963.

Dittman, Laura L., editor. *Early Child Care: The New Perspectives.* New York: Atherton Press, 1968.

Eells, K. W., et al. *Intelligence and Cultural Differences: A Study of Cultural Learning and Problem Solving.* Chicago: University of Chicago Press, 1951.

Ginzberg, E., and Bray, D. W. *The Uneducated.* New York: Columbia University Press, 1953.

Gross, M. *Learning Readiness in Two Jewish Groups: A Study in "Cultural Deprivation."* New York: Center for Urban Education, 1967.

Haywood, H. C., editor. *Social-Cultural Aspects of Mental Retardation.* New York: Appleton-Century-Croft, 1970.

Hellmuth, J., ed. *Disadvantaged Child, Vol. 3, Compensatory Education: A National Debate.* Seattle: Special Education Publications, 1970.

Hersch, C. "Child Guidance Services to the Poor." *Journal of the American Academy of Child Psychiatry* 7 (1968): 223-42.

Hess, R. D., and Shipman, V. "Early Blocks to Children's Learning." *Children* 12 (1965): 189-94.

Hurley, R. L. *Poverty and Mental Retardation—A Causal Relationship.* New York: Random House, 1969.

Jensen, A. R. "Intelligence, Learning Ability, and Socioeconomic Status." *Journal of Special Education* 3 (1969): 23-35.

John, Vera. "The Intellectual Development of Slum Children: Some Preliminary Findings." *American Journal of Orthopsychiatry* 33 (1963): 813-22.

Kirkland, Marjorie H. *Retarded Children of the Poor: A Casebook, Social, and Rehabilitation Service.* Washington, D.C.: U.S. Department of Health, Education, and Welfare, 1971.

Kugel, R. B., and Parsons, Mabel H. *Children of Deprivation: Changing the Course of Familial Retardation.* Washington, D.C.: Children's Bureau, U.S. Department of Health, Education, and Welfare, 1967.

Lapouse, R., and Weitzner, M. *"Epidemiology."* In *Mental Retardation: An Annual Review*, Vol. 1, edited by J. Wortis, pp. 197-221. New York, Grune & Stratton, 1970.

Lewis, H. *Deprived Children*. London: Oxford University Press, 1954.

Mercer, C. V., and Newbrough, J. R. "The North Nashville Health Study: Research into the Culture of the Deprived." Nashville, Tennessee: Institute on Mental Retardation and Intellectual Development, *IMRID Behavioral Science Monograph*, No. 8, 1967.

Miles To Go. Hartford: Connecticut Mental Retardation Project Report, March 1966.

Olshansky, S; Schonfield, J.; and Sternfeld, L. "Mentally Retarded or Culturally Different?" *Training School Bulletin* 59 (1962): 18-21.

President's Committee on Mental Retardation. *The Six-Hour Retarded Child*. Washington, D.C.: U.S. Department of Health, Education, and Welfare, 1970.

Reissman, F. *The Culturally Deprived Child*. New York: Harper and Row, 1962.

———. "The Culturally Deprived Child: A New View." *School Life* 45 (1963): 5-7.

Roswell, Daphne. "Some Characteristics of a Group of Deprived Subnormal Young Men." *Nursing Mirror* 120 (1965): 353-54.

Roucek, J. S., editor. *The Slow Learner*. New York: Philosophical Library, 1969.

Sarason, S., and Gladwin, T. "Psychological and Cultural Problems in Mental Subnormality." *American Journal of Mental Deficiency* 62 (1958): 1172-201.

Skeels, H. M., and Fillmore, Eva A. "Mental Development of Children from Underprivileged Homes." *Journal of Genetic Psychology* 56 (1937): 427-39.

Spodek, B. "Poverty, Education, and the Young Child." *Educational Leadership* 22 (1965): 593-604.

Teele, J. E. "Socio-Cultural Factors Relating to Mild Mental Retardation." *Social Science and Medicine* 3 (1970): 363-69.

Witmer, Helen. "Children and Poverty." *Children* 11 (1964): 207-13.

Young, W. M. "The Retarded Victims of Deprivation." *President's Committee on Mental Retardation Message* 7 (1968): 1-8.

———. "Poverty, Intelligence, and Life in the Inner City." *Mental Retardation* 7 (1969): 24-29.

Zigler, E. "Familial Mental Retardation: A Continuing Dilemma." *Science* 155 (1967): 292-98.

LESSON NINE
The Heredity-Environment Controversy

A review of the literature regarding attitudes about the inheritance of mental retardation might be traced to Sir Francis Galton, who is considered by many to be the "father of the eugenics movement." As early as 1865 he held to the idea of a systematic effort to improve or upgrade the human race by checking the birthrate of the "unfit" and furthering the procreation of the healthy individuals in our society.

Following Galton, Dr. Henry Goddard, in 1912, further advanced the theory that inheritance was a primary factor contributing to intelligence. The question of heredity versus environment as the cause of mental retardation has occupied varying degrees of prominence in the literature since Goddard's relatively famous study in which he followed the two lines of descent from Martin Kallikak, a soldier in the American Revolution who had cohabited with a mentally retarded girl. Goddard then followed the offspring of that illicit affair and compared these individuals with the offspring of Kallikak's marriage to a girl with an apparently normal background. As a result of his findings, which can be questioned in terms of modern-day design and research acceptability, Goddard believed there were overwhelming indications that inheritance was the primary factor contributing to intelligence.

In 1915 Arthur Estabrook succeeded Goddard with a follow-up study of the Jukes family, which had been surveyed in 1877 and found to have a high incidence of criminality, mental retardation, and pauperism. Estabrook was able to locate over 1,250 living members of this family, half of whom were found to be mentally retarded. Heredity apparently did play a part in the appearance of retardation in this family, but Estabrook made no clear-cut statements about the results of his study other than to indicate that both heredity and environment appeared to be involved in the causation of mental retardation.

As the result of such studies by Goddard, Estabrook, and others, an awakening concern was created in the minds of those who believed that mental retardation was an hereditary condition. Around the beginning of the twentieth century, this concern was voiced by a few well-intentioned people who felt that the solution to the problem of mental retardation was to isolate and, in many cases, sterilize the retarded so that they could not continue to produce offspring who would also be retarded.

Through the years, the controversy has raged concerning whether heredity or environment contributes more to mental deficiency. Estimates of heredity as the causative factor in mental retardation have varied from a high of 90 percent to a low of 1.7 percent. With each shift in outlook, as either heredity or environment has taken prominence, attitudes toward the retarded also have changed. By the 1930s, the heredity scare had become so pervasive that people everywhere were considering the only answer to the problems of the retarded to be institutionalization and sterilization. In part, this attitude was a reaction to earlier beliefs that the retarded could be "cured" if given adequate and proper training and education. Unfortunately, the cure did not occur because the bulk of the retarded for whom there had been a concentration of training and education up to that time had made little progress because they were primarily from groups of the seriously handicapped individuals and from groups of those less capable of responding to help.

Today, the controversy still rages, and many experts hold firmly to the opinion that if we could identify a vulnerable retarded child early enough and provide him with appropriate educational opportunities and experiences, he could be helped to achieve a relatively normal life. They argue that there is firm evidence that early detrimental surroundings and experiences may have a seriously adverse effect upon intellectual development. They believe that those retarded individuals found in residential programs and special-education classes support their claim because a large majority of these individuals come from the poor and culturally deprived areas where children have had neither the opportunity nor the stimulus to improve their functioning. Thus, those authorities who believe that environment plays a major part in causing retardation feel that the family and school must properly reinforce each other as well as the child for the child to develop to his highest potential.

One author whose research findings in support of the environmentalist point of view are most impressive is Bernadine Schmidt. Her 1946 study showed that retarded children who had spent three years in a special teaching center had made remarkable IQ improvements. Following such schooling, approximately 60 percent of the children had made IQ gains sufficient to classify them as falling within normal IQ ranges; 81 percent of the children gained at least thirty IQ points. In contrast to the group that had received special training, children in the control group had a small drop in average IQ.

Two other researchers, Skeels and Dye, reported in 1942 that they moved thirteen retarded children from an orphanage to an institution for the retarded where much attention was given to them. After two years, the median increase in IQ was approximately twenty-seven points, with the range of IQ increases extending from seven to fifty-eight points. By comparison, a group of children who remained at the orphanage and did not receive much attention were found to have a median decrease in IQ of twenty points. In addition, after the children were grown, it was discovered that those who had been given special attention in the institution were self-supporting while those who had remained in the orphanage were still living in institutions. This study tends to support the environmentalists' arguments that a good environment fosters a higher level of individual functioning.

As with other controversial matters there is disagreement among some workers in the field of mental retardation with the findings of authors such as Schmidt, and Skeels and Dye. Both of the studies have come under rather harsh criticism from some workers, who claim that neither piece of research was sufficiently controlled to provide valid results.

Those who presently expound the heredity philosophy, on the other hand, do so, in part, on the basis of some controversial research by Dr. Arthur Jensen and others which shows that biological factors are related to the level of intelligence at which a person functions. Jensen has concluded from his studies that there is a high level of probability that intelligence is inherited. His findings indicate that genetic factors are much more important than environmental factors in producing IQ differences.

The answer as to whether it is environment or heredity that is the primary causative factor of mental deficiency probably lies somewhere between these two extreme views. There is little doubt that many socially deprived children have been kept from falling into the retarded category by appropriate early intervention; the records of many agencies indicate that this is true. On the other hand, it is equally true that there are children who are only partially responsive to changes that occur in their environment and who cannot progress beyond the range of the mentally retarded in terms of intellectual achievement, even with expert help. Therefore, it appears that neither heredity nor environment alone can account for the whole of human behavior or development. There seems to be an extremely complex interaction which occurs between these two factors and which has not been completely identified as yet. Heredity cannot be denied; on the other hand, environment may also be an important factor contributing to the causation of mental retardation.

OBJECTIVES

The purpose of this lesson is to familiarize you with the three major general opinions that have been presented by researchers regarding the causation of mental subnormality as it relates to the heredity-environment controversy.

When you have completed this lesson, you will be able to accomplish the following tasks:

1. Given the name of a researcher, identify the position regarding mental retardation causation that the researcher's studies tend to substantiate.
2. Given a statement regarding mental retardation causation and a list of substantiations, identify those that substantiate the given statement.
3. Given different statements regarding mental retardation causation, decide which is the most acceptable statement in light of our present knowledge of the subject.

Please begin the programmed material now by turning to the next page.

QUESTIONS

Please answer each of the following questions carefully. After each possible answer, you will be referred to a frame in the section beginning on p. 155 where you will be told whether or not your choice is correct. If the alternative you have selected is correct, you will be told in the answer frame which frame in the "Questions" section to turn to next. If your choice is incorrect, your answer will tell you to return to the question frame you have just answered to review and to try again. Please note that you will always be given your instructions according to frame number. Frames designated with "Q" indicate a frame in the "Questions" section (e.g., "Q-1, Q-2"). Frames designated with an "A" indicate answers. Only occasionally will you be given a page number to which to turn. It is most important that you follow the instructions for *each individual question or answer frame* most carefully.

EARLY STUDIES ON INTELLIGENCE

Q-1   It had long been assumed that intelligence was inherited along with all other human attributes and, therefore, that subaverage intelligence was due, for the most part, to genetics. The first major study supposedly substantiating this assumption was Dr. Henry Goddard's research on the Kallikak family in 1912. By following the descendants of a retarded woman and those of a "normal" woman who had both borne children by the same man, Dr. Goddard concluded that there was an overwhelming indication that inheritance was the primary factor contributing to intelligence.

In 1915, Arthur Estabrook published a follow-up (*The Jukes in 1915*) of R. L. Dugdale's 1877 study *The Jukes*. Estabrook located 1250 descendants of the Jukes family and found half of these descendants to be retarded. Estabrook concluded that both heredity and environment had led to the causation of mental retardation.

As a result of these studies and many others, a controversy, which still continues today, began regarding which factor contributed the most to retardation—heredity or environment.

Dr. Henry Goddard's study lent substance to the belief that:

a. Heredity is the major cause of retardation.   Turn to A-6.
b. Environment is the major cause of retardation.   Turn to A-3.
c. Both heredity and environment are causative
   factors in retardation.   Turn to A-9.

Substantiation for the Heredity Argument

Those who believe that heredity is the primary cause of retarda-   Q-2
tion back up their argument with studies such as Dr. Goddard's
and the more recent studies of Dr. Arthur Jensen. In 1969, Dr.
Jensen presented his research, which he believed showed that
biological factors are the major cause of the level of intelligence at
which a person functions.

Those who argue that heredity is the primary factor in the causation of mental retardation can cite which of the following?

a. Jensen's studies.   Turn to A-5.
b. Goddard's studies.   Turn to A-1.
c. Both of the above.   Turn to A-8.

Substantiation for the Environmental Viewpoint

At different times during the twentieth century, the environmen-   Q-3
talists (those who argue that environmental factors are the primary
cause of intellectual functioning) have been more persuasive than
those who have propounded the heredity argument.

The environmentalist believes that there is substantial evidence
pointing to the fact that if the early environment of the retarded
child could be changed, the child would be able to live a relatively
normal life.

The environmentalist backs up his viewpoint by referring to:

1. Research such as the results obtained by Schmidt, and Skeels
   and Dye. Schmidt showed in 1946 that retarded children improved their IQs remarkably after spending three years in a
   special teaching center. In contrast, a control group which
   received no special treatment had a small drop in average IQ.

   Skeels and Dye reported that a group of retarded children who
   were sent to an institution from an orphanage and given a great
   deal of attention had a median increase in IQ of approximately
   twenty-seven points after two years, while those who remained
   in the orphanage had a median decrease of twenty points.

2. The large number of retarded individuals from poor and culturally deprived areas who are found in residential programs and in special-education classes have had neither the opportunity nor the encouragement to improve their intellectual functioning. Without such opportunity, the potential intelligence with which the child was born is not allowed to develop properly.

3. The records of many social agencies indicate that retardation has been ameliorated or eliminated with appropriate intervention at the proper time.

If you wished to argue that *environmental* conditions are the major causes of retarded intellectual development, to which of the following sources would you refer? Circle the letters of the proper sources and then turn to A-4.

a. Goddard's studies.
b. Estabrook's studies.
c. Some agency records dealing with early training.
d. Skeel's and Dye's study.
e. Jensen's studies.
f. The background of children in special-education classes.
g. The deprived conditions from which many children in residential programs come.
h. Schmidt's study.

Q-4   From our study in this lesson, we would have to conclude that subaverage intellectual functioning most often results from:

a. The early environment.   Turn to A-7.
b. Heredity.   Turn to A-2.
c. A combination of heredity and environment.   Turn to A-10.

Please follow the same instructions as those you were given on page 152 in working with this section. It is most important that you remember to follow the individual instructions in each answer frame.

Yes, Dr. Goddard's research did lend substance to the belief that inheritance plays the primary role in determining intelligence. However, this is only one of the possible sources given by those arguing that heredity is the key to intelligence.

A-1

Return to Q-2 and select the correct answer.

Although heredity has been shown to be an important factor in the causation of intellectual development and functioning, it has not been shown to be the only possible cause. Environmental influences also have been shown to be powerful determining factors.

A-2

Return to Q-4 and make another choice.

No, Dr. Goddard's research in the early 1900s lent substance to the belief that heredity and not environment was the primary factor contributing to the determination of intelligence.

A-3

Return to Q-1 and make another choice.

The letters you should have circled are c, d, f, g, and h.

A-4

Continue now with Q-4.

A-5   Dr. Jensen did conclude that the most important factor in producing differences in intelligence is inheritance. However, this is only one of the correct answers.

Return to Q-2 and select the correct answer.

A-6   Exactly! The results of Dr. Goddard's research lent substance to the hypothesis that heredity plays a major role in the causation of mental retardation.

Continue now with Q-2.

A-7   Although early environmental conditions seem to be important factors in the causation of mental deficiency, they are probably not the only causative factors. Heredity may also play a part.

Return to Q-4 and make another choice.

A-8   Exactly! The research of both Dr. Jensen and Dr. Goddard lent substance to the belief that inheritance is the primary factor in the causation of intellectual functioning.

There are many other studies and presentations that may be cited to back up this side of the controversy.

Continue now with Q-3.

No, Dr. Goddard's research in the early 1900s lent substance to   A-9
the belief that heredity alone was the major factor contributing to
an individual's intelligence. It was believed that environment had
little to contribute.

Return to Q-1 and make another selection.

This is correct. It is probably some combination of heredity and   A-10
environment that is evident in causing most cases of mental retardation.

Turn now to the conclusion on the following page.

CONCLUSION

The *Primary Cause of Mental Deficiency*

The answer to the question of whether environment or heredity is the primary cause of mental deficiency has yet to be settled. If there is an answer, it probably lies somewhere between the two extremes for it seems that both heredity and the influences of the early childhood environment combine to enhance or reduce the level of intellectual functioning of the individual. Neither environment nor heredity alone probably accounts for the intellectual development of any individual. There appears to be a highly complex interaction of these two factors.

Therefore, what is important for those involved with the retarded is not which one of these two factors is more important. Rather, they should try to discover what combination of circumstances and what specific factors lead to mental retardation and how these may be ameliorated or eliminated.

Please turn now to the review questions for this lesson to see if you have everything firmly in mind.

Circle the *letter* corresponding to the answer of your choice.

1. Cultural factors in mental retardation are:

   a. Negligible.
   b. Forces in the social environment.
   c. Not involved in the higher levels of retardation.
   d. Limited to prenatally caused factors.

2. Which of the following statements is most correct?

   a. All retardation has hereditary causation.
   b. All retardation is environmentally caused.
   c. All retardation is caused by a combination of either heredity or environment or both.
   d. None of the above are correct since no one knows what causes retardation.

3. Goddard's study focused attention on the _____ aspects causing mental retardation.

   a. Environmental.
   b. Nutritional.
   c. Medical.
   d. Hereditary.

4. Some people felt after hearing about Goddard's and Estabrook's studies that the solution to the problem of what to do with the mental retarded was to:

   a. Sterilize retardates so they could not reproduce.
   b. Segregate retardates and keep them away from society.
   c. Institutionalize retardates because they needed to be protected and kept away from others.
   d. All of the above.

5. Estimates by professional workers in the field of retardation show that there is a _____ level of agreement as to the incidence of retardation where the causation is hereditary.

   a. Very high.
   b. Somewhat high.
   c. Somewhat low.
   d. Very low.

6. Those who believe that early detrimental surroundings and experiences may have a strongly adverse effect upon intellectual development would be known as:

a. Detrimentalists.
b. Environmentalists.
c. Intellectualists.
d. Developmentalists.

7. Which of the following individuals would argue that the surroundings of a child are more important as a cause of retardation than heredity would be?

a. Arthur Jensen.
b. Kallikak.
c. Goddard.
d. Schmidt or Skeels and Dye.

8. Arthur Jensen's findings show that the major causes of retardation are:

a. Sociological.
b. Biological.
c. Environmental.
d. None of the above.

Answers

The answers to the preceding questions are:

1. b.
2. c.
3. d.
4. d.
5. d.
6. b.
7. d.
8. b.

Allen, G. "Intellectual Potential and Heredity." *Science* 133 (1961): 378-79.

Anastasi, A. "Heredity, Environment, and the Question 'How?'" *Psychological Review* 65 (1958): 197-208.

Anastasi, A., and Foley, J. P. "A Proposed Reorientation to the Heredity Environment Controversy." *Psychological Review* 55 (1948): 239-49.

Burks, B. S. "The Relative Influence of Nature and Nurture upon Mental Development: A Comparative Study of Foster Parent-Foster Child Resemblance and True Parent-True Child Resemblance." *National Society for the Study of Education Yearbook, Part 1* 27 (1928): 219-316.

Burt, C. "The Genetic Determination of Differences in Intelligence: A Study of Monozygotic Twins Reared Together and Apart." *British Journal of Psychology* 57 (1966): 137-53.

_____. "Inheritance of Mental Ability." *Eugenics Review* 49 (1957): 137-39.

_____. "Intelligence and Social Mobility." *British Journal of Statistical Psychology* 14 (1961): 2-24.

Burt, C., and Howard, N. "Heredity and Intelligence: A Reply to Criticisms." *British Journal of Statistical Psychology* 10 (1957): 33-63.

Carter, H. D. "Ten Years of Research on Twins: Contributions to the Nature-Nurture Problem." *National Society for the Study of Education Yearbook, Part 1* 39 (1940): 235-55.

Coleman, R. W., and Provence, S. "Environmental Retardation (Hospitalism) in Infants Living in Families." *Pediatrics* 19 (1957): 285.

Conant, J. B. *Slums and Suburbs.* New York: McGraw-Hill, 1961.

Conway, J. "The Inheritance of Intelligence and Its Social Implications." *British Journal of Statistical Psychology* 11 (1958): 171-90.

Davies, S. P. and Ecob, E. G. *The Mentally Retarded in Society*, 2nd ed. New York: Columbia University Press, 1959.

Dobzhansky, T. "Heredity, Environment, and Evolution." *Science* 111 (1950): 161-66.

Doll, E. A., "The Inheritance of Social Competence." *Journal of Heredity* 28 (1937): 153.

Dugdale, R. L. *The Jukes.* New York: Putnam, 1910.

Eckland, B. K. "Genetics and Sociology: A Reconsideration." *American Sociological Review* 32 (1967): 191-94.

Erlenmeyer-Kimling, L., and Jarvik, Lissy F. "Genetics and Intelligence: A Review." *Science* 142 (1964): 1477-78.

Estabrook, A. H. *The Jukes in 1915.* Washington, D.C.: Carnegie Institute, 1915.

Fehr, F. S. "Critique of Hereditarian Accounts." *Harvard Educational Review* 39 (1969): 571-80.

Fuller, J. L. *Nature and Nurture: A Modern Synthesis.* New York: Doubleday, 1954.

Goddard, H. H. *Feeblemindedness: Its Causes and Consequences.* New York: Macmillan, 1914.

_____. *The Kallikak Family.* New York: Macmillan, 1912.

Gunsberg, H. C. and Gunsberg, A. L. *Mental Handicap and Physical Environment.* Baltimore: Williams and Wilkens, 1973.

Humphreys, L. G., and Dachler, H. P. "Jensen's Theory of Intelligence." *Journal of Educational Psychology,* Part 1 60 (1969): 419-26.

Jensen, A. "How Much Can We Boost IQ and Scholastic Achievement?" *Harvard Educational Review* 39 (1969): 1-123.

Jervis, G. A. "Genetic Factors in Mental Deficiency." *American Journal of Human Genetics* 4 (1952): 260.

John, V. P. "The Intellectual Development of Slum Children: Some Preliminary Findings." *American Journal of Orthopsychiatry* 33 (1963): 813-22.

Jones, H. E. "Environmental Influences on Mental Development." In *Manual of Child Psychology,* edited by L. Carmichael. New York: John Wiley and Sons, 1946.

Kirk, S. A. *Early Education of the Mentally Retarded Child: An Experimental Study.* Urbana: University of Illinois Press, 1958.

Knobloch, H., and Pasamanick, B. "Some Thoughts on the Inheritance of Intelligence." *American Journal of Orthopsychiatry* 31 (1961): 454-73.

Leahy, A. M. "Nature-Nurture and Intelligence." *Genetic Psychology Monographs* 17 (1935): 236-308.

McCandless, B. R. "Relation of Environmental Factors to Intellectual Functioning." In *Mental Retardation,* edited by H. A. Stevens and R. Heber. Chicago: University of Chicago Press, 1964.

Montagu, A., ed. *Race and IQ.* New York: Oxford University Press, 1975.

Newman, H. H.; Freeman, F. F.; and Holzinger, K. J. *Twins: A Study of Heredity and Environment.* Chicago: University of Chicago Press, 1937.

Reed, E. W., and Reed, S. C. *Mental Retardation: A Family Study.* Philadelphia: W. B. Saunders, 1965.

Sarason, S. B., and Gladwin, T. "Psychological and Cultural Problems in Mental Subnormality: A Review of Research." *American Journal of Mental Deficiency* 62 (1958): 1115-307.

Schmidt, B. G. "Changes in Personal, Social, and Intellectual Behavior of Children Originally Classified as Feebleminded." *Psychological Monographs* 60 (1946): 1-144.

Shields, J. "Twins Brought Up Apart." *Eugenics Review* 50 (1958): 113-23.

Skeels, H. M. "Effects of Adoption on Children from Institutions." In *The Disadvantaged Child,* edited by J. J. Frost and G. R. Hawkes. Boston: Houghton-Mifflin, 1966.

Skeels, H. M., and Dye, H. B. "A Study of the Effects of Differential Stimulation on Mentally Retarded Children." *Proceedings of the American Association on Mental Deficiency* 44 (1939): 114-36.

Skodak, M., and Skeels, H. M. "A Final Follow-up Study of 100 Adopted Children." *Journal of Genetic Psychology* 75 (1949): 85-125.

Smith, R. T. "A Comparison of Socio-Environmental Factors in Monozygotic and Dizygotic Twins, Testing an Assumption." In *Methods and Goals in Human Behavior Genetics,* edited by S. G. Vandenburg. New York: Academic Press, 1965.

Spicker, H. H.; Hodges, W. L.; and McCandless, B. R. "A Diagnostically Based Curriculum for Psycho-Socially Deprived Preschool Mentally Retarded Children." *Exceptional Children* 33 (1966): 215-20.

Stinchcombe, A. L. "Environment: The Cumulation Effect Is Yet to Be Understood." *Harvard Educational Review* 39 (1969): 511-22.

Vandenburg, S. G. "Contributions of Twin Research to Psychology." *Psychological Bulletin* 66 (1966): 327-52.

Woodbury, R. S. *Heredity and Environment.* New York: Social Science Research Council, 1941.

UNIT 3

LESSON TEN
Special Problems Faced by the Family with a Retarded Child

There are few misfortunes which can befall the modern family that are more difficult to cope with than the arrested development of a child's mind. The crippling of an arm or leg is a tangible defect that most parents can understand and accept with relative ease, but the improper functioning of the brain often seems to be an unknown and, certainly, an unexpected affliction. It is not difficult to understand, therefore, why parents have difficulty in comprehending just what mental retardation means and the effects which such a condition will have upon their child.

Considerable confusion for parents is created by the fact that there is a bewildering array of known and unknown causes of retardation. (Remember in Lesson Seven you learned there are over 100 causes of retardation.) The family will often find that they have great difficulty in trying to understand the many causes of retardation and especially those causes that are specific to their own child. Parents of retarded children are also faced with problems that result in part from the inadequacy of our present knowledge for accomplishing clear-cut diagnosis. This problem is compounded because in the majority of cases, there is no specific (causal) diagnosis which can be made.

In addition, the problem is a difficult one with which families must cope because the retarded vary so much in degree of intellectual and social functioning. Sometimes the degree of retardation is clear-cut, and the parents can be informed with some degree of certainty what they can expect their child to achieve. But when diagnosis cannot be accurately made, levels of functioning cannot be anticipated, and the parents can only wait and watch the development of their child as he grows and changes. With counseling, they should be made aware of the varying levels of achievement of retarded children. They should know, for example, that there are some retarded children who will need total care for their entire lives and that there are others who can become quite independent—those who as adults will blend into society without any special concerns on the part of social agencies.

In some cases, there are parents who try to deny that their child is retarded and feel that unless the child is physically impaired or deformed, he may not be retarded. The fact that their child is retarded may not be recognized or accepted by such parents until the child's inability in the most obvious developmental activities, such as crawling, walking, and talking, has persisted long beyond the average age. Often, when a child is not attaining even the minimal level of development, there is a gnawing fear that something serious is wrong and a simultaneous unwillingness to accept retardation. This occurs for the most part because the child may still be within the wide range of possible normal development. Thus, for many parents, a high level of anxiety centers on their retarded child, and this anxiety often has adverse effects on family relationships.

There are also parents who, depending upon their emotional make-up, may begin quite early to search for medical attention through repeated examinations of their child. These are the parents who are "shopping around" in the hope that some physician, therapist, or other professional person will tell them that their child is not retarded.

Because the most obvious evidence indicating the possibility of mental retardation probably is a lack of language development, many parents will say that if their child could speak he would be normal. Caution is advised, however, in counseling such parents as it must be ascertained that the child is not suffering from a hearing loss or from some other physical problem that could prevent development of language skills. What the parents probably are saying is that if the child could only communicate, his management and total adjustment would be less complex, less slow in development, and, perhaps, a lesser problem for them to handle.

The growth and development of the retarded child tends to be slow and uneven in particular areas of functioning (e.g., speaking and reading). On the other hand, he may develop, however, in much the same manner as an average or bright child but present a combination of deficiencies caused by problems in learning which then result in lower levels of functioning. Parents become confused by this fact and by the fact that some retarded children may show quite high ability in certain specific areas.

The role of the family is central to the entire problem of the retarded child's functioning. The retarded child is basically a *child*, subject to human emotions and requiring the fulfillment of basic needs. The literature contains a great deal of information derived from studies which demonstrate that the family is a key factor in the development of any child. These studies indicate that the family assumes even greater importance when there is a mentally retarded child in the home.

There are two reasons for the importance of the role of the retarded child's family. In the first place, the retarded tends to be subject to more stress, both inside and outside the home, than the normal child. The retarded child meets greater frustration, tends to have less ability to maintain a companionship role with other children, and is not able to compete intellectually to the same degree as other children. These differences can produce an extreme emotional reaction by the parents which runs the gamut from severe overprotection to rejection. Second, it is important to note that despite the fact that a retarded child is in dire need of family surroundings which are emotionally well balanced and stable, the very nature of the child's retardation tends to create the converse of his needs; it is often found that the retardation produces a highly charged emotional situation within the family which creates an unstable situation for the child.

Although the retarded child may not be able to function in later life as a completely independent adult, some retardates approach a greater degree of independence than others. The levels and differences of performance and competence among the retarded are as varied as those existing within the normal population. Under these circumstances, there is no single approach in planning for a retarded child which will be adequate or appropriately applicable to all retarded children; consequently, no one approach will produce the same effect upon the family of every child.

When a child is retarded, family activities tend to be curtailed—often because of the amount of care which the child requires and because parents tend to become frustrated or despondent. Some parents have said that the experience of finding they had a retarded child was like living for a period of time in a great void. Some have said that they felt that they had nothing to live for, and some have even wished for their own deaths or the death of the child. There is no doubt that almost every parent of a retarded child asks the question, "How did this happen to us?" or "Why did this happen to me?" Very often, these feelings of self-doubt, depression, and even bitterness adversely influence the entire family's way of life. These negative feelings are not easily handled by members of the family and, frequently, there is even difficulty in discussing them with professional workers. But, in time, most parents are able to live with the problems presented by their child.

Thus, in every family, certain attitudes are taken toward the child and his problems in accordance with the capacities of the family. Those attitudes may range from healthful to destructive.

The most difficult problem for the parents probably centers around the question of whether to place the child in a residential care program or to continue to care for him in the home. Many parents say that they could never consider residential care for their child, and, perhaps, some of these feelings have been generated by an overemphasis on the value of community services. A little over a decade ago, the major resources for the care and training of the retarded child were the state residential facilities, and the entire direction of family planning revolved around such facilities. But as community services have developed for the retarded, the idea of keeping the child at home has become so prevalent and has weighed so heavily on the minds of many parents that even the possibility of considering institutionalization has created a considerable amount of guilt. The earlier emphasis on residential care is now being replaced with strong emphasis on the use of community services. However, many parents are beginning to realize that in certain instances and circumstances their child cannot be cared for through available community resources and may need residential care instead. Professional workers in the field should realize the importance of permitting parents to consider plans that will include both residential care as well as home care without overrating the merits of either.

Most parents of a retarded child are confronted with a persistent worry about the future of the child. This concern often takes the form of the question, "What will happen to my child when I'm no longer able to care for him?" This is a subject that both parents need to discuss openly. When parents submerge their attitudes and feelings, resentment toward each other may lead to marital problems or to a lack of harmony in the parents' relationships.

There is no best age to arrange for the child's admission to residential care. Parents must consider the child himself, the community resources, their own feelings, and the availability of residential care in making a decision about placement. Some years ago, in working with parents of retarded children, especially where the child appeared to fall intellectually at the more retarded levels, the usual recommendation by professional workers was to suggest immediate institutional care. This approach has now changed considerably, and professional people today usually suggest to parents that they consider residential care only when the need for such care appears to be most appropriate. If the child is quite physically handicapped or is severely or profoundly retarded, the need for residential care may come earlier. Each case should be treated individually. Although a given child in one family might require early removal and placement in a residential care program, in another family, the same child might be able to adjust satisfactorily without undue emotional strain on the family situation.

Generally, although not always, parents tend to go through certain common stages leading toward the acceptance of their retarded child. The first period is an awareness that their child is different. The second period is one of recognition that they, as parents, are faced with a problem that must be dealt with. The third phase is a search for the cause of the problem, and the fourth phase is looking for some means of curing the retardation. The fifth and last phase is an acceptance of the retarded child while recognizing his limitations.

This lesson is only meant to introduce the student to the complex area of special problems faced by the family. Some of the authors listed in the selected readings have gone into great depth on specific topics. The work of Bernard Faber on family integration, stresses, and strains is one example.

In this lesson we are concerned with the special problems confronting families who have retarded children. Some of the major problems which members of such families are likely to seek professional help are included. Upon completion of this lesson, you will be able to accomplish the following tasks:

1. Name or identify the five phases through which many parents of retarded children proceed as they adjust to the fact that their child is handicapped.
2. Explain or identify a description of the parents' typical reactions while they are progressing through each of the five phases.
3. Explain or identify a description of six typical problems which are particularly troublesome to the parents of a retarded child.

Please turn now to the next page.

QUESTIONS

Please answer each of the following questions carefully. After each possible answer, you will be referred to a frame in the section beginning on p. 179 where you will be told whether or not your choice is correct. If the alternative you have selected is correct, you will be told in the answer frame which frame in the "Questions" section to turn to next. If your choice is incorrect, your answer will tell you to return to the question frame you have just answered to review and to try again. Please note that you will always be given your instructions according to frame number. Frames designated with "Q" indicate a frame in the "Questions" section (e.g., "Q-1, Q-2"). Frames designated with an "A" indicate answers. Only occasionally will you be given a page number to which to turn. It is most important that you follow the instruction for *each individual question or answer frame* most carefully.

Please begin the programmed lesson on the following page.

THE PARENTAL PROBLEM OF ADJUSTMENT IN FACING
THE FACT THAT THE CHILD IS MENTALLY RETARDED

Q-1

In facing the fact of retardation, there is often a common parental pattern of behavior; however, the five phases of the usual pattern are not common to all parents. Every parent, like every other individual, is unique. Even those parents who follow the patterns to be described may be and often are involved in more than one phase during any one period of time.

Depending upon the strength of their mechanisms for coping, parents of retarded children may need either a little or a great deal of help in progressing through any or all of the five stages. Parents of children who are able to achieve a degree of independence are also likely to view their situation with less fear or anxiety.

The adjustment process usually begins with an awareness of the problem. This is often the first phase in adjustment.

Many parents, even when the facts are conclusive, tend to deny that their child is retarded, and when this denial is carried to extremes, it can become harmful to all concerned.

It is often the family doctor who discovers the severely, profoundly, or moderately retarded child. The kindergarten teacher, first-grade teacher, or possibly a counselor often discovers the mildly retarded child. However, no matter what professional person is involved, he must be aware of the possibility of the parents' initial denial and be sure to present information about the child's retardation with gentleness and patient understanding.

Parents of a retarded child often tend to _____ the fact that their child is retarded in order to avoid facing the fact of having borne a retarded child. This phase is termed _____ of the problem.

After filling in the blanks above, check your answers by turning to A-3.

Q-2   The second phase of the process of adjustment for parents is a recognition of the basic problem. Once the parents have become aware of the existence of retardation in their child, they often experience a profound sense of shock and become withdrawn and preoccupied with their own sense of inadequacy and sorrow. At this point, the counselor should help the parents face their worries and fears.

The second phase of the process for parents of facing the fact that their child is retarded is:

a. A recognition of the basic problem.   Turn to A-6.
b. Awareness of the problem.   Turn to A-9.

Q-3   Once the parents of a retarded child recognize that the problem of retardation exists, they often experience a _____ which, in some cases, can be quite profound, and they begin to withdraw and become preoccupied with a sense of inadequacy and sorrow.

Once you have filled in the blank above, go on to A-14 and check your answer.

The third phase in the process of adjustment occurs when the Q-4 parents begin to search for a cause of the condition.

The parents are often motivated in this search by one or all of the following wishes:

1. A desire to prevent having a second retarded child.
2. A desire to find a way to relieve themselves of the responsibility of having to care for the child throughout their lives.
3. A desire to find a way to relieve themselves about their concern for having borne a retarded child.

After recognizing the problem of retardation, the parents of a retarded child often begin to search for the _____ of the condition.

Fill in the blank above and then turn to A-5.

Once the parents have discovered the cause or have come to accept Q-5 the fact that there is no known cause, they often begin searching for a cure. This period of search is the fourth phase of the adjustment process.

Although there are no miraculous cures, medical science is advancing so rapidly that many parents need never lose hope for a breakthrough. However, at this point in the process, the parents must begin to accept the fact that there are no cures for their child and that they themselves must begin to learn as best they can to help their child develop to the limit of his capacities.

During the fourth phase of the process of facing the fact that their child is retarded, parents begin searching for a:

a. Cause.   Turn to A-8.
b. Cure.   Turn to A-12.

Q-6 When the parents are able to switch their energies from searching for a cure to searching for realistic ways of helping their child to develop, they have entered the fifth and final phase in the process of facing the problem. They are on their way toward acceptance of the child.

Acceptance of the retarded child, just as of normal children, involves such feelings as warm appreciation of his individuality, pride in his assets, and tolerance for his shortcomings. During this phase, the professional must be able to help the parents understand the fact that there is little difference between a retarded child and a normal child when it comes to acceptance. If anything, the retarded child may need to be accepted more than does his normal sibling.

As a method for checking yourself, list below the five phases of the adjustment process for parents of retarded children.

Then turn to A-1.

1. _____ .

2. _____ .

3. _____ .

4. _____ .

5. _____ .

SIX TYPICAL PROBLEMS FACED BY
FAMILIES WITH A RETARDED CHILD

The six problems presented here are common enough so that Q-7 almost every person who has worked with the retarded and their families will recognize them.

The first problem is that many families attempt to overprotect the retarded child. This stems from a perfectly normal desire to protect someone younger or weaker than oneself, but families often have ambivalent emotions regarding the retarded child which they express through overprotection. Although this may be an easier method of coping with the child and at the same time salving wounded egos for the parents, it will result in failure to encourage the retarded child to achieve his maximum growth and independence.

One problem which often occurs in families with a retarded child is a tendency toward _____ .

Fill in the blank and then turn to A-11.

The second problem that typically develops is a weakening of Q-8 family integration. The presence of the retarded child creates psychological and emotional conditions which can literally tear the family apart. Family integration and cohesion as a unit can be seriously undermined by the constant demands put on it by the needs of the retarded child.

The third problem common among families having the combination of both normal and retarded children in the home is the possible development of adverse effects on the normal siblings.

There are indications that most children can adapt themselves to the presence of the retarded brother or sister. Only when they are pushed aside or expected to assume maturity and responsibility beyond their years are they likely to suffer serious consequences.

Please fill in the blanks below and then turn to A-4.

For your review, list below the three typical problems that have been discussed so far that commonly occur in families with retarded children.

1. _____.
2. _____.
3._____.

Q-9   The fourth typical problem is limitation of family activities. Parents often find that they are unable to go out together because of excessive concern about the child's welfare, even when a competent baby-sitter can be found. Taking the child with them is also difficult since families may be embarrassed or fear public reactions—especially in cases where there is an obviously abnormal appearance.

As society matures and becomes more accepting of differences, it is to be hoped that this problem will be greatly reduced.

Fill in the blanks below and then turn to A-7.

A fourth typical problem experienced by families with a retarded child is _____ of family_____.

The fifth typical problem is the necessity of constant supervision of the child's activities for fear the child might hurt himself or damage home furnishings. Some children need continuous nursing care if they are severely retarded.

Overexhaustion of the mother and sometimes of the father may result from this physical necessity. The only remedy often is to remove the child or the parents temporarily. In this case, even if professional services are available, the cost of bringing in a competent professional caretaker for even a short time may be outside the family's financial reach. When this is true, removal of the child to a temporary foster home or other institutional setting may be required.

Which of the following are possible solutions to the problem of constant supervision of the child?

a. Remove him from the home temporarily.   Turn to A-13.
b. Bring in a professional caretaker
   to give the parents a rest.   Turn to A-10.
c. Both of the above.   Turn to A-2.

Q-11   The sixth and last typical problem is the burden on the family of additional expenses.

Since retardation is a life-long condition, parents often must anticipate expenditures greater than those needed for normal children. Although there are many more services available now at a reasonable cost, the total cost for the length of time that they are needed may be large indeed. It is also true that in many geographic areas there is a lack of services so that parents must bear the entire burden without any assistance from society.

This lesson has discussed six major common problems of parents of retarded children. List these six problems below and then turn to A-15.

1. _____.

2. _____.

3. _____.

4. _____.

5. _____.

6. _____.

Please follow the same instructions as those you were given on page 170 in working with this section. It is important that you remember to follow the individual instructions in each answer frame.

A-1

The five phases in adjustment are:

1. Awareness of the problem.
2. Recognition of the basic problem.
3. Search for a cause.
4. Search for a cure.
5. Acceptance of the child.

Proceed now to Q-7.

A-2

You have chosen the correct answer. Both solutions are possible. Parents can either remove the child or remove themselves; either way they will be able to obtain a needed rest from constant care and supervision of the child.

Continue now to Q-11 for the sixth common problem.

A-3

The blanks should have the words "deny" and "awareness." Parents tend to *deny* the fact of their child's retardation during the first phase of adjustment, which is termed *awareness* of the problem. Awareness may bring about this denial.

Now turn back to Q-2 to learn about the second phase of the parent's adjustment process.

A-4   Three of the problems typically found in families with a retarded child are:

1. Tendencies toward overprotection of the retardate.
2. Weakening of family integration or cohesiveness.
3. Adverse effects on normal siblings.

Go on now to Q-9.

A-5   The blank should have been filled in with the word "cause." After recognition of the problem, parents often begin to search for a *cause* of the condition. This search is the third phase of the adjustment process.

Continue now with Q-5.

A-6   Yes, recognizing the basic problem of retardation is the second phase through which many parents of retarded children progress when adjusting to the fact that their child is different.

This is the correct answer; go on now to Q-3.

A-7   The blanks should have been filled in with the words "limitation" and "activities." Thus, *limitation* of family *activities* is the fourth in the list of typical problems experiences by parents of a retarded child.

Continue now to Q-10.

Parents are in the third phase when they begin searching for a   A-8
cause of their child's condition.

Return to the second paragraph on page 168 for a review before
answering Q-5 correctly.

Awareness of the problem is the first phase of the process of   A-9
adjustment for parents of retarded children.

Return to Q-2 since you had trouble with this question and review
the material presented there.

This is correct in part. Giving the parents a rest from the   A-10
exhausting task of constantly supervising the activities of the
retarded child can be accomplished by bringing in a competent
caretaker. However, a homemaker service may not be available or
they may be too expensive a solution for many parents. But there
is also another alternative.

Return to page 177 and review the material presented there before
answering Q-10 correctly.

You should have filled in the blank with the word "overprotec-   A-11
tion." Parents of a retarded child often develop tendencies toward
overprotection of the retarded child.

When parents overprotect a child, especially a retarded child, he
becomes more dependent on them, thus exaggerating his inability
to cope with his environment.

Go right on to Q-8.

A-12   This is correct. Parents begin to search for a cure during the fourth phase of adjustment.

During this phase, the counselor must help the parents to accept the fact that there are no known cures and to realize as well that they are capable of helping their child reach his potential limits.

Go on now to Q-6.

A-13   Yes, this is one possible solution to the problem of constant supervision. However, it is not the only solution.

Return to Q-10 and review the material presented there.

A-14   The blank should have been filled in with the word "shock." Parents of retarded children often experience a *shock* upon recognizing that their child is retarded. Withdrawal often follows, and a sense of inadequacy and sorrow may result.

Turn to Q-4 for a brief description of the third phase of adjustment.

If you have written all six items correctly, they should look similar to the following:

1. Tendencies toward overprotection of the retardate.
2. Weakening of family integration or cohesiveness.
3. Adverse effects on the normal siblings, if there are both normal and retarded children in the family.
4. Limitation of family activities.
5. Constant supervision and care of the retardate.
6. Additional expenses which often last for the entire lives of the parents.

Were all six items correct? If you can answer affirmatively, you should proceed to the review questions on the next page. However, if the answer is "no," please return to page 175 and review the lesson before going on to the next page.

REVIEW QUESTIONS—LESSON TEN

Questions

Circle the *letter* corresponding to the answer of your choice.

1. The second phase that many parents go through in facing the fact that their child is retarded is referred to as:

    a. Awareness of the problem.
    b. Search for a cause.
    c. Recognition of the problem.
    d. Search for a cure.

2. Parents are involved in the fourth phase of the process of facing the fact that their child is retarded when they begin to:

    a. Search for a cure.
    b. Search for a cause.
    c. Accept the child as he is.
    d. Temporarily reject the child.

3. In which phase of the process of facing the fact that their child is retarded are the parents when they are searching for a cause of the condition?

    a. First.
    b. Second.
    c. Third.
    d. Fourth.

4. Parents often begin to search for a cause of their child's retardation in order to:

    a. Relieve their feelings of anxiety and concern.
    b. Prevent having another retarded child.
    c. Relieve their burden of responsibility.
    d. b and c above.
    e. a, b, and c above.

5. Which of the following problems occur more often in families with a retarded child than in families without such a child?

    a. Parental tendencies toward overprotectiveness.
    b. Adverse effects on the normal siblings.
    c. Weakening of family integration or togetherness.
    d. a and c above.
    e. a, b, and c above.

6. Of the following, which is not one of the most troublesome problems of everyday life cited by parents of retarded children?

    a. Additional expenses.
    b. Inability to communicate with the child.
    c. Limitation of family activities.
    d. Constant supervision of the child.

Answers

The answers to the preceding questions are:

1. c.
2. a.
3. c.
4. e.
5. e.
6. b.

SELECTED READINGS

Bernstein, N. R., ed. *Diminished People: Problems and Care of the Mentally Retarded.* Boston: Little, Brown & Co., 1970.

Boyd, D. "The Three Stages in the Growth of a Parent of a Mentally Retarded Child." *American Journal of Mental Deficiency* 55 (1951): 608-11.

Dittman, L. L. *The Mentally Retarded Child at Home.* Children's Bureau Publication Number 374. Washington, D.C.: U.S. Department of Health, Education, and Welfare, 1959.

Drayer, C., and Schlesinger, E. G. "The Informing Interview." *American Journal of Mental Deficiency* 65 (1960): 363-70.

Ehlers, W. H. *Mothers of Retarded Children: How They Feel, Where They Find Help.* Springfield, Illinois: Charles C. Thomas Co., 1966.

Farber, B. "Effects of a Severely Mentally Retarded Child on Family Integration." *Monographs of the Society for Research in Child Development* 24 (1959): 1-112.

_____. "Family Organization and Crisis: Maintenance of Integration in Families with a Severely Mentally Retarded Child." *Monographs of the Society for Research in Child Development* 25 (1960): 1-95.

_____. "Perceptions of Crisis and Related Variables in the Impact of a Retarded Child on the Mother." *Journal of Health and Human Behavior* 1 (1960): 108-18.

Farber, H.; Jenne, W. C.; and Toigo, R. "Family Crisis and the Decision to Institutionalize the Retarded Child." *Council for Exceptional Children Research Monograph* Series A, Number 1 (1960): 1-66.

Forbes, L. M. "Some Psychiatric Problems Related to Mental Retardation." *American Journal of Mental Deficiency* 62 (1958): 637-41.

Fowle, C. M. "The Effect of the Severely Mentally Retarded Child on His Family." *American Journal of Mental Deficiency* 73 (1968): 468-73.

Gordon, E. W., and Ullman, M. "Reactions of Parents to Problems of Mental Retardation in Children." *American Journal of Mental Deficiency* 61 (1956): 158-63.

Grebler, A. M. "Parental Attitudes toward Mentally Retarded Children." *American Journal of Mental Deficiency* 56 (1952): 475-83.

Heilman, A. E. "Parental Adjustment of the Dull Handicapped Child." *American Journal of Mental Deficiency* 54 (1950): 556-62.

Kanner, L. "Parents' Feelings about Retarded Children." *American Journal of Mental Deficiency* 57 (1953): 375-83.

Kennedy, J. "Maternal Reactions to the Birth of a Defective Baby." *Social Casework* 51 (1970): 410-16.

Klebanoff, L. "Parental Attitudes of Mothers of Schizophrenic, Brain-Injured and Retarded, and Normal Children." *American Journal of Orthopsychiatry* 29 (1959): 445-54.

Krishef, C. H. "State Laws on Marriage and Sterilization of the Mentally Retarded." *Mental Retardation* 10 (1972): 36-38.

Kvaraceus, W. C. "Acceptance-Rejection and Exceptionality." *Exceptional Children* 22 (1956): 328-31.

Lethberthson, E. "Helping Families Live with and for the Mentally Retarded Child." *Journal of Rehabilitation* 34 (1968): 24-26.

Levy, D. J. *Maternal Overprotection.* New York: Columbia University Press, 1943.

Lobo, E. de H., and Webb, A. "Parental Reactions to Their Mongol Baby." *The Practitioner* 204 (1970): 1221.

Mercer, J. R. "Patterns of Family Crisis Related to Reacceptance of the Retardate." *California Mental Health Research Digest* 3(1965): 112-14.

Metheny, A. P., Jr., and Vernick, J. "Parents of the Mentally Retarded Child: Emotionally Overwhelmed or Informationally Deprived?" *Journal of Pediatrics* 74 (1969): 954-59.

Meyerowitz, J. H. "Parental Awareness of Retardation." *American Journal of Mental Deficiency* 71 (1967): 637-43.

Olshansky, S. "Chronic Sorrow: A Response to Having a Mentally Defective Child." *Social Casework* 43 (1962): 190-93.

Owens, C. "Parents' Reactions to Defective Babies." *American Journal of Nursing* 64 (1964): 83-86.

Patterson, L. L. "Some Pointers for Professionals." *Children* 3 (1956): 13-17.

Peck, J. R., and Stephens, W. B. "A Study of the Relationships between the Attitudes and Behavior of Parents and That of Their Mentally Defective Child." *American Journal of Mental Deficiency* 64 (1960): 839-43.

Rheingold, H. "Interpreting Mental Retardation to Parents." *Journal of Consulting Psychology* 9 (1945): 142-48.

Rosen, L. "Selected Aspects in the Development of the Mother's Understanding of Her Mentally Retarded Child." *American Journal of Mental Deficiency* 59 (1955): 522-28.

Schild, S. "Counseling with Parents of Retarded Children Living at Home." *Social Work* 9 (1964): 86-91.

Schonell, F. J., and Watts, B. H. "A First Survey of the Effects of a Subnormal Child on the Family Unit." *American Journal of Mental Deficiency* 61 (1956): 210-19.

Stone, N. D., and Parnicky, J. J. "Factors in Child Placement: Parental Response to Congenital Defect." *Social Work* 11 (1966): 35-43.

Waterman, J. H. "Psychogenic Factors in Parental Acceptance of Feeble-minded Children." *Diseases of the Nervous System* 9 (1948): 184-87.

Wolfensberger, W., and Kurtz, R. A., editors. *Management of the Family of the Mentally Retarded.* Chicago: Follett Educational Corporation, 1969.

Worchel, P., and Worchel, T. L. "The Parental Concept of the Mentally Retarded Child." *American Journal of Mental Deficiency* 65 (1961): 782-88.

Zuk, G. H. "The Religious Factor and the Role of Guilt in Parental Acceptance of the Retarded Child." *American Journal of Mental Deficiency* 64 (1959): 139-47.

Zwerling, I. "Initial Counseling of Parents with Mentally Retarded Children." *Journal of Pediatrics* 44 (1954): 469-79.

UNIT 3

LESSON ELEVEN
Counseling the Parents of Retarded Children

Because the problem of mental retardation is very complicated, there are numerous elements that contribute to its profound personal and social impact. Among these are the generally negative attitudes which have prevailed in the past and which to some extent carry through into today's world. Caught in this web of complexities and misunderstandings is the retarded person himself and his family. What needs to be done to help them both? How should the family be counseled in order to assist them in rising above the stigma of retardation and its accompanying problems?

All parents show one of three basic responses toward their retarded child. First, the child is accepted for what he is as he is, and the parents, recognizing the child's limitations, try to the best of their abilities to provide the most wholesome environment possible in which the child can achieve his highest possible level. Second, the parents either accept or reject the child, with possible shadings of both of these two reactions, but decide to institutionalize him. Third, they reject the child either in part or in whole.

These categories often overlap from one to the next. Some parents have particular difficulty in establishing realistic levels of aspiration for their retarded child; some suffer inordinately from outside pressures caused by relatives, neighbors, and community where there is an unsympathetic attitude about the child who is "different." All of these responses, and, perhaps, many more frequently create a need for counseling services.

It can be stated unequivocally that parents never wish for the birth of a retarded child; they are generally ill-prepared for the presence of such a problem, and the counselor needs to help them understand and, to the greatest extent possible, accept the child.

Usually, parents want and need help. They may not understand why their child is retarded, and they may feel that in some way they are to blame for something they did or did not do. They may react to these feelings by rejecting the child or by being over-protective or overdemanding. These parents need help in solving the problems with which they are confronted. They need to know what type of home atmosphere and training the child will require in order to fully develop his limited capabilities.

In working with parents, the counselor should remember that parents are important in the lives of their children. They live with their retarded child and maintain closer ties to him than does anyone else. Whether the parents appear adequate or inadequate to the counselor, whether they seem to have unusual insight or are totally uninformed about the problems of their children, whether they are deeply interested or entirely superficial in their attitudes, they are the parents and, as such, enjoy more opportunities, responsibilities, and privileges than anyone else in the child's world.

Always keeping in mind the parents' point of view, the counselor should attempt to direct discussion to those problems that seem to be of the greatest importance to the parents. When parents seek professional help, counseling should be directed toward:

1. Helping them to be more objective about their child.
2. Helping them to learn about behavior their child will outgrow and behavior they can expect to continue.
3. Helping them to assimilate ideas about handling various problem situations common to families of a retarded child.
4. Advising them about the help books and pamphlets can provide and making these materials available for their study and use.

5. Assisting them in learning how to handle their retarded child more successfully and with greater acceptance, understanding, and knowledge.
6. Aiding them in helping the child engage in leisure-time pursuits and other constructive activities which may result in a happier child and, therefore, a happier family.
7. Advising them regarding the community resources which are available (e.g., clinics, evaluation centers, parents' groups, sheltered workshops, and educational institutions for the retarded).

Those who work as counselors with parents of retarded children should understand the difficulties which these parents must face. Parents have suddenly been confronted with an overwhelming problem, and they may feel that they are uniquely alone and isolated. They may feel more alone than they have felt or will feel at any other time in their lives.

Perhaps the greatest need of parents, especially when they first learn that they have a retarded child, is to have someone with whom they can talk, someone who will understand their feelings, someone familiar with the field of retardation, someone with whom they can share their fears and concerns; that someone can be the counselor.

A source of ongoing help for many parents may exist in the form of an association for retarded children. Such organizations often stimulate services for the retarded and enable parents to offer support to one another.

The objective of this lesson is to acquaint you with some of the major principles that a professional counselor should bear in mind when counseling parents of a retarded child. When this lesson is completed, you will be able to accomplish the following tasks:

1. Identify the foundation upon which all counseling, including counseling parents of a retarded child, is based.
2. State in your own words the two steps involved in developing a foundation in counseling.
3. Describe in your own words the basic fact that the counselor must keep in mind when working with parents of a retarded child.
4. State in your own words at least seven of the nine principles of counseling that are of particular significance when counseling parents of a retarded child.
5. Identify the possible consequences when the principles are not followed by the counselor.

When filling in blanks or writing answers to questions remember that the goal is to understand the idea and not just memorize words. Therefore, as long as your answers are similar to the ones presented in the lessons, they are completely acceptable.

QUESTIONS

Please answer each of the following questions carefully. After each possible answer, you will be referred to a frame in the section beginning of p. 200 where you will be told whether or not your choice is correct. If the alternative you have selected is correct, you will be told in the answer frame which frame in the "Questions" section to turn to next. If your choice is incorrect, your answer will tell you to return to the question frame you have just answered to review and to try again. Please note that you will always be given your instructions according to frame number. Frames designated with "Q" indicate a frame in the "Questions" section (e.g., "Q-1, Q-2"). Frames designated with an "A" indicate answers. Only occasionally will you be given a page number to which to turn. It is most important that you follow the instructions for *each individual question or answer frame* most carefully.

THE FOUNDATION OF COUNSELING

Q-1   Although the following statement may be perfectly evident, it needs to be repeated often. The foundation upon which all counseling rests, including counseling the retarded and their parents, is competency in counseling.

Competency in counseling involves two factors:

1. Gaining a basic knowledge of the principles of counseling.
2. Applying these principles directly in field experience.

Choose the best answer to complete the following statement.

The foundation of counseling, including counseling parents of retarded children, is developed by:

a. Learning the principles of counseling only. Turn to A-6.
b. Learning the principles of counseling
   and then applying them in practice. Turn to A-14.

COUNSELING PARENTS OF A RETARDED CHILD

Q-2

Before discussing those principles of counseling which are significant when counseling parents of a retarded child, we should emphasize the immensity of the shock upon the parents when they find out that their child is retarded. Even parents who have had close contact with retarded children often find themselves in a state of shock when told that their own child is retarded.

A cognizance on the part of the counselor of this shock factor and learning to deal with it is what separates the counseling of parents with a retarded child from the counseling of most other clients.

In the space below, state the basic fact that separates counseling parents of retarded children from counseling all other clients. Then turn to A-10 to check your answer.

_____

_____

_____

NINE BASIC PRINCIPLES

Q-3

Of the many principles of counseling, nine should be kept uppermost in mind when counseling parents of a retarded child.

First, the counselor should go out of his way if necessary to involve both parents in the counseling process.

When the counselor fails to include both parents, distortions in behavior of child or parent and marital friction may result. Parents may come to disregard the findings of the counselor. Above all, involving both parents often serves the unique function of alleviating the anxiety of each parent by focusing on the mutuality of feelings and responsibility.

Fill in the blanks below and then turn to A-15.

In order to help avoid friction and distortions of parent or child behavior and help to alleviate anxiety feelings by focusing on the mutuality of feelings and responsibility, the counselor should try his utmost to _____ _____ _____ in the counseling process.

Q-4   During the first interview with the parents the counselor should be sure to apply the following additional principles:

1. Give a great deal of support and understanding. Since this period usually is an extremely sensitive time for the parents they may easily develop rigid defense mechanisms which will be difficult to dispel later on if they are not given initial support and understanding.
2. Emphasize the value of the feedback interview (question-and-answer interview) and subsequent follow-up interviews.
3. Urge parents to take advantage of whatever other kind of help and service they may need from community service agencies for the mentally retarded. (You will learn about many of the services for the retarded in Lesson Thirteen.) Without such follow-up services, diagnosis alone can be frustrating and valueless.

For review now ask yourself, "What are the three principles that the counselor should remember to apply during the first interview with the parents of a retarded child?"

Check your answers by turning to A-3.

_____

_____

_____

Q-5   By giving the parents more support and understanding than usual during the first interview, what may be avoided?

See A-19 to check your answer.

_____

_____

_____

To review then:

What are the four principles mentioned so far?

Fill in the blanks and then turn to A-7.

1. _____

_____

2. _____

_____

3. _____

_____

_____

4. _____

_____

The next five principles apply to the feedback and subsequent
follow-up interviews.

The first of these principles is that the counselor should never
initiate an interview, especially the feedback interview with the
parents, until he has gathered and understands all of the relevant
facts concerning the retarded child.

Test yourself with this question:

What should the counselor do before initiating a feedback
interview as well as any other interview with parents of a retarded
child?

Fill in the blanks and then turn to A-17 to check your answers.

_____

_____

_____

_____

Q-8   During either the feedback or the first follow-up interview with the parents of a retarded child, the counselor should give a prognosis of the child's future functioning. This is the sixth significant principle of such counseling.

The counselor must be sure to base his prognosis on an accurate, carefully conducted individual diagnostic evaluation. He should base the prognosis on the child himself and not on the general stereotype of the child's condition. Emphasis should be placed on what the child will be able to do rather than on what he will be unable to do.

When parents are given incorrect or stereotyped prognoses, they may not only lose faith in all professional practice but also find it more difficult to accept their child's retardation.

Now check yourself by answering the following question.

When giving the parents of a retarded child a prognosis, the counselor should base it on which of the following?

a. The basic stereotype of the child's condition.   Turn to A-11.
b. The diagnostic evaluation.   Turn to A-4.
c. What the child will be unable to do.   Turn to A-1.
d. b and c above.   Turn to A-16.

Q-9   Before the close of the feedback interview, the parents should be given some written feedback, such as descriptions of their child's condition and of problems that may develop, to which they can refer in order to reduce the chances of distorting and misunderstanding the findings concerning the child. This material should be clearly written and easily understandable by the parents.

In order to reduce the chances of distorting or misunderstanding the findings concerning their child, parents should be given some type of _____ _____ to which they can refer whenever the need arises.

Check your answers by turning to A-8.

During the feedback and all subsequent follow-up interviews, the   Q-10
counselor should remember to apply the eighth principle of
counseling parents of retarded children. This principle is to focus
in an objective manner on the problems of the parents as they
attempt to deal with the child on a day-by-day basis. Some of the
major problems were presented in Lesson Ten. Before going on,
see if you can recall these problems. Write down what you
remember regarding the typical problems faced by parents.

1. _____
2. _____
3. _____
4. _____
5. _____
6. _____

To see how well you did turn to A-12.

The counselor must be objective when focusing on the parents'   Q-11
problems and he also must help them learn to become more objective. The ultimate goal embodied in this eighth principle is to
help the parents learn how to solve their problems by using all of the
resources available, including their own strengths as well as community social services.

Test yourself with this question:

What is the eighth and most important principle that the counselor
should apply when counseling parents of retarded children?

_____
_____
_____

Check your answer by turning to A-18.

Q-12   What is the ultimate goal of the eighth principle of counseling the parents of a retarded child?

_____

_____

_____

After filling in the blanks turn to A-9.

Q-13   The last significant principle of counseling parents of a retarded child concerns agency policy. Agencies should make every effort to preserve the continuity of the relationship between one main contact person and the parents.

The parents may become confused and frustrated if they are subjected to differing viewpoints concerning their child's condition and/or potential. This situation often occurs when multiple counseling is employed.

Concerning the counseling of parents of a retarded child, agency policy should be to:

a. Employ multiple counseling whenever possible.   Turn to A-2.
b. Preserve the continuity of relationship between
    one counselor and the parents.   Turn to A-5.

To review the nine principles, please state in the space below and Q-14 in your own words the principles of counseling that are of particular significance in counseling parents of a retarded child.

1. _____.

2. _____.

3. _____.

4. _____.

5. _____.

6. _____.

7. _____.

8. _____.

9. _____.

Now check your answers by turning to A-13.

ANSWERS

Please follow the same instructions as those you were given on page 192 in working with this section. It is most important that you remember to follow the individual instructions in each answer frame.

A-1 Some counselors erroneously base their prognosis of a retarded child on what he will be unable to do. This is not a constructive approach. Being positive in revealing the capabilities of the child is far more helpful than listing all the things that the child will be unable to do.

Return to Q-8 on page 196 and review the material presented there; then select the correct answer for Q-8.

A-2 You may be able to come up with some plausible reason for employing multiple counseling with the parents of a retarded child, but it would probably apply in an unusual case or situation.

For the present moment, return to Q-13 and choose the other answer.

A-3 1. The counselor should be sure to give the parents a great deal of support and understanding during the first interview.
2. He should also help them to realize the value of the feedback and subsequent follow-up interviews.
3. He should make sure that they take advantage of other services they may need.

Continue now with Q-5.

Quite right! The prognosis should be based on the diagnostic   A-4
evaluation of the retarded child. Emphasis should be placed on
what he will be able to do rather than on what he will be unable to
do.

Continue now with Q-9.

Yes, this is the most feasible policy that an agency should try to   A-5
employ. One counselor within each agency should be the contact
person for the parents of a retarded child.

Continue now with Q-14.

Although learning the principles of counseling is the first step   A-6
toward competency in counseling, it is not the only step.

Return to page 192 and review the material presented there before
trying to answer Q-1 again.

The first four principles of counseling parents of retarded children   A-7
include:

1. Involving both parents in the counseling process.
2. Giving the parents a great deal of support and understanding,
   especially during the first interview.
3. Relating the value of feedback and follow-up interviews during
   the first interview if possible.
4. Making sure the parents take advantage of other community
   services they may need.

Continue now with Q-7.

A-8   You should have filled in the blanks with the words "written" feedback." Parents of a retarded child should be given some type of *written feedback* concerning their child in order to avoid misunderstanding or distortions.

Continue now with Q-10.

A-9   The ultimate goal is to help parents utilize all available personal and community resources for the solution of the problems.

Continue now with Q-13.

A-10   The basic fact that separates the counseling of parents of retarded children from the counseling of most other clients is that when parents find out their child is retarded, they usually experience a severe shock. The counselor, in order to be effective, must be cognizant of this reaction and learn to deal with it.

Continue now with Q-3.

A-11   No, the prognosis should never be based on the stereotype of the child's condition.

Return to page 196 and review the material presented there; then select the correct answer for Q-8.

Some of the major problems that are typical of families with   A-12
retarded children include:

1. Tendencies toward overprotection.
2. Weakening of family integration.
3. Adverse effects on normal siblings.
4. Limitation of family activities.
5. Constant supervision.
6. Additional expenses.

Did you get all of these items right? If not, you may want to
review Lesson Ten.

Continue now with Q-11.

The following principles are of particular significance for the   A-13
counselor of parents of a retarded child.

1. Involve both parents in the counseling process.
2. During the first interview give the parents a great deal of
   support and understanding.
3. Help the parents during the first interview to realize the value of
   the feedback and subsequent follow-up interviews.
4. During the first interview also make sure that the parents take
   advantage of other community services they may need.

   (The remaining five principles apply especially to the feedback
   and follow-up interviews.)

5. Gather and understand all of the relevant facts concerning the
   retarded child.
6. Base the child's prognosis on an accurate diagnostic evaluation
   emphazing what the child will be able to do.
7. Give the parents clear and concise written feedback.
8. Focus on the parents' problems in an objective manner and
   work toward their solution.
9. Preserve the continuity of the relationship between the main
   counselor and the parents.

If you have satisfactorily stated at least seven of these principles
you have completed this lesson. If not, you need to reread the
material before continuing. If you are ready for the review
questions turn to page 206.

A-14   Right you are! One develops competency in counseling by first learning the principles of counseling and then applying them in practice.

Continue now with Q-2.

A-15   Did you write in "to involve both parents"? By involving both parents in the counseling process, the counselor may help them to avoid marital friction and distortions of findings as well as help to alleviate feelings of anxiety and self-doubt.

Continue now with Q-4.

A-16   Although you are partially correct, you will only be partially effective with the parents of a retarded child. The prognosis should be based on an accurate diagnostic evaluation, but listing the things that the child will be unable to do may do more harm than good.

Return to page 196 and review the material presented there; then select the correct answer for Q-8.

A-17   The counselor should gather and understand all the available relevant facts regarding the retarded child before initiating a feedback or any other interview with the parents.

Continue now with Q-8.

The eighth and most important principle is to focus on the actual   A-18
problems being experienced by the parents and to help them work
toward their solution.

Continue now with Q-12.

If the parents are given a great deal of support and understanding,   A-19
we may be able to avoid the development of rigid defense
mechanisms which will be very difficult to dispel later.

Continue now with Q-6.

REVIEW QUESTIONS—LESSON ELEVEN

Questions

Circle the *letter* corresponding to the answer of your choice.

1. One major organization which is a source of ongoing help offering opportunities for many parents of retarded children to seek support and assistance from others who have similar problems is:

   a. The American Association on Mental Deficiency.
   b. The Associations for Retarded Children.
   c. The Council for Exceptional Children.
   d. All of the above.
   e. None of the above.

2. The counselor of the retarded and their families should cultivate the belief in the right of self-determination with no limitations for the retarded individual. This statement is:

   a. Correct in all respects.
   b. Incorrect; this is not an attitude that a counselor needs to cultivate.
   c. Correct, except that the limitations should be the same as for a normal individual.
   d. Incorrect; the counselor must consider whether or not it is diagnostically sound to allow the retarded person to determine what is best for him.

3. Which of the following choices is considered to be the foundation of counseling, including counseling the parents of retarded children?

   a. The development of tolerance to the problem of retardation.
   b. The development of competency in counseling.
   c. The development of special attitudes toward the retarded and their parents.
   d. None of the above.

4. The best way to develop competency in counseling is by:

   a. Learning the basic principles of counseling.
   b. Counseling many other types of handicapped individuals and their families.
   c. Learning the principles of counseling and then applying them in practice.
   d. Working with simulated situations similar to those the counselor will work with in reality.

5. Counselors must be able to develop skills in helping the parents of retarded children with their concerns about:

   a. The availability and use of appropriate community resources.
   b. The anxiety and concern which center around their child's retardation.
   c. Present and future planning for the retarded child.
   d. All of the above.

6. The application of which of the following principles is most helpful in alleviating the feelings of anxiety and concern of parents of retarded children?

   a. Being straightforward and abrupt if necessary.
   b. Handling the parents with special care.
   c. Obtaining and understanding all the relevant facts concerning the problems of mental retardation.
   d. Involving both parents in the counseling process.

7. Which of the following is not one of the principles to be applied during the first interview?

   a. Helping the parents to realize the value of feedback and follow-up interviews.
   b. Making sure the parents take advantage of other community services they may need.
   c. Giving a prognosis of the child's condition.
   d. Giving the parents a great deal of support and understanding.

8. The most common wholesome reaction of parents to their retarded child is to:
   a. Provide a high level of protection in order to keep the child secure from the harsh adversities of life.
   b. Offer a gentle but continuous forcing of the child to master tasks which are only slightly beyond his ability.
   c. Accept the child for what he is, recognizing the child's limitations and helping him to achieve his highest possible level of functioning.
   d. All of the above.

9. When giving a prognosis to the parents of a retarded child, the counselor should base his prognosis on:

   a. The stereotype of the child's general condition.
   b. The child's diagnostic evaluation.
   c. What the child will be able to do.
   d. a and c above.
   e. b and c above.

10. Which of the following principles is/are applicable to counseling the parents of retarded children?

    a. Involving only the parent asking for help in the counseling process.
    b. Using different counselors whenever possible during the counseling process.
    c. Preserving the continuity of the relationship between the main counselor and the parents.
    d. a and b above.
    e. a and c above.

Answers

The answers to the preceding questions are:

1. b.
2. d.
3. b.
4. c.
5. d.
6. d.
7. c.
8. c.
9. e.
10. c.

Ayers, G. E., and Dugray, R. A. "Critical Variables in Counseling the Mentally Retarded." *Rehabilitation Literature* 30 (1969) 42-44, 50.

Begab, M. J. "Counseling Parents of Retarded Children." *Canada's Mental Health* 12 (1964): 2-5.

Bryant, K. N., and Hirschberg, J. C. "Helping the Parents of a Retarded Child: The Role of the Physician." *American Journal of Diseases of Children* 102 (1961): 52-66.

Campanelle, T. C. *Counseling Parents of Mentally Retarded.* Milwaukee, Wisconsin: The Bruce Publishing Co., 1962.

Cohen, P. C. "The Impact of the Handicapped Child on the Family." *Social Casework* 43 (1962): 137-42.

Dalton, Juanita, and Epstein, Helene. "Counseling Parents of Mildly Retarded Children." *Social Casework* 44 (1963): 523-30.

Disner, E. "Reporting to Parents." *American Journal of Mental Deficiency* 61 (1956): 362-367.

Drayer, C., and Schlesinger, E. "The Informing Interview." *American Journal of Mental Deficiency* 65 (1960): 363-70.

Dybwad, G. "Group Approaches in Working with Parents of the Retarded: An Overview." In *Challenges in Mental Retardation.* New York: Columbia University Press, 1964.

Fine, Marvin J. "Counseling with the Educable Mentally Retarded." *Training School Bulletin* 66 (1969): 105-10.

Giannini, M. J., and Goodman, L. "Counseling Families during the Crisis Reaction to Mongolism." *American Journal of Mental Deficiency* 67 (1963): 740-47.

Goodman, L. "Continuing Treatment of Parents with Congenitally Defective Infants." *Social Work* 9 (1964): 92-97.

Goodman, L., and Rothman, R. "The Development of a Group Counseling Program in a Clinic for Retarded Children." *American Journal of Mental Deficiency* 65 (1961): 789-95.

Hanaschaka, Evelyn D. "Reporting to Parents." *American Journal of Mental Deficiency* 61 (1956): 362-67.

Koch, R. and Dobson, J. *The Mentally Retarded Child and the Family: A Multi-disciplinary Approach.* New York: Brunner-Mazel, 1971.

Mahoney, S. C. "Observations concerning Counseling with Parents of Mentally Retarded Children." *American Journal of Mental Deficiency* 63 (1958): 81-86.

McDonald, E. T. *Understand Those Feelings.* Pittsburgh: Stanwix House, 1962.

Mental Retardation: A Handbook for the Primary Physician. Report of the American Medical Association Conference on Mental Retardation. Reprinted from the *Journal of the American Medical Association* 191 (1965): 183-232.

Motulsky, A., and Hecht, F. "Genetic Prognosis and Counseling." *American Journal of Obstetrics and Gynecology* 90 (1964): 1227-241.

Murray, Dorothy G. "Needs of Parents of Mentally Retarded Children." *American Journal of Mental Deficiency* 63 (1959): 1078-088.

Nadal, R. M. "A Counseling Program for Parents of Severely Retarded Preschool Children." *Social Casework* 42 (1961): 78-83.

Noland, R. L. *Counseling Parents of the Mentally Retarded.* Springfield, Ill.: Charles C. Thomas, 1970.

Popp, Cleo E.; Ingram, Viven; and Jordan, P. H. "Helping Parents Understand Their Mentally Handicapped Child." *American Journal of Mental Deficiency* 58 (1954): 530-34.

Raech, H. "A Parent Discusses Initial Counseling." *Mental Retardation* 4 (1966): 25-26.

Roos, P. "Psychological Counseling with Parents of Retarded Children." *Mental Retardation* 1 (1963): 345-50.

Schild, Sylvia. "Counseling with Parents of Retarded Children Living at Home." *Social Work* 9 (1964): 86-91.

Sheimo, S. L. "Problems in Helping Parents of Mentally Defective and Handicapped Children." *American Journal of Mental Deficiency* 56 (1951): 42-47.

Solomons, G. "What Do You Tell the Parents of a Retarded Child: Some Personal Experiences and Reflections?" *Clinical Pediatrics* 4 (1965): 227-32.

Stacey, C. L., and DeMartino, M. F., editors. *Counseling and Psychotherapy with the Mentally Retarded.* Glencoe, Illinois: The Free Press, 1957.

Stubblefield, H. W. *The Church's Ministry in Mental Retardation.* Nashville, Tennessee: Broadman Press, 1965.

Thornton, E. E. *Theology and Pastoral Counseling.* Englewood Cliffs, New Jersey: Prentice-Hall, 1964.

Waskowitz, Charlotte H. "The Parents of Retarded Children Speak for Themselves." *Journal of Pediatrics* 54 (1959): 319-29.

Watts, Evadean M. "Family Therapy: Its Use in Mental Retardation." *Mental Retardation* 7 (1969): 41-44.

Weingold, J.T., and Hormuth, R.P. "Group Guidance of Parents of Mentally Retarded Children." *Journal of Clinical Psychology* 9 (1953): 118-24.

Wolfensberger, W. "Counseling the Parents of the Retarded." In *Mental Retardation: Appraisal, Education, Rehabilitation*, edited by A. Baumeister, pp. 329-400. Chicago: Aldine Publishing Co., 1967.

Yates, Mary L., and Lederer, Ruth. "Small, Short-Term Group Meetings with Parents of Children with Mongolism." *American Journal of Mental Deficiency* 65 (1961): 467-72.

Zook, Linn, and Unkovic, Charles. "Areas of Concern for the Counselor in a Diagnostic Clinic for Mentally Retarded Children." *Mental Retardation* 6 (1968): 19-24.

Zwerling, I. "Initial Counseling of Parents with Mentally Retarded Children." *Journal of Pediatrics* 44 (1954): 469-79.

UNIT 3

LESSON TWELVE
Counseling the Mentally Retarded

Counselors who work with the mentally retarded must realize that the primary objective in counseling such a person is to help him recognize his potential for achievement. The counselor should strive to help the retarded person learn to develop confidence in his own abilities and to become as self-reliant as possible.

One of the major difficulties in aiding the retarded is communication. Although they possess only limited language skills and limited comprehension, the retarded may give the impression of fully understanding the conversation taking place. However, unless the communication is geared to the retardate's level of understanding, he may develop a misconception about the counseling relationship and his role in it. In addition, despite limited communications skills, it is known that the retarded individual has an active emotional life and reactions. Even though he may not show his reactions or verbalize them effectively, he is, nonetheless, affected by the attitudes of the counselor toward him.

In a counseling relationship, it is, therefore, essential to hold firmly to the belief that retardates, except perhaps for the most severely afflicted, have the ability to react to the way they are treated. The counselor needs to be concerned with the most effective means by which he can communicate to the retarded person better ways of adapting to his present circumstances. In order to accomplish this, the counselor must make the retarded person feel that he can place his trust in the counselor. The counselor should remember that it is important for him to earn this trust which can only be built through verbal understanding and nonverbal supportive behavior on his part. Without a sense of trust, warmth, giving, and mutual respect, the counseling effort will not be successful.

The counselor should be alert to the fact that the retarded individual has limited foresight about his needs for tomorrow and that he should not necessarily be expected to define an appropriate future role for himself. Instead, he probably will need help in planning for the future. The counselor also may find that initial discussion with a retarded individual may be difficult because of the individual's previous experiences with rejection. To repeat, the retarded person needs understanding and reassurance if the counseling process is to be meaningful or successful.

Above all, the counselor who works with the retarded should keep continuously in mind that retarded individuals have a need for success and for successful experiences. Unfortunately, the retarded person has too often had a long history of being conditioned to accepting himself as a failure. To break this cycle of defeatism, the counselor should help the retarded person to locate himself in an environment in which he will be more successful in both social and interpersonal experiences as well as in vocational and recreational activities.

If the worker is to establish a good counseling relationship, the following general attitudes and beliefs must prevail in order to assist the retarded individual to achieve an optimal level of happiness and satisfaction:

1. The counselor must accept the retarded individual and must accord him the same basic human rights he would any non-retarded person.
2. The retarded person should be treated with dignity and respect.
3. The retarded person should be permitted to participate, to the extent that he is able, in decisions which affect his circumstances.
4. The retarded person should have the right to develop his abilities and potential to the fullest possible extent, regardless of the degree of his handicap.

5. The counselor must have a firm belief in the value of social services and their use in the prevention or amelioration of the problems that a retarded person faces.
6. The counselor must have an appreciation for the importance of suggesting appropriate services based on extensive study, diagnosis, and treatment.

The intent of this lesson is to help you become more aware of basic attitudes which underlie competent counseling of the mentally retarded.

OBJECTIVES

Upon completion of this lesson, you will be able to identify the following items which are of specific relevance when counseling the retarded individual.

1. Identify and elaborate on the basic attitude regarding the dignity of the individual which should be cultivated by every counselor of the retarded.

2. Identify and elaborate on the right of individuals to have the opportunity of meeting their basic needs.

3. Identify and elaborate on the right of self-determination.

4. Identify and elaborate on the individual's potential for growth.

5. Identify and elaborate on the value of those basic services appropriate to prevention, protection, and amelioration.

6. Identify and elaborate on the factors involved in learning to use services for referral purposes.

Please answer each of the following questions carefully. After each possible answer, you will be referred to a frame in the section beginning on p. 219 where you will be told whether or not your choice is correct. If the alternative you have selected is correct, you will be told in the answer frame which frame in the "Questions" section to turn to next. If your choice is incorrect, your answer will tell you to return to the question frame you have just answered to review and to try again. Please note that you will always be given your instructions according to frame number. Frames designated with "Q" indicate a frame in the "Questions" section (e.g., "Q-1, Q-2"). Frames designated with an "A" indicate answers. Only occasionally will you be given a page number to which to turn. It is most important that you follow the instructions for *each individual question or answer frame* most carefully.

Q-1

The first important attitude which should be cultivated by the counselor and the families of the retarded is a belief in the dignity of the human personality. This means that every individual, no matter what his problems or condition, should be accorded equal and sincere respect by the counselor.

The mentally retarded person is no less a human being than his "normal" contemporaries. If anything, because of his condition, he is more in need of the respect and warmth of those he encounters. Without the counselor's belief in the dignity of the retardate, the development of trust and, therefore, the creation of a meaningful relationship with him and his family will be impeded. Without such a relationship, the counselor becomes ineffectual.

What attitude is a person revealing if he is able to show every individual with whom he comes in contact a warm feeling of respect? Write your answer below and then turn to A-3.

_____

_____

Q-2   A second pertinent attitude is the belief in the right of every human being to have the opportunity to meet his basic needs.

The mentally retarded person is no different than anyone else in this respect. His need for love and affection is often greater than the need of normal individuals, for his opportunities for fulfilling these needs are often inhibited by his condition.

Test yourself with the following exercise.

State in your own words the second pertinent attitude that the counselor must exhibit when working with the retarded.

_____

_____

Turn to A-8 to check your answer.

Q-3   The third attitude which underlies competent counseling of the retarded is the belief in the right of self-determination for the retarded individual insofar as this is diagnostically sound.

When counseling the retarded, the counselor should remember that the severity of the retardate's condition has an important bearing on his ability to determine for himself what is best for him. Often the counselor, together with the family, must make relevant decisions that the retardate is not capable of making.

Test yourself with the following exercise.

The counselor, when dealing with the mentally retarded, must temper his belief in the _____ _____ _____ in accordance with the retardate's diagnosis.

Fill in the blanks and then turn to A-11.

The fourth attitude is the belief that the retarded individual has   Q-4
the potential for growth and change. If belief that everyone has
the potential for growth and change is not fundamental, the
counselor may as well forget about his work. However, for the
retarded individual, the limits of his potential are set by the degree
of his retardation and by the opportunities for change offered by
his environment, including his family and community.

Of the two basic attitudes that are tempered by the fact that the
client is retarded, which one is limited by the diagnosis?

a. The belief that the retarded individual
   has the potential for growth and change.   Turn to A-2.
b. The belief in the right of self-determination.   Turn to A-10.

The fifth basic attitude to be cultivated by the counselor is the   Q-5
belief in and use of appropriate preventive, protective, and ameliorative social service resources. Ameliorative resources are those
measures which help the retarded and their families to cope with
their problems.

Since mental retardation decreases social functioning, social
service intervention is almost always appropriate. This intervention, if needed, may extend over the individual's entire life,
especially if it is used as a protective function.

In regard to the mentally retarded, social services should be viewed

by the counselor as_____,_____, and _____
resources.

Fill in the blanks above and then turn to A-7.

Q-6   In the case of the mentally retarded, intervention should never be viewed as being likely to last throughout the individual's entire life.

a. This is a true statement.   Turn to A-4.
b. This is a false statement.   Turn to A-6.

Q-7   The sixth attitude basic to counseling the retarded is the belief that the determination and provision of appropriate services for the retarded individual and his family should be based on the extensive study, diagnosis, and treatment that characterize counseling any other client or client group.

Which of the following factors should determine the provision of appropriate services for the retarded individual and his family?

a. Extensive study.   Turn to A-1.
b. Diagnosis.   Turn to A-12.
c. Treatment.   Turn to A-9.
d. All of the above.   Turn to A-5.

ANSWERS

Please follow the same instructions as those you were given on page 215 in working with this section. It is most important that you remember to follow the individual instructions in each answer frame.

The determination and provision of appropriate services for the retarded and his family should be based on extensive study, but these decisions should also be based on other criteria.

Return to Q-7 and review the material presented there; then answer this question correctly.

A-1

The extent to which the retarded individual has the potential for growth and change is limited by the degree of retardation and the environment, not by the diagnosis.

Return to Q-4 for a brief review; then answer Q-4 correctly.

A-2

The person who shows respect to every individual has a belief in the dignity of the human personality. No counselor should attempt to help another individual unless he holds this belief to be of prime importance.

Continue now with Q-2.

A-3

Not so. Social services, especially as protective resources, should be viewed as lifelong measures when dealing with many of the mentally retarded. For example, in most cases of profoundly and severely retarded individuals, lifelong protection is a necessity.

Return to page 217, Q-5 and review the material presented there; then see if you can answer Q-6 correctly.

A-4

A-5   Yes, the answer should be "all of the above." The determination and provision of appropriate services for the retarded should be based on the same extensive study, diagnosis, and treatment that characterize any other client or client group.

Continue now with the review questions on page 222.

A-6   The statement is correct. Social services for many of the mentally retarded should be viewed as lifelong, especially as a protective resource. In most cases of profoundly and severely retarded individuals, lifelong protection is a necessity.

Continue now with Q-7.

A-7   Social services should be viewed by the counselor of the retarded and their families as preventive, protective, and ameliorative resources.

Continue now with Q-6.

A-8   Did you indicate that the belief in the right of every individual to have an opportunity to meet his basic needs is the second pertinent attitude?

If you did, then move along to Q-3.

The determination and provision of appropriate services is based   A-9
partially on the treatment aspect of the case, but such decisions
are also based on other aspects.

To find out what these factors are, return to Q-7 and review the
material presented there.

The belief in the right of self-determination is limited by the diag-   A-10
nosis. You've got it right!

Continue now with Q-5.

Yes, when counseling the retarded and their families, the coun-   A-11
selor must temper his belief in the *right of self-determination* in
accordance with the retardate's diagnosis.

Continue now with Q-4.

You're partially correct; the determination and provision of appro-   A-12
priate social services should be based on the retardate's diagnosis,
but this is only one of the aspects that should be taken into
consideration.

Return to Q-7 and review the other aspects; then answer the question correctly.

Questions

Now, for a quick review of the six basic attitudes relevant to counseling the mentally retarded and their families, test your memory by completing the following statements.

1. Belief in the _____ of the _____ .

2. Belief, insofar as it is diagnostically sound, in the right of _____ for the mentally retarded individual.

3. Belief in the right of the _____ to have the opportunity for meeting _____ .

4. Belief that, like everyone else, the retarded person has the potential for _____ and _____ .

5. Belief in the appropriateness of social services as _____ , _____ , and _____ resources, sometimes lasting a lifetime.

6. Belief that the determination and provision of social services for the retarded and their families, as with any other client or client group, should be based on extensive _____ , _____ and _____ .

Answers

1. Belief in the *dignity* of the *human personality*. (If you missed this question, return to page 215 for a review.)
2. Belief, insofar as it is diagnostically sound, in the right of *self-determination* for the mentally retarded individual. (If you were unable to answer this question correctly return to page 216 for a review.)
3. Belief in the right of the *human personality* to have the opportunity for meeting *basic needs*. (Did you miss this one? If so, return to page 216 and review the material presented there.)
4. Belief that, like everyone else, the retarded person has the potential for *growth* and *change*. (How did you do? If you need a review return to page 217.)

5. Belief in the appropriateness of social services as *preventive*, *protective*, and *ameliorative* resources, sometimes lasting a lifetime. (For a review, if it is needed, return to page 217.)
6. Belief that the determination and provision of social services for the retarded and their families, as with any other client or client group, should be based on extensive *study*, *diagnosis*, and *treatment*. (If you need a review here return to page 218.)

SELECTED READINGS

Bruno, A. "Counseling Suggestions." *Special Education Review* 10 (1953): 26-30.

DiMichael, S. G., and Terwillinger, W. B. "Counselors' Activities in the Vocational Rehabilitation of the Mentally Retarded." *Journal of Clinical Psychology* 9 (1953): 97-106.

Fine, M. J. "Counseling with the Educable Mentally Retarded." *Training School Bulletin* 66 (1969): 105-10.

Goldstein, H., and Heber, R. *Preparation of Mentally Retarded Youth for Gainful Employment*, Bulletin 1959, No. 28. Washington, D.C.: U.S. Department of Health, Education, and Welfare, 1959.

Menzel, Mariella, Z. "Psychotherapeutic Techniques among the Mentally Deficient: Occupational Therapy." *American Journal of Mental Deficiency* 56 (1952): 796-802.

Miezio, S. "Group Therapy with Mentally Retarded Adolescents in Institutional Settings." *International Journal of Group Psychotherapy* 17 (1967): 321-27.

Nitzberg, J. "Training and Counseling Retarded Adults." *Canada's Mental Health* 14 (1966): 14-20.

Rosen, H. G., and Rosen, Susan. "Group Therapy as an Instrument to Develop a Concept of Self-Worth in the Adolescent and Young Adult Mentally Retarded." *Mental Retardation* 7 (1969): 52-55.

Stacey, C. L., and De Martino, M. F. *Counseling and Psychotherapy with the Mentally Retarded.* Glencoe, Illinois: The Free Press and The Falcon's Wing Press, 1957.

Thorne, F. C. "Counseling and Psychotherapy with Mental Defectives." *American Journal of Mental Deficiency* 52 (1948): 263-71.

Thorne, F. C., and Dolan, Katherine M. "The Role of Counseling in a Placement Program for Mentally Retarded Females." *Journal of Clinical Psychology* 9 (1953): 110-13.

Thorne, G. D. *Understanding the Mentally Retarded.* New York: McGraw-Hill, 1965.

Woody, R. H. "Counseling the Mentally Abnormal: An American Model." *Journal of Mental Subnormality* 127 (1966): 73-79.

Woody, R. H., and Billy, J. J. "Counseling and Psychotherapy for the Mentally Retarded: A Survey of Opinions and Practices." *Mental Retardation* 4 (1966): 20-23.

Woody, R. H., and Herr, E. L. "The School Counselor's Responsibility to the Slow Learner." *School Counselor* 13 (1965): 6-13.

Yepsen, L. N. "Counseling the Mentally Retarded." *American Journal of Mental Deficiency* 57 (1952): 205-13.

LESSON THIRTEEN
Community Services

The challenge to those concerned with community programs for the retarded begins with the identification of individuals who may be mentally retarded and their guidance to appropriate diagnostic facilities and continues through the gamut of community services which exist to enable such individuals and their families to use fully their personal abilities and the resources of the community.

There are a number of program areas to be considered in assessing the presence or lack of community services to meet the needs of the individual retarded person. Although this lesson does not describe all of the possible services for the retarded, even the most minimal program of community service should include the following resources:

1. *Diagnostic and Evaluation Services.* Generally, these services are obtainable from professional private or public out-patient clinics. Within this grouping of services, programs for early detection of retardation should exist. In addition, counseling should be available to help families and relatives with long-term planning and guidance.

2. *Special Education.* The availability of schooling opportunities for school-aged retarded children is the responsibility of the public school system. Educational programs should be developed in order to meet the needs and abilities of each retarded child and to help him develop to his optimum level of functioning. Teachers of the retarded should be well-qualified professionals who have been specifically trained to teach the retarded. School systems should provide educational experiences for the full range of retardates, including the mild and moderately retarded. The school should make available programs which provide close linkage of school, vocational training, and ultimate employment.

For retarded children of preschool age, well-operated nursery schools or kindergartens with a balanced curriculum and qualified teachers are of invaluable importance. Preschool programs are especially important where the cause of retardation has been socioeconomic deprivation; preschool programs open new horizons for such children and motivate them to learn.

3. *Vocational Habilitation Programs.* Vocational habilitation is the means by which the retarded can be ensured opportuni ies for remunerative employment and economic independence. Habilitation services improve the skills of retarded individuals and thus make it possible for them to take advantage of a wider range of job opportunities. Included with habilitative services should be programs of pre-employment and evaluation, placement services for those capable of competitive employment, and sheltered workshops for providing continuing training as well as long-term employment for those persons unable to work in other than protected, noncompetitive settings. Activity programs established for those who are unable to work in a sheltered workshop are also included. Such programs help the retarded to learn hobbies and to engage in simple constructive activities for which they may or may not be paid.

4. *Social Services.* Services provided by social agencies for the retarded are many and varied. They include homemaker services, foster-care placement, guardianship programs, financial assistance, protective services, long- and short-term counseling for the retarded person and his family, and home training programs. Since many retarded individuals need these services, it is important that such services not only be available to them but also that programs be organized and provided in a manner which will meet the special needs of the retarded. Social services should be available with qualified staff to handle problems

which fall under each of the areas of program services listed. Information and referral services as well as financial assistance programs should also be available for the retarded and their families. Child-placement programs offering carefully selected substitute homes as well as programs for the return of a child to his own home and community should also be provided. In addition, there should be day-care programs available which are suitably licensed and supervised. Lastly, social services should coordinate clinical and program services for the retarded individual in order to help the child and his family to attain a maximum level of social functioning.

5. *Recreational Programs.* The mentally retarded obtain important physical, social, and educational benefits from involvement in suitable recreational activities. These services are important to retardates because they aid them in socializing with others, thereby making them more socially astute and more capable of independent functioning. Recreation provides the means to success through the valuable use of leisure time. The kinds of programs in which retarded individuals can become reasonably involved depend upon the educational level, severity of retardation, and physical capabilities of the individual. Generic recreation programs, when modified, can often fulfill the special need for recreational pursuits by those who are retarded.

Retarded children can be quite lonely unless there are recreational opportunities available which allow them to socialize and enjoy the company of those who are their physical and intellectual peers. The retarded should be helped to engage only in those activities which do not tax them to the point of frustration. For those who are not well coordinated or who have some type of physical handicap, being a spectator at a sporting event can often be just as enjoyable as being a participant. Most important of all, it should be kept in mind that recreational activities should be conducive to enjoyment, entertainment, and socialization.

A balanced community recreation program for the mentally retarded should consist of some or all of the following activities: scouting, camping, social development programs, physical education, swimming, hobby groups, teen-age clubs, dancing, softball, volleyball, tennis, bowling, tours, picnics, arts and crafts, and some quiet types of games. For the more severely retarded, special attention should be paid to the organization of activities suitable to their limited abilities. It should not be assumed that they are unable or unwilling to participate in any recreational activities.

6. *Religious Programs.* The church and clergy are able to serve the mentally retarded and their families in ways which differ from most other community programs. First, the church can interpret the problems and needs of the retarded to members of each congregation as well as to the community at large. Second, the church can minister to the families of the retarded by involving them in church activities and by offering pastoral counseling. Third, the church can offer special religious education programs geared to meet the spiritual needs of the children.

Both religious and lay leaders generally believe that the spiritual part of life may be even more meaningful to the retarded person than to the average individual. It has been found that the retarded are frequently quite responsive to opportunities for religious nurture and guidance. Today, many churches operate nursery schools, kindergartens, and Sunday school classes for the retarded, and some are even offering their classrooms and playgrounds for weekday use by day schools or other similar programs of service to the retarded.

Religious leaders also have become aware of the importance of pastoral counseling for parents of the retarded. Sometimes parents are unwilling to turn for help to such professional disciplines as social work, medicine, nursing, or education, but they will seek out guidance and counsel from their religious leader. The clergy have found that they can be of great help to parents in rearing a retarded child and in learning to better understand their problems and fears.

7. *Residential Programs.* Residential facilities should be available to serve all retarded children and adults who are in need of long- or short-term care. Such facilities should be equipped to provide a therapeutic environment to meet the needs of the resident. Residential services should be community-based and limited to those retarded whose specific needs can best be met by this type of program. There are seven basic concepts which all residential programs should follow if they are to be good programs for the retarded:

   a. The residential facility should have a balanced program in which each and every resident receives a "fair share" of service.
   b. The facility should have a staff and program oriented to treatment, education, and habilitation.
   c. The physical plant of the facility should be maintained at a maximum level of utility as well as attractiveness of appearance.

d. The facility should place emphasis upon return of the resident to his family and community so long as it is in the best interest of the retarded individual and in keeping with existing community resources and services.

e. The facility should work cooperatively with related public and private health, education, and welfare agencies.

f. The facility should be cognizant of the major importance of the resident's relationship with his parents, relatives, and friends who should be involved, as is appropriate, with planning for the resident's present situation as well as future goals.

g. The facility should be adequately staffed with sufficient numbers of qualified professional and attendant personnel to provide adequate services to those in residence.

Most specialists in the field of mental retardation agree that residential facilities for the retarded should not be large, isolated, and inaccessible to parents and relatives. On the contrary, facilities should be community-based and accessible to the community. They should be small, homelike programs designed to provide service to each resident as an individual so that he is known and treated with dignity and respect.

Often, residential facilities are thought of only in terms of state or private institutions for the care of the retarded. Descriptions of several other types of residential programs follow:

a. *Halfway Houses.* These are short-term treatment facilities for persons who no longer require institutionalization but are in need of further supervision and treatment prior to their re-entry into the community. The programs usually provide a temporary group-living situation while the retarded individual acquires the necessary social and vocational skills for successful functioning within the community.

b. *Group-Care Facilities.* These are generally group-care residence programs which are licensed, community-based, family-type programs for the retarded who need twenty-four-hour-a-day supervision. Retarded individuals using these types of facilities are usually capable of some degree of self-care but are not capable of independent living. These individuals need close but flexible supervision and are able, for the most part, to participate in community activities.

c. *Boarding Houses.* These are generally facilities for the retarded which have no organization or administration per se. Occupants have no set rules or regulations except those arbitrarily decided upon by the management. There is no direct supervision, and the retarded individual may leave the facility at any time he desires. These programs are for the mildly retarded, competently functioning individual.

8. *Day-Care Programs.* Day care first originated for normal children who needed to be cared for away from their own homes during some part of the day when the situation called for help outside the ordinary care which could be given in their homes. These programs were established primarily for working mothers, and they placed emphasis on substitute care.

With the retarded, however, the definition of day care is not as clear-cut. Day care has been interpreted as being any one of a combination of the following three types of programs for those who are retarded:

a. A program established to care for the child during the day and to provide relief for the parents from the twenty-four hour-a-day stress and strain in caring for their retarded child.
b. A preparatory day program designed to help the retarded child move into the public school.
c. A day program designed to offer after-hours care for children who attend public schools and whose parents are not able to provide care for them between the time that school closes for the day and suppertime.

Day-care programs for the retarded must be more than just baby-sitting programs. Such programs should include within their activities specific educational, recreational, and health services which have been designed to serve the best interests of the retarded child.

This lesson concerns the services provided by society for the mentally retarded. At present, services are not uniformly available or of a consistent quality. At the local level, some parents of the retarded strive to assure that adequate services are made available. But in areas without active associations for retarded children, there are often only limited services.

After completing this lesson, you will be able to accomplish the following tasks:

1. Identify the services offered by different agencies serving the mentally retarded.
2. Cite or identify the agency offering each kind of service.
3. Identify services that are most helpful to specific mentally retarded persons.
4. Recognize the services that are most helpful to different retarded individuals.
5. Given descriptions of mentally retarded individuals, make referrals to appropriate agencies.

QUESTIONS

Please answer each of the following questions carefully. After each possible answer, you will be referred to a frame in the section beginning on p. 241 where you will be told whether or not your choice is correct. If the alternative you have selected is correct, you will be told in the answer frame which frame in the "Questions" section to turn to next. If your choice is incorrect, your answer will tell you to return to the question frame you have just answered to review and to try again. Please note that you will always be given your instructions according to frame number. Frames designated with "Q" indicate a frame in the "Questions" section (e.g., "Q-1, Q-2"). Frames designated with an "A" indicate answers. Only occasionally will you be given a page number to which to turn. It is most important that you follow the instructions for *each individual question or answer frame* most carefully.

DIAGNOSTIC AND EVALUATION SERVICES

Q-1   Although there may be many agencies providing services for the mentally retarded who live in the community, one of the first agencies that a mentally retarded individual should be taken to is the diagnostic and evaluation clinic.

The purpose of this clinic is to provide coordinated medical, psychological, and social functioning appraisals in order to evaluate the mentally retarded individual's strength, skills, abilities, and potentials and to develop recommendations for a special treatment plan and services related to his individual needs.

The purpose of the diagnostic and evaluation clinic is:

a. To provide medical and physical diagnosis.   Turn to A-5.
b. To evaluate the social functioning of the
   retarded individual.   Turn to A-8.
c. To provide coordinated medical, psycho-
   logical, and social functioning appraisals
   and to recommend a special treatment plan.   Turn to A-3.

There are two major types of school-related services for the men-   Q-2
tally retarded—preschool programs and special-education classes.

The goal of the preschool is to prepare the retarded child as well as
possible for school participation. These services may be found in
day-care programs or in educational facilities designed specifically
for the preschool child.

A word of caution is needed here, for the terms "day-care program" or "preschool nursery" sometimes are used interchangeably
to imply that an educational program is offered for the young
retarded child. This may or may not be true. Each program must
be examined on its individual merits. The worker should be
aware of the criteria for determining what an educational program
is and then recommend only those preschool programs that meet
the needs of the individual child.

Preschool programs are especially helpful for the socioeconomically deprived mildly retarded children, mainly because they help
to provide motivation for learning by introducing these children
to many concepts that they have not encountered in their homes.

The goal of a preschool program is to _____ the retarded child
for school participation.

Fill in the blank and turn to A-13.

Which of the following groups of retarded children would benefit   Q-3
most from preschool programs?

1. Severely retarded.   Turn to A-1.
2. Mildly retarded, especially the socioeconomically deprived.   Turn to A-15.
3. Profoundly retarded.   Turn to A-18.

Q-4   The other type of school-related services provided for the mentally retarded includes public and private special-education classes for school-aged retardates who are able to benefit from special-education programs. Both the educable and the trainable retarded can benefit from special-education programs.

Public and private schools offer _____ _____ _____
for educable or trainable retarded individuals of school age.

Fill in the blanks and then turn to A-11.

Q-5   List below the names of the three services (to retardates living in the community) that have been mentioned so far:

1. _____

2. _____

3. _____

Please fill in the blanks and then turn to A-14.

The next services to be described in this lesson are available for the mentally retarded who are beyond school age.

State vocational rehabilitation agencies provide one example of a post-school type of service. These government-supported, nation-wide agencies are organized to provide vocational training and to help disadvantaged and handicapped individuals find suitable jobs in the community. The services provided by vocational rehabilitation agencies include:

1. Vocational evaluation and guidance.
2. Vocational training.
3. Job placement in community businesses.

Test yourself with the following example.

Name the three services that are offered by state vocational rehabilitation agencies to the adult retardate.

1. _____

2. _____

3. _____

Fill in the blanks and then check your answer by turning to A-16.

Q-7   Private organizations, such as Goodwill Industries, the Salvation Army, the Associations for Retarded Citizens, and others, also offer services in the area of vocational habilitation.

The services offered by such private organizations usually include:

1. Vocational evaluation and guidance.
2. Vocational training.
3. Employment in sheltered workshops.

Sheltered workshops provide supervised work with remuneration aiming toward habilitation of the retarded individual. They serve those retarded who are able to work under noncompetitive conditions; some of these persons will be able to accept employment within the community after training.

Test yourself with the next exercise.

Private organizations, such as Goodwill Industries, the Salvation Army, and Associations for Retarded Citizens, usually offer three types of services. What are they?

1. _____

2. _____

3. _____

Fill in the blanks and then turn to A-9.

There are several types of leisure-time services which are often available in the community for retardates of all ages. Some examples are:

1. Camping programs.
2. Scouting programs.
3. Teen-age clubs.
4. Hobby groups.
5. Arts and crafts groups.
6. Various ball games.

All of these programs provide opportunities for social interaction as well as the development of manual skills through such activities as arts and crafts and other hobbies.

If parents of a retarded child wanted to know about available programs that would give their child a chance to socialize and enjoy himself with other children who have similar handicaps, what programs would you suggest for them?

1. _____
2. _____
3. _____
4. _____
5. _____
6. _____

Fill in the blanks and then turn to A-6.

RESIDENTIAL PROGRAMS

Q-9 Although state residential care programs have been the major societal service to the mentally retarded for a long period of time, there is promising evidence that this emphasis is shifting to the offering of nonresidential programs for the large majority of retarded individuals who are able to live in the community. Public awareness of the value of community care has been responsible for this change.

Residential care is important, however, for those retarded individuals in any classification who either have difficulty in social adjustment or whose care in the community poses a considerable problem. Those who are mildly retarded may need a period of institutionalization because of community adjustment problems, while the profoundly or severely retarded may need to be placed in residential facilities because they require such constant care and supervision that they cannot continue to be cared for in their own homes.

Experience has shown that assistance in the form of services given the parents and guardians will make community living more possible for the retarded, will reduce the need for residential care, and will thereby reduce the costs and increase the benefits to the larger society.

Agencies offering twenty-four-hour-a-day care include state and private facilities for the mentally retarded as well as many state and a few private facilities for the mentally ill.

Test yourself with the following example.

Circle the letters below that identify agencies which offer twenty-four-hour-a-day, long-term care for the mentally retarded. Then turn to A-12 to check your answers.

a. Day-care programs.
b. State residential facilities for the mentally retarded.
c. Welfare agencies.
d. State residential facilities for the mentally ill.
e. Sheltered workshop programs.
f. Private residential facilities for mentally retarded.

Circle the letters below which correspond to the classifications of   Q-10
retarded individuals who may need to be given twenty-four-hour-
a-day care.

a. Profoundly retarded.
b. Severely retarded.
c. Moderately retarded.
d. Mildly retarded.

Turn to A-2 to see if you answered correctly.

Other Residential Facilities

In addition to the full-time care agencies just described, there are   Q-11
other types of residential facilities that provide a more short-term
care for the mentally retarded.

Group-Care Facilities. These agencies provide twenty-four-hour-
a-day care and relatively close supervision. The retarded in these
programs are capable of some degree of self-care and can participate in supervised community activities.

Halfway Houses. These facilities provide short-term treatment
and care for persons generally needing further temporary supervision and treatment after leaving an institution and before reen-
tering the larger community. The care and supervision required in
such facilities is usually modest.

Boarding Houses. These re-entering facilities provide minimal
supervision over the boarders who are in residence; the length of
stay in these facilities is generally of limited duration and entirely
dependent upon the boarder's wishes whether to stay or leave.

Test yourself with the following exercise.

Which of the following residential programs provide twenty-four-
hour-a-day care for those retarded who are capable of some self-

care and are able to participate in closely supervised community activities?

a. Halfway houses.   Turn to A-7.
b. Boarding houses.   Turn to A-4.
c. Group-care facilities.   Turn to A-17.

RELIGIOUS PROGRAMS

Q-12   The church and clergy can and often do serve the retarded and their families in unique ways which include:

1. Interpreting the problems and needs of the retarded to other parishioners and to the community at large.
2. Ministering to the retarded and their families through church activities and through pastoral counseling.
3. Sponsoring activities and programs of an educational or quasi-educational nature (e.g., nursery school, kindergartens, Sunday school classes, special classes, camping, etc.)
4. Sponsoring legislation which is in the best interest of the retarded.

Test yourself with the following question.

Circle the letters below which correspond to the services that the church and clergy are very often able to offer the retarded and their families:

a. Vocational training.
b. Interpreting the problems of the retarded to the community.
c. Spiritual counseling.
d. Special educational and quasi-educational programs.
e. Sponsoring or running kindergartens.
f. Sponsoring legislation needed for aid to the retarded.
g. Providing twenty-four-hour-a-day care.

Turn to A-10 to check your answers.

Please follow the same instructions as those you were given on page 232 in working with this section. It is most important that you remember to follow the individual instructions in each answer frame.

Although the severely retarded may benefit from a preschool program, they would benefit far less than the socioeconomically deprived, mildly retarded child.

Return to Q-3 and answer the question correctly.

A-1

You should have circled all the letters. Individuals in all four classifications may need to be offered twenty-four-hour-a-day care. Although the majority of the profoundly and severely retarded need close care and supervision, many moderately and midly retarded persons who are physically handicapped or are unable to adjust to society may also need institutional care for a period of time.

Continue now with Q-11.

A-2

The *diagnostic and evaluation clinic* must make a comprehensive analysis of the retardate's physical, psychological, and social situation and then recommend a well-rounded treatment plan. Right you are.

Continue now with Q-2.

A-3

A-4   A *boarding house* for the mentally retarded provides a minimum of supervision and permits considerable freedom in community activities. Because this question related to closely supervised activities, you did not answer it correctly.

Return to Q-11 and select another response.

A-5   You said, "to provide medical and physical diagnosis." This is only a portion of the purpose.

Please return to Q-1, review the material, and then make another selection.

A-6   The parents wishing social activities for their retarded child should be referred to any available recreation program, including camping, scouting, teen-age clubs, hobby groups, arts and crafts groups, and other similar types of programs.

Continue now with Q-9.

A-7   *Halfway houses* usually provide temporary and modest amounts of supervision. They offer short-term intermediate care for persons who have left institutional care but are not yet ready for community living.

Since the question related to close supervision, you did not answer correctly. Return to Q-11 and select another answer.

To evaluate *social functioning* is only one aspect of the purpose of   A-8
the diagnostic and evaluation clinic.

Please return to Q-1, review the material, and make another selection.

Private habilitation organizations usually offer 1) vocational evalua-   A-9
tion and guidance, 2) vocational training, and 3) employment in
sheltered workshops.

Continue now with Q-8.

You should have circled all of the letters except a and g. Most   A-10
church-oriented programs do not get involved in vocational training or in offering twenty-four-hour-a-day care. All of the other
programs may be offered by church groups, although it is a rare
group that would offer the wide gamut of services listed.

Continue now with the conclusion on p. 246.

You should have filled in the blank with "special–education   A-11
classes." Public and private schools offer *special-education* classes
for both the trainable and the educable retarded who are of school
age.

Continue now with Q-5.

A-12   The three agencies that take care of the mentally retarded on a twenty-four-hour-a-day basis are: state residential facilities for the mentally retarded and the mentally ill, and private residential facilities for the retarded. The letters you should have circled are: b, d, and f.

Continue now with Q-10.

A-13   You should have filled in the blank with the word "prepare." The goal is to *prepare* the retarded child for school participation.

Continue now with Q-3.

A-14   The three services thus far mentioned include:

1. Diagnostic and evaluation clinics.
2. Preschool programs.
3. Special-education programs for the school-aged child.

Review if you need to, then turn to Q-6.

A-15   This is correct. The mildly retarded, especially those who are socioeconomically deprived, would obtain the most benefit from preschool programs, primarily because of the motivation that these programs provide as well as because of the opportunities available to open new horizons to the child.

Turn now to Q-4.

Vocational habilitation offers 1) vocational evaluation and guidance as well as 2) vocational training and 3) job placement.   A-16

Continue now with Q-7.

The group-care facility would be the correct answer from the   A-17
choices given since it alone can be regarded as a care program for
those who are capable of some self-support and are able to participate in closely supervised community activities.

Continue now with Q-12.

No. The profoundly retarded individual would benefit little, if at   A-18
all, from a preschool program.

Return to page 233 and review the material presented there before
answering Q-3 correctly.

CONCLUSION

From the discussion in this lesson, you should now be aware that there are quite a few community organizations and facilities providing services for the mentally retarded and that these services are increasing as they must do if society expects families of retarded individuals living in the community to be able to cope with their problem.

It should be remembered as a concluding note that one of the major weapons in the arsenal of the professional worker is his knowledge of community agencies and facilities and the services provided by each. A listing of agencies providing services for the mentally retarded can usually be obtained from the individual state's division of mental retardation or from state or local chapters of the Associations for Retarded Children. Some welfare departments may also possess such lists. If you are to be an effective force in helping the retarded and their families, it would be to your benefit to know the location and services offered by all the agencies in your community.

Please test yourself using the review questions on the following page. If you are satisfied with your progress, go on to the next lesson.

1. In helping the young child enhance his learning abilities workers have generally found that preschool programs for those who come from socioeconomically deprived areas are of:

    a. Great importance.
    b. Some importance.
    c. Very little importance.
    d. No importance.

2. Which of the following services would most appropriately aid the retarded in developing and improving work skills in preparation for employment?

    a. Vocational habilitation programs.
    b. Recreation programs.
    c. Diagnostic and evaluation clinics.
    d. Residential programs.

3. Most workers in the field of retardation agree that residential facilities for the retarded should be:

    a. Inaccessable to parents in order to break family ties.
    b. Isolated so as not to cause disturbances to those living near the facility.
    c. Community based and small enough to offer individualized attention to each resident.
    d. Large and multi-purpose in order to achieve the least cost of operation and assurance of being able to recruit adequately qualified staff.

4. Boarding homes are generally facilities for the retarded with:

    a. Little or no organization or administrative structure within the facility.
    b. Few, if any, rules or regulations except those established by the management.
    c. No direct supervision and the resident can come and go as he pleases.
    d. All of the above.

5. One thing that an institution for the retarded should not do is:

    a.   Emphasize return of the resident to his family.
    b.   Let the facility decline and become unattractive in appearance.
    c.   Work cooperatively with community agencies.
    d.   Provide a "fair share" of service to each and every resident.

6. Which of the following programs is not considered to be residential in nature:

    a. A state institution for the retarded.
    b. A day-care program
    c. A boarding home.
    d. A group-care facility.

7. In general, the use of the term "day care" for the retarded includes which of the following services:

    a. Relief to parents in caring for their retarded child.
    b. Preparation of the retarded child for public school.
    c. After-hours care for children in attending school.
    d. All of the above.

8. Services such as foster care placement, financial assistance, protective services, long- and short-term counseling, guardianship programs and provision of homemaker services would all be included in which of the following:

    a. Education services.
    b. Social services.
    c. Habilitation services.
    d. Diagnostic services.

9. Which of the following are generally considered to be part of habilitation services:

    a. Sheltered workshops.
    b. Activity programs.
    c. Child-placement programs.
    d. a and b above.

10. Which of the following agencies would be primarily concerned with a coordinated medical, psychological, and social service in order to develop recommendations for a special plan of help for the retarded individual:

a. Private schools.
b. Diagnostic and evaluation clinics.
c. City parks and recreation programs.
d. Private habilitation organizations.

11. If you are working with a child who is suspected of being retarded, to which agency would you refer the parents and why?

a. Preschool program for intensive counseling.
b. Day-care center for a recommended plan of action.
c. Diagnostic and evaluation clinic for a diagnosis of the child's condition.
d. Recreation program to learn self-help skills.

Answers

The answers to the questions for Lesson Thirteen are:

1. a.
2. a.
3. c.
4. d.
5. b.
6. b.
7. d.
8. b.
9. d.
10. b.
11. c.

SELECTED READINGS

Adams, Margaret. "Community Organization in the Field of Mental Retardation." In *Mental Retardation and Its Social Dimensions*, edited by Margaret Adams, pp. 248-85, Chapter 10. New York: Columbia University, 1971.

Ames, T. "Independent Living for the Mentally Handicapped: A Program for Young Adults." *Mental Hygiene* 53 (1969): 641-42.

Begab, M. J. *The Mentally Retarded Child . . . a Guide to Services of Social Agencies.* Children's Bureau Publication No. 404. Washington, D.C.: U.S. Department of Education, and Welfare, 1963.

_____. "Unmet Needs of the Mentally Retarded in the Community." *American Journal of Mental Deficiency* 62 (1958): 712-23.

Boggs, E. M. "State Programming for the Mentally Deficient." In *National Conference on Social Welfare: Community Organization*, pp. 130-39. New York: Columbia University Press, 1958.

Chope, H. D. "The Organization of Community Services for the Mentally Retarded." In *Prevention and Treatment of Mental Retardation*, edited by I. Philips. New York: Basic Books, Inc., 1966.

Crawford, D. "Retarded and the Community." *Australian Children Limited* 3, (1969): 199-222.

Doll, E. A. "Programs for the Adult Retarded." *Mental Retardation* 6 (1968): 19-21.

_____. "Total Program for the Mentally Retarded." *Training School Bulletin* 60 (1963): 13-22.

Dupont, H. "Community Mental Health Centers and Services for the Mentally Retarded." *Community Mental Health Journal* 3 (1967): 33-36.

Dybwad, G. "Community Organization for the Mentally Retarded." In *National Conference on Social Welfare: Community Organization*, pp. 108-21. New York: Columbia University Press, 1959.

Ehlers, W. H. *Mothers of Retarded Children.* Springfield, Illinois: Charles C. Thomas, 1966.

Extending Clinical Services for the Mentally Retarded Children at the Community Level. Washington, D.C.: U.S. Department of Health, Education, and Welfare, Children's Bureau, 1965.

Gardner, W. I., and Nisonger, H. W. "Manual on Program Development in Mental Retardation: Guidelines for Planning, Development, and Coordination of Programs for the Mentally Retarded at State and Local Levels." *American Journal of Mental Deficiency Monograph Supplement* 66 (1962): 1-192.

Hutchison, A. "Community Care Services for the Mentally Retarded in Britain." *American Journal of Public Health* 60 (1970): 56-63.

Jaslow, R. I. "A Modern Plan for Modern Services to the Mentally Retarded: Expanding Community Services to the Mentally Retarded." *Clinical Pediatrics* 7 (1968): 80-82.

Katz, E. *The Retarded Adult in the Community.* Springfield, Illinois: Charles Thomas, 1968.

Krishef, C. "Community and State Responsibility toward the Mentally Retarded." In Mental Retardation—A Basic Guide, edited by H. D. Love. Berkeley, California. McCutchan Publishing Co., 1968.

Ottenstein, D., and Cooper, S. "A Community Mental Health Program for Mental Retardation: Community and Planning Aspects." *Journal of the American Academy of Child Psychiatry* 7 (1968): 536-47.

Pense, A. W. 'How to Insure a Satisfactory Building Program." *American Journal of Mental Deficiency* 58 (1953): 236-38.

The President's Panel on Mental Retardation. *A Proposed Program for National Action to Combat Mental Retardation.* Washington, D.C.: U.S. Government Printing Office, 1962.

Scheerenberger, R. C., editor. *Mental Retardation: Selected Conference Papers.* Springfield: Illinois Mental Health Department, 1965.

Shafter, A. J., and Fraenkel, W. A. "Services to Mentally Retarded Children and Youth in Rural Areas." In *Rural Youth in Crises,* edited by L. B. Burchard. Washington, D.C.: U.S. Department of Health, Education, and Welfare, 1965.

Soforenko, A. A., and Stevens, H. A. "The Diffusion Process: A Model for Understanding Community Program Development in Mental Retardation." *Mental Retardation* 6 (1968): 25-27.

Stedman, D. J. "Intermediate Step Planning for Mentally Retarded Programs." *Mental Retardation* 5 (1967): 28-29.

Talkington, L. W., and Chiocario, S. J. "An Approach to Programming for Aged Mentally Retarded." *Mental Retardation* 7 (1969): 29-30.

Tisdall, W. J., and Moss, J. W. "Total Program for the Severely Mentally Retarded." *Exceptional Children* 28 (1962): 357-62.

Tudyman, A. "A Realistic Total Program for the Severely Mentally Retarded." *American Journal of Mental Deficiency* 59 (1955): 574-82.

White, W. D. *Planning and Programming for the Retarded: Yesterday, Today and Tomorrow.* New York: National Association for Retarded Children, 1969.

Yannet, H. "The Community Management of the Mentally Retarded." *Journal of the Louisiana Medical Society* 107 (1955): 291-95.

UNIT 4

LESSON FOURTEEN
Vocational Rehabilitation and Employment Services for the Retarded

DEINSTITUTIONALIZATION

Only a few short years ago, most people had little optimism that the retarded had any potentiality for development. The answer in the past was to isolate and abandon the retarded in institutions far from communities in which others lived. In 1960 well over 200,000 retarded individuals were housed in public institutions throughout the United States. The approximate cost for the care of these individuals was well over a billion dollars a year.

In 1971 the President of the United States accepted a proposed plan which established a goal of returning to useful community living at least one-third of the retarded who were living in public institutions. The term *deinstitutionalization* was adopted about that time to connote a concept emphasizing removal of retarded individuals from nonproductive lives in institutions and arranging for them to lead productive and useful lives in the community.

In 1975 the National Association of Superintendents of Public Residential Facilities for the Mentally Retarded reported the results of a survey in which projected estimates showed a nine-year decline in the number of public institution residents, from 190,000 in 1969 to 176,000 in 1974, or about 14,000 fewer residents.

Thus the effort to reduce the numbers of public institution residents appears to be gaining some degree of success and the traditional approach of institutional care for the retarded is being challenged.

In order to accomplish a continuing program of deinstitutionalization for the retarded, a number of conditions need to be safeguarded. The National Association of Superintendents of Public Residential Facilities for the Mentally Retarded has suggested that the process which should be followed in order to attain the goal of deinstitutionalization encompasses three interrelated processes: (a) averting admission to institutions by locating or developing alternative community methods of care and training, (b) returning to the community all institutional residents who have been prepared through rehabilitation, habilitation, and training programs to function adequately outside of the institution, and (c) establishing and maintaining residential programs that assure protection of the retarded person's civil human rights and speedy return, whenever possible, to normal community living. On the other hand, for those residing in institutions for long-term periods, deinstitutionalization also means that both the attitudes of staff and the policies which regulate the institutions must be improved. Every resource available should be used to help retarded individuals reach their optimum level of functioning whether it be in the institution or in the community. In any case, the retarded person should be allowed to reside in the least restrictive environment which it is possible for him to attain.

Caution must be exercised, however, to be sure that community "back wards" are not substituted for institution "back wards" in the deinstitutionalization programs for the retarded. For far too long, many retarded individuals were "warehoused" in institutions where they were essentially stored away from society. Although deinstitutionalization seeks to avert institutional warehousing, simply placing the retarded into community warehouses serves no better purpose. All programs must strive to make sure that the rights of the retarded are protected wherever they may live and that programs which serve these individuals are continuously being improved.

Deinstitutionalization is worthwhile and possible. In order for such programs to be successful, new attitudes must be developed and improved programs must be initiated within institutional programs. The community must also change its attitudes by becoming more willing to accept and include the retarded in the mainstream of general society. The community must make every effort to provide the type of services necessary to help the retarded person to sustain himself in community life.

EMPLOYMENT SERVICES FOR THE RETARDED

The idea of helping a person return to gainful employment after losing his or her job because of some physically handicapping condition began with legislation in 1920 that provided for both State and Federal rehabilitation programs. The mentally retarded were not given consideration as eligible clients for such programs until 1943. Unfortunately, even then little was done to help the retarded until the 1960s.

The number of retarded who were given training through vocational rehabilitation agencies increased from 106 in 1945 to 5,909 in 1963. During the year 1971, it was estimated that 52,520 mentally retarded persons had been served by vocational rehabilitation agencies.[1] Not only had there been a dramatic increase in the number of retarded served by rehabilitation programs, but these agencies, within recent years, have even begun to focus their attention on the more severely handicapped and more difficult to rehabilitate retarded person.

Most of us recognize that there are fewer things in life that are more important than the opportunity to work. Work helps a person to be independent and to feel some sense of pride and accomplishment. Work becomes exceedingly important for the retarded because it helps to keep them constructively occupied. Rather than being a liability they become an asset to our society.

The National Association for Retarded Citizens estimates that about 87 percent of the retarded could support themselves to some degree providing they were able to receive adequate vocational training services.[2] However, helping the retarded become economically productive requires more than just training in job-related skills. Training for employment should also help the retarded person to become more knowledgeable about adequate skills to perform on the job, and also skills to help prepare him socially and psycholog-

---

[1] President's Committee on Mental Retardation, *Mental Retardation: the Known and the Unknown,* DHEW Publication #OHD 76-21008. Washington, D.C., 1975, p. 54.
[2] *The Mentally Retarded: Their Special Training Needs.* Manpower Research Bulletin, No. 6, October 1964. U.S. Department of Labor, Manpower Administration, p. 2.

ically for work. Thus, the following represents the vocational services which should be provided to the retarded.

Vocational Services Needed by the Retarded

1. *Vocational Counseling.* There are some retarded individuals who may not take a realistic view of their future vocational goals or they may misunderstand the nature of certain jobs. Job titles can be confusing. The author knows of one young retarded man who wanted to be a "busboy" so that he could help people on and off the bus. Another was interested in bookkeeping because he liked to keep his own books neatly in a row and well dusted, and he believed this to be the nature of the bookkeeper's position. The counselor must help the retarded person to establish a reasonable plan for future employment, taking into consideration the retarded person's limitations and strengths.

2. *Work Evaluation.* Sometimes it is necessary for the retarded person to be evaluated in preparation for determining his future job plans. Such factors as desire to work, degree of disability, personality characteristics, personal and work habits, previous training and education, and influences of the family are all observed and assessed by the evaluator. When this evaluation is completed, it will provide a realistic plan for preparing the retarded individual for future employment.

3. *Personal Adjustment Training.* After the retarded person has been evaluated, it may be necessary to provide some personal training which will help him present a better appearance and be more acceptable for employment. This training should include such things as conduct in social situations, the importance of regularity in attendance and punctuality, and other areas which are part of work preparation.

4. *Vocational Training.* Those who receive vocational training are being specifically prepared for work. Some actual vocational training may be provided in the classroom. In other cases specific tasks may be taught which are closely related to a particular type of job. One way that has been found to be very useful in job training for the retarded is by the use of "sheltered workshop" programs. These workshops provide both work training and employment opportunities for the retarded. For those not capable of competing for jobs in the labor market, the sheltered workshop is designed to assign work in an employment-simulated setting to train these individuals until they have reached the point of being acceptable for competitive employment in the labor market.

For whatever reasons, there are a few retarded individuals who, regardless of the degree of their training, will not be capable of competing in the open labor market. Many of them become reliable workers but they must still remain in a sheltered work environment. These individuals, however, can work along with those who are in the sheltered workshop program and who are being trained for eventual placement into community jobs.

Another vocational program which serves the retarded is known as an "activity program." While sheltered workshops are mainly for those who are mildly and moderately retarded, the activity program is primarily designed to serve the more severely retarded individual who may not yet be ready either for advanced job training or sheltered employment in a workshop. Activity programs provide beginning training in basic skills, such as grooming, personal deportment, and how to travel in the real world. The most current information available on these programs is for the year 1971, when a survey by Arnold Cortazzo located 706 activity programs for the retarded throughout the United States. It was estimated that about 18,000 retarded persons were being served by these programs, and the major thrust of the training was to help prepare retarded persons for employment and to aid them in their social development.

5. *On-the-Job Training.* It can hardly be disputed that the best type of training is that which takes place on the job. For those who are able to tolerate and withstand normal work pressures under supervision, on-the-job training may be the best approach.

EMPLOYMENT POSSIBILITIES FOR THE RETARDED

Research has shown that the mentally retarded may be more successful in their work if they enter into certain types of jobs for which they appear to be best suited. Obviously there are individual differences among the retarded but certain jobs, such as clean-up people, kitchen helpers, janitors, stock clerks, truck-driver helpers, and assemblers, seem to be the types of positions in which the retarded are often found. The retarded can perform well in a wide variety of unskilled and semiskilled jobs. The above listing is by no means exhaustive.

One interesting phenomenon about the mildly retarded is the fact that, although they are usually identified during their school years, they seem to disappear and become unidentifiable as adults. This most likely means that those at the higher levels of retardation are able to enter the labor market, be mostly self-sustaining, and blend into society.

In this lesson you will be introduced to the types of vocational services needed to help the majority of retarded individuals become productive members of society. When you have completed this lesson, you will be able to:

1. Define, in your own words, the term "deinstitutionalization."
2. Identify the three processes needed to attain deinstitutionalization.
3. Identify the types of retarded persons now being served by vocational rehabilitation agencies.
4. Cite the approximate percentage of retarded individuals who can support themselves to some degree in society, providing they are able to receive adequate vocational training services.
5. List the five vocational services needed by the retarded.
6. Given a description of one of the vocational services needed by the retarded, identify the service.
7. Given a list of jobs, identify those for which a retarded individual could be trained to fill.
8. State one possible conclusion that could be reached to explain why the mildly retarded are identifiable during their school years but become unidentifiable during their adult years.

QUESTIONS

Please answer each of the following questions carefully. After each possible answer, you will be referred to a frame in the section beginning on page 268, where you will be told whether or not your choice is correct. If the alternative you have selected is correct, you will be told in the answer frame which frame in the "Questions" section to turn to next. If your choice is incorrect, your answer will tell you to return to the question frame you have just answered to review and to try again. Please note that you will always be given your instructions according to frame number. Frames designated with "Q" indicate a frame in the "Questions" section (e.g., "Q-1, Q-2"). Frames designated with an "A" indicate answers. Only occasionally will you be given a page number to which to turn. It is important that you follow the instructions for *each individual question or answer frame* most carefully.

DEINSTITUTIONALIZATION

Q-1   Until recently, the major method for dealing with the retarded has been to isolate and abandon them in public institutions far from local communities. In 1971 a plan aimed at deinstitutionalizing the retarded was accepted by the President of the United States. Deinstitutionalization refers to a process for removing retarded individuals from institutions and arranging for them to live far more productive lives in the community.

Describe in the space below and in your own words the meaning of deinstitutionalization as related to the retarded, and then turn to A-9.

_____

_____

_____

_____

_____

_____

According to the National Association of Superintendents of Public Residential Facilities for the Mentally Retarded, there are three processes which must be followed if the goal of deinstitutionalization of the retarded is to be effectively accomplished. These three interrelated processes include:

1. Locate and establish community methods of care and training other than public institutions.
2. Return to the community those retarded persons best able to function in these community settings.
3. Establish and maintain residential programs which provide protection of the retarded person's human rights, and help him or her to become prepared for normal community living.

Identify the processes which must be followed in order for deinstitutionalization to be effectively accomplished by placing a checkmark in the spaces beside those processes described below which apply and then turn to A-32.

A. ___ Return all retarded individuals to the community as soon as possible.

B. ___ Identify and establish alternate methods of care and training of the retarded in the community.

C. ___ Improve public institutions and the services they provide.

D. ___ Return those retarded persons to the community who are best prepared to function in the settings provided for them.

E. ___ Establish residential programs in the community which expect a high level of functioning for their clients.

F. ___ Establish residential programs which provide protection for the retarded and training to help them become prepared for normal community living.

RETARDED INDIVIDUALS SERVED BY
VOCATIONAL REHABILITATION AGENCIES

Q-3   Until the 1960s, vocational rehabilitation agencies were reluctant to provide services to retarded individuals. Since then, there has been a dramatic increase in the number of retarded served by these agencies. In addition, there has been a change in focus from serving mainly the easier-to-rehabilitate, mildly retarded person, to also serving moderately and even severely retarded individuals.

Vocational rehabilitation agencies now provide services to which of the following?

a. Mildly retarded.	Turn to A-1.
b. Moderately retarded.	Turn to A-6.
c. Severely retarded.	Turn to A-11.
d. Profoundly retarded.	Turn to A-17.
e. a and b above.	Turn to A-21.
f. a, b, and c above.	Turn to A-25.
g. All of the above.	Turn to A-30.

VOCATIONAL SERVICES NEEDED BY THE RETARDED

Q-4   There are five major types of vocational services needed to help most retarded individuals become productive members of society. A small percentage of the retarded are unable to function on their own and need constant supervision throughout their lives. In this lesson we are not referring to those individuals, but to those who have the potential to make a contribution to society if given the necessary assistance.

The five major vocational services needed by most of the retarded include:

1. Vocational counseling.
2. Work evaluation.
3. Personal adjustment training.
4. Vocational training.
5. On-the-job training.

Which of the following is a true statement?

a. All the retarded, given the proper assistance,
   can become productive members of society.   Turn to A-3.
b. All but a small percentage of the retarded
   can become productive members of society
   given the necessary assistance.   Turn to A-10.

Three of the five major vocational services needed by the retarded   Q-5
are listed below. Add the other two services and then turn to A-12.

1. Vocational counseling.
2. Vocational training.
3. On-the-job training.
4.
5.

VOCATIONAL COUNSELING AND WORK EVALUATION

Q-6   Vocational counseling is one type of rehabilitation service that may be of assistance to the retarded. The vocational counselor can help the retarded individual better understand the nature of different jobs and develop a realistic plan for future employment by taking the retarded individual's strengths and limitations into consideration. In addition, in order to most effectively help the retarded individual develop a realistic future employment plan, a work evaluation may be needed. This evaluation should include, at a minimum, the retarded individual's:

1. Desire to work (motivation).
2. Degree of disability.
3. Personality characteristics.
4. Personal and work habits.
5. Previous training and education.
6. Family influences.

Once an employment plan is developed, the next step is to identify the training needed, if any, to help prepare the retarded person for a job or related group of jobs.

Which of the following services does the vocational counselor provide the retarded individual?

a. Help him or her establish a reasonable plan
   for future employment.   Turn to A-2.
b. Help him or her learn how to perform a job.   Turn to A-8.
c. Help him or her better understand the nature
   of different jobs.   Turn to A-14.
d. a and c above.   Turn to A-23.
e. a, b, and c above.   Turn to A-28.

A work evaluation helps identify the retarded individual's strengths and limitations related to obtaining and retaining a job on the labor market. Such an evaluation should include which of the following? Circle the letters corresponding to those which apply and then turn to A-19.

Q-7

a. Personality characteristics.
b. Family influences.
c. Friends.
d. Degree of disability.
e. Motivation.
f. Personal habits.
g. Job openings.
h. Work habits.
i. Previous training.
j. Educational background.
k. Location of job.
l. Desire to work.

THREE TYPES OF TRAINING FOR THE RETARDED

In addition to vocational counseling and a work evaluation, three types of training should be made available in a community to help the retarded prepare for a productive job in the labor market or under supervised conditions. These include personal adjustment, vocational, and on-the-job training.

Q-8

Personal Adjustment Training

Personal adjustment training should be provided to those retarded persons who have not learned or have learned but do not apply basic social skills related to work. Such skills should include, among others:

1. Personal hygiene
2. Getting along with others (communication skills, acceptable social behaviors, appropriate control of emotions, and so on.
3. Arriving on time for work and for appointments while at work.
4. Reporting to work regularly.
5. Informing employer whenever absent for legitimate reasons.

Vocational Training

There are, at present, two major programs used by different agencies to provide vocational training for the retarded. These include sheltered workshops and activity programs.

The sheltered workshop is a place where the mildly and moderately retarded receive both job training and employment opportunities under close supervision. It is a training ground for those who are eventually able to seek and obtain employment in the labor market. While receiving this special training, that could be obtained in no other setting, these people are also paid for their work. For those individuals who, for any reason, are unable to function without close supervision, the sheltered workshop provides permanent employment opportunities.

The activity program is designed for the more severely retarded individual who is not ready for advanced job training or sheltered employment in a workshop. Thus, these programs primarily provide beginning job training along with training in social skills and skills in the psychological aspects of work.

On-the-job Training

On-the-job training is the most effective vocational training. However, this requires that the retarded person be able to tolerate normal work pressures, and most of the retarded are unable to do this. For those who have demonstrated an ability to handle this stress, on-the-job training with some supervision would be the best approach.

If a retarded person has trouble getting along with others in a work situation, which service would probably benefit him/her the most?

a. Work evaluation.   Turn to A-4.
b. Vocational counseling.   Turn to A-13.
c. On-the-job training.   Turn to A-20.
d. Personal adjustment training.   Turn to A-26.

If a mildly retarded individual is able to withstand a normal amount of stress in vocational situations, he would probably obtain the most benefit from which services?

Q-9

a. Sheltered workshop.   Turn to A-5.
b. Activity program.   Turn to A-16.
c. On-the-job training.   Turn to A-27.

Circle below those letters corresponding to statements which describe the services provided by sheltered workshops and then turn to A-15.

Q-10

a. Rudimentary skills in personal appearance.
b. Supervised job training.
c. Permanent employment.
d. Temporary employment.
e. Preparation for activity program.
f. Preparation for eventual placement in the labor market.

If a retarded individual needed training for placement in a sheltered workshop, he/she could receive this training in what program? State your answer below and then turn to A-18.

Q-11

Q-12   Not unlike everyone, the retarded appear to be most successful in work which is best suited for them. Some of the many jobs that are well-suited for them include unskilled and many semiskilled jobs, such as:

1. Laundry workers.
2. Factory helpers.
3. Busboys.
4. Truck driver helpers.
5. Janitors.
6. Dishwashers.
7. Stock clerks.
8. Assemblers.
9. Clean-up people.
10. Maids.
11. Farm hands.

It would appear that at least one category of the retarded, namely the mildly retarded, are able to blend into society when they become adults and become unidentifiable, even though they may have been identifiable during their school years. The major reason for this appears to be that most of them are able to obtain gainful employment and live relatively normal lives. With the aid of vocational rehabilitation agencies, the same result might also be accomplished by retarded individuals in other categories.

The retarded are able to perform which of the following jobs if they receive appropriate guidance?

a. Managerial.   Turn to A-7.
b. Skilled.   Turn to A-22.
c. Semiskilled and unskilled.   Turn to A-31.

List below ten jobs that would be best suited for retarded in-   Q-13
dividuals and then turn to A-29.

1.
2.
3.
4.
5.
6.
7.
8.
9.
10.

Explain below one possible reason why the mildly retarded usually   Q-14
become unidentifiable during their adult life, even though they
were readily identifiable during their school years. Turn to A-24
to check your answer.

ANSWERS

Please follow the same instructions as those you were given on page 258 in working with this section. It is most important that you remember to follow the individual instructions in each answer frame.

A-1   Yes, vocational rehabilitation agencies do provide services to the mildly retarded. However, individuals from other categories are also provided such services, so your answer is only partially correct. Review the material in Q-3 before answering this question correctly.

A-2   Yes, the vocational counselor does help the retarded individual establish a reasonable plan for future employment, but he/she usually also provides other services to the retarded. Return to the material in Q-6 if you need a review and then answer this question again.

A-3   This is incorrect. The profoundly retarded and many of the severely retarded must have constant supervision throughout their lives and will not become productive members of society no matter how much assistance they receive. Return to Q-4 and select the correct answer.

A-4   No, a work evaluation is designed to match the individual with a future job and therefore helps reveal the retarded individual's material in Q-8 for a review before correctly answering this question.

Although a mildly retarded person who can tolerate stressful situations would be helped in a sheltered workshop, he/she would probably obtain greater benefit from on-the-job training in an unsheltered setting. If there is no such service available, then the sheltered workshop would be a second choice until such an opportunity became available. Return to Q-9 and select the correct answer.

A-5

Yes, the moderately retarded are provided services by vocational rehabilitation agencies, but these agencies also provide services to retarded individuals in other categories. Return for a review of the material in Q-3 before selecting another answer to this question.

A-6

Although this may be a fantasy of some people, managing is usually beyond the capacity of the retarded. Return to Q-12 for a review before selecting another answer to this question.

A-7

No, helping the retarded individual learn to perform on a job is usually not one of the services provided by the vocational counselor. Return to the material in Q-6 for a review and then answer this question correctly.

A-8

Deinstitutionalization refers to a process aimed at removing the retarded from nonproductive lives in public institutions to more productive lives in the community.

A-9

If you wrote something similar to the above, give yourself a pat on the back and move on to Q-2. If you had trouble defining this term, return for a review to Q-1 before moving on to Q-2.

Return to the material in Q-6 for a review before answering this question again.

A-10   This is correct. All but the profoundly retarded and many of the severely retarded can become productive members of society and function on their own with minimal supervision. Well done. Continue now with Q-5.

A-11   Yes, some severely retarded individuals are now being provided services by vocational rehabilitation agencies. However, many other retarded individuals are also being served by these agencies. Return to Q-1 and select the more complete answer. If you need a review, reread the material presented in Q-3.

A-12   The two services needed by the retarded, but not listed, include work evaluation and personal adjustment training. Did you write down both of these services? If so, go on to Q-6. If not, review the material in Q-5 before moving on to Q-6.

A-13   Vocational counseling may be of some help but another service would be more beneficial to a retarded person in learning to function more effectively with others. Return to Q-8 and select the best answer.

Yes, this is one of the services provided by the vocational counselor A-14
but there may be others. Return to the material in Q-6 for a review
if necessary before answering this question correctly.

The answers include b, c, d, and f. Sheltered workshops provide A-15
supervised job training, preparation for placement in the labor
market, and both temporary and permanent employment for the
retarded.

If you had any trouble answering this question correctly, return for
a review to the material in Q-8 before moving on to Q-11. If you
had no trouble, congratulations. Move right on to Q-11.

An activity program would be of little, if any, benefit to a mildly A-16
retarded person who can tolerate normal amounts of stress. Return to the material in Q-8 for a review before answering Q-9
correctly.

No, the profoundly retarded are the only individuals who would A-17
not benefit from vocational rehabilitation services. Return to the
material in Q-3 for a much needed review before selecting the
correct answer to this question.

The *activity program* provides preparation for retarded individuals A-18
to enter a sheltered workshop. Such preparation includes beginning
job training and training in personal adjustment skills. Return now
to Q-12 for a look at job opportunities for the retarded.

A-19   The answers are a, b, d, e, f, h, i, j, and l. How well did you do? If you missed or added any components, you may need a review of the material in Q-6. If you identified all the above, well done! Go right on to Q-8.

A-20   On-the-job training may not be the most effective service to use to help improve a retarded individual's ability to get along with others. It may even aggravate his or her problems in this area and having adequate social skills should precede on-the-job training. Return to Q-8 for a review before answering this question correctly.

A-21   This answer is two-thirds correct. Vocational rehabilitation agencies do provide services to the mildly and moderately retarded. However, these agencies are also providing services to people in another category. Return to Q-3 and select the correct answer.

A-22   No, even the mildly retarded have usually been incapable of developing the skills necessary for functioning effectively in skilled jobs. It would probably be a mistake to expect any retarded individual to reach this goal. Return to the material in Q-12 for a review and then answer this question correctly.

A-23   Well done! The vocational counselor usually helps the retarded develop reasonable plans for future employment based on the individual's strengths and limitations, as well as clarifies any misunderstandings they may have about the nature of different jobs. Continue now to Q-7.

One of the most plausible reasons why the mildly retarded blend   A-24
into society and become unidentifiable as adults is that they become
self-sustaining and productive members of their communities. You
may have stated a similar or even more plausible reason. If so, you
are using your mind well. Keep it up!

You have now completed the programmed material for this lesson.
Please turn to the conclusion on page 276.

You have arrived at the most complete answer. Yes, vocational re-   A-25
habilitation agencies provide services to the mildly, moderately
and some of the severely retarded. Only the profoundly retarded
require constant supervision throughout their lives and, therefore,
cannot benefit from vocational services. Continue now with Q-4.

Right you are! Personal adjustment training is designed to help the   A-26
retarded learn social skills, including grooming, communication,
manners, and so forth, which improve their ability to get along
with other people, especially in work-related situations. Continue
now with Q-9.

Yes, the most effective vocational training for anyone is on-the-job   A-27
training. However, the person receiving this training must be able
to function under a normal amount of stress and possess social
skills related to work situations. A mildly retarded person who
demonstrates his or her ability to function under stress would,
therefore, obtain the most benefit from receiving this type of
training. Continue now with Q-10.

A-28   This answer is partially correct. Although the vocational counselor helps retarded individuals understand the nature of different jobs and helps them develop realistic plans for future employment, the counselor is usually not involved in direct vocational training. Return to the material in Q-6 for a brief review before answering this question correctly.

A-29   Some of the many jobs best suited for the retarded include:

1. Gardener.
2. Janitor.
3. Stock clerk.
4. Busboy.
5. Truck driver helpers.
6. Maids.
7. Farm hands.
8. Assemblers.
9. Dishwashers.
10. Clean-up people.
11. Laundry workers.
12. Factory helpers.
13. Gas station attendants
14. Delivery people.
15. Sanitation engineers.

How well did you do? You may have thought of other unskilled or semiskilled jobs not listed above. If so, you may be a prime candidate for vocational counselor of the retarded. Continue now with Q-14.

A-30   This answer is incorrect in one aspect. Vocational rehabilitation agencies do not provide services for the profoundly retarded since these people require constant care and supervision and are unable to perform even the most menial tasks without assistance. Return to Q-3 and select the best answer to this question.

This is correct. The retarded are capable of performing both unskilled and many semiskilled jobs effectively with proper training.
Continue now with Q-13 and list some of these jobs.

A-31

The best answers are B, D, and F. If you identified these three processes, you are to be congratulated. Go on to Q-3. If you had any
trouble here, return to Q-2 for a review before moving on to Q-3.

A-32

CONCLUSION

You have now acquired a basic understanding of the services provided by vocational rehabilitation agencies to retarded individuals. These services help prepare the majority of the retarded to become self-sustaining, productive members of society and are a valuable part of our society.

This is the end of this lesson. Before you move on to Lesson Fifteen, remember to answer the questions on the following pages and then check your answers with those provided at the end of the lesson.

Questions

1. About ___% of the retarded could learn to support themselves to some degree if they were provided the appropriate vocational services.

    a. 13%.
    b. 35%.
    c. 65%.
    d. 87%.
    e. 96%.

2. If a retarded individual is unable to take a realistic view of his future vocational goals, he needs:

    a. Personal adjustment training.
    b. Vocational counseling.
    c. Vocational training.
    d. Work evaluation.

3. If a retarded individual is often late for appointments and has little regard for others, he or she could benefit from which of the following services?

    a. Personal adjustment training.
    b. Sheltered workshop.
    c. Vocational counseling.
    d. On-the-job training.

4. If a retarded person needs to develop self-help skills in personal deportment, grooming, and how to travel in society, which would be the best service for him?

    a. Sheltered workshop.
    b. Vocational counseling.
    c. On-the-job training.
    d. Activity program.

5. If a mildly retarded individual needs training to develop work skills and develop a higher level of tolerance to stress, he should be sent to:

    a. An activity program.
    b. A vocational counselor.
    c. A sheltered workshop.
    d. On-the-job training.

6. A retarded individual, who has demonstrated his or her ability to tolerate stress in a work situation, would be helped the most if given:

    a. Vocational counseling.
    b. On-the-job training.
    c. Vocational training in a sheltered workshop.
    d. A work evaluation.

7. If a retarded individual is able to work but only under close supervision, he should be sent to:

    a. A sheltered workshop.
    b. An activity program.
    c. A vocational counselor.
    d. A business needing an unskilled laborer.

8. Deinstitutionalization requires:

    a. Establishment of alternate methods of providing care for the retarded in the community.
    b. Returning those retarded persons best prepared to function in the community setting to which they are sent.
    c. Establishment of residential programs to protect and provide proper training for community living.
    d. d. a and c above.
    e. e. a, b, and c above.

9. Most of the _____ retarded are able to blend into society and become unidentifiable during their adult years.

    a. Profoundly.
    b. Severely.
    c. Moderately.
    d. Mildly.
    e. All of the above.

The answers to the review questions for Lesson Fourteen are:

1. d.
2. b.
3. a.
4. d.
5. c.
6. b.
7. a.
8. e.
9. d.

SELECTED READINGS

Brolin, D. E. *Vocational Preparation of Retarded Citizens.* Columbus, Ohio: Charles E. Merrill, 1976.

Browning, P. L. *Mental Retardation: Rehabilitation and Counseling.* Springfield, Illinois: Charles C. Thomas, 1974.

Cobb, H. "The Forecast of Fulfillment: A Review of Research on the Predictive Assessment of the Adult Retarded for Social and Vocational Adjustment." New York: Teachers' College Press, 1972.

Conley, R. *The Economics of Mental Retardation.* Baltimore: Johns Hopkins Press, 1973.

Cortazzo, A. "Activity Center for Retarded Adults." Washington, D.C.: President's Committee on Mental Retardation, 1972.

Eagle, E. "Prognosis and Outcome of Community Placement of Institutionalized Retardates." American Journal of Mental Deficiency 72 (1967): 232-43.

Fulton, R. W. "Job Retention of the Mentally Retarded." Mental Retardation 13 (1975): 26.

Gold, M. "Research on the Vocational Habilitation of the Retarded: The Present, the Future." In Ellis, N. R., ed., *International Review of Research in Mental Retardation,* vol. 6. New York: Academic Press, 1973.

Goldstein, H. "Social and Occupational Adjustment." In Stevens, H. A. and Heber, R., eds., *Mental Retardation: A Review of Research.* Chicago: University of Chicago Press, 1964.

Hardy, R. and Cull, J., eds., *Modification of Behavior of the Mentally Retarded.* Springfield, Illinois: Charles C. Thomas, 1974.

Kolstoe, O. P. and Frey, R. M. *A High School Work-Study Program for Mentally Subnormal Youth.* Carbondale, Illinois: Southern Illinois Press, 1965.

Krishef, C. H. and Hall, M. A. "Employment of the Mentally Retarded in Hennepin County, Minnesota." *American Journal of Mental Deficiency* 60 (1955): 182-89.

National Association of Superintendents of Public Residential Facilities for the Mentally Retarded. *Contemporary Issues in Residential Programming.* Washington, D.C. President's Committee on Mental Retardation, 1974.

Santiestevan, Henry. *Out of Their Beds and into the Streets.* Washington, D.C.: American Federation of State County and Municipal Employees, 1975.

Scheerenberg, R. C. A Model for Deinstitutionalization. *Mental Retardation,* 1974.

Walthall, J. E. and Love, H. D. *Habilitation of the Mentally Retarded Individual.* Springfield, Illinois: Charles C. Thomas, 1974.

Wolfensberger, W. "Vocational Preparation and Occupation." In Baumeister, A., ed., *Mental Retardation, Appraisal, Education and Rehabilitation.* Chicago: Aldine Publishing Co., 1967.

LESSON FIFTEEN
Special Education for the Retarded

In American society, so much importance has been placed on education that it has become more than a system of imparting certain skills and information and has become as well a symbol of status. The desirability of being "educated" is assumed, and the assumption of this value so pervades our society that it has begun to reach the point where individuals are evaluated primarily on the basis of the number of years they have attended school or the number of degrees they have obtained.

Going to school is probably the most common cultural experience the American child engages in away from his family. When a child is admitted to school, it is an exciting event for child and parents alike. Consequently, when the child does not gain admission because of mental or physical defects, the situation can have a catastrophic effect on the whole family. The idea of an "equal opportunity" to go to school is so generally accepted that rejection from school is psychologically damaging to the entire family.

Most people see the school as the agency through which the child will learn the specific skills necessary to maintain himself as a contributing adult member of society. In general, people place great confidence in the school's role in teaching children values, such as independence, leadership, rearing a family, and good citizenship. The child who cannot learn these skills or whose beliefs are different from the norm is devalued, and this lowering of regard and concern is experienced not only by the child but by the family as well.

Until quite recently, schools have appeared to hesitate in developing educational programs for the retarded child. This attitude has stemmed from the following factors:

1. A general defensiveness among educators regarding the adequacy of school programs for the "normal" child and the feeling that starting programs for the retarded might jeopardize those programs currently in existence.
2. A lack of information about the development of retarded children and how to design school programs to serve them best.
3. Divergent philosophical orientations regarding the definition and goals of education.

HISTORY AND PROBLEMS RELATED TO PROVIDING EDUCATION FOR THE EDUCABLE RETARDED IN PUBLIC SCHOOLS

Special classes for educable retarded children have been organized for many years in countries throughout the world; the first special education program for the retarded was established in this country before 1900. It is helpful then to note some of the historical changes in emphasis which have taken place in classes for the educable retarded child in the United States during the course of the last century.

In the twenties, retarded youngsters were placed in "subnormal rooms," and considerable stress was placed upon the development of useful skills. The presence of big looms characterized most of the classes. Sewing, cooking, and simple carpentry were taught, while little attention was given to reading, writing, and arithmetic. In general, there was no academic curriculum or, if one did exist, it was exceptionally meager.

Under strong educational leadership in the thirties, most programs swung to an emphasis on reading and other academic skills. The looms gradually disappeared as teachers who had been trained in newer methods found the day too short for children to spend endless hours on repetitive weaving. With teachers motivated by a driving conviction that these children could be taught to read, wide adoption of individualized work materials became the norm. Every child was provided with reading materials at his own level and with keyed objective tests that could be checked by helpers. These were the days of the "nonoral" reading methods. Although some of the teachers did continue with a program of social studies, speech improvement, nature study, job preparation, and other elements, there generally came to the classrooms for the retarded a monotonous round of paper work. A method of teaching reading, excellent as a part of a total program, became an end in itself in many classes.

Since the middle forties, a generally broader program has been stressed. Lively, cheerful classrooms with many activities in progress have come to be the rule. Music and art enrich many learning experiences, while such traditional courses as social studies, science, oral language, the three "Rs," and physical education are also emphasized. For the older retarded child, most classroom teachers attempt to teach some prevocational skills, citizenship, preparation for community living, home-making skills, and understanding of problems of family living and job adjustment. By 1956, forty-six of the forty-eight states either permitted or required special facilities for the education of the mentally retarded.

In an unpublished report in 1965 by Dr. Edward LaCross, who was with the National Association for Retarded Children at that time, it was stated that during the period from 1952-1953 to 1964-1965, the total public school enrollment for all children increased by 50 percent, from approximately twenty-seven million to about fifty million. During the same period, the number of educable retarded children in public schools increased about 250 percent, from 108,903 to 413,760. The amazingly large increase came, however, because of public school attendance for those within the trainable ranges. In 1952-1953, there were only 4,659 trainable-level children in the public schools. By 1964-1965, the number had increased by 35,816 to 40,475 for a total increase of 850 percent.

Mental retardation covers a wide range of abilities and characteristics and is far from a unitary condition. In school, the largest group within the mentally retarded range, comprising about two percent of the school-aged population, is called "educable." The educable retarded child eventually is able to learn to read usefully and will be able to achieve social and vocational skills adequate to self-maintenance as an adult. For the most part, the educable are those children who will progress slowly through the school program, but by approximately the age of sixteen, they will only be able to perform at an academic level equivalent to an individual in the fourth to sixth grade.

Today, every educator, every school administrator, and every school system is faced with the problem of providing optimally for these youngsters. Yet they must do so in a manner which does not penalize other children. And they must remember that the problem does not "evaporate" because a school has "no facilities." The children will still be there and will still need to have the benefits of an educational program from which they can profit to the greatest possible extent.

After all of the past experiences, both in this country and abroad, in teaching retarded children through special-education programs, there still remain two conflicting points of view with regard to the effectiveness of special classes for educable retarded children. These include:

1. Those in favor of special-education classes in the public schools who believe that with individual attention in classes of small membership, the educable retarded child can be helped to make optimum progress in academic skills.

2. Those opposed to special-education classes in public schools who are convinced that educable children learn best in regular classrooms because of the stimulation of children brighter than themselves. In addition, there are those who oppose special classes because they believe that retarded children develop feelings of inferiority and rejection as a result of being segregated in special classes.

Until the present time, there has been a general lack of adequate research demonstrating the effectiveness of special-education programs for the educable retarded. The results of research in this area have been summarized by Kirk (1964); Goldstein, Moss, and Jordan (1964); and Dunn and Capobianco (1965). This research indicates practically nothing that is of a uniquely positive nature when special-education classes are compared to programs in which the educable retarded are in regular classes. There seems to be no difference as far as academic achievement is concerned. However, the results of almost all studies in this area can be seriously questioned on three major points:

1. Most of the special-class children who were studied had been in regular classes before entering special classes, and many of these children had no doubt been "failed" from regular classes into these special classes. This fact introduces an automatic bias into the populations of almost all of the studies.

2. The lack of a definitive concept as to what constitutes a "special class" and what skills are required of a special-education teacher is very evident. "Special classes" may not be special at all. Or they may be special only in that they are receiving a subsidy from the state for their operation. No one has developed a successful method to measure teacher qualifications or characteristics as they influence a given special-education program. Both teacher and pupil characteristics need to be studied to determine whether certain kinds of teachers are more effective in special classes and whether special classes may be more effective for certain types of retarded individuals.

3. The general lack of validity and reliability of the bulk of the instruments used in the various research efforts hinders drawing conclusions. A number of the studies used improvised scales which had not been adequately standardized and only served to reflect the particular bias of the experimenter since there was no control that could be placed against the instrument.

In 1968 Lloyd Dunn wrote an article entitled "Special Education for the Mildly Retarded—Is Much of it Justifiable?" in which he questioned the labeling and segregation of the educable retarded child and emphasized the growing disillusionment with special education programs. There were many who rallied behind Dunn's concerns. Essentially, the purpose for special education classes was questioned and the idea of abolishing such classes for all but the severely retarded was suggested. It was argued that special education classes had been created for problem children because they could not be handled in regular classes. The main interest of many school systems seemed to be the removal of these children so they would not be disruptive in regular classes. However, there was little provision for them in special classes which would truly enhance their educational competencies. The approach of "get them out of the regular classroom so they won't bother the teacher and the other kids" tended to perpetuate an institutional prejudice within the schools, since a preponderant number of minority children eventually ended up in special education programs.

It took only a short time, however, for proponents of special education programs to state their case convincingly. They presented evidence that certain schools attended predominantly by minority children produced a large percentage of nonreaders. Other professional workers said that, because evidence on the value of special education programs was inconclusive, it was shortsighted to abolish already existing and organized special education classes on the basis of inadequate research evidence.

Probably the best index for ascertaining whether a special education program has been successful is to view the productivity level of those who have been involved in a special education program. It would seem that if the individual is a productive and contributing citizen, the special education classes he or she attended can be surmised to have been beneficial for him. There have been a number of studies on sociovocational adjustment, and all of these have shown that the educable retarded are able to make acceptable adjustments in their communities. Nonetheless, the questions still remain unanswered concerning the best type of educational program for these individuals.

The question of the advantages and disadvantages of special education programs for the educable retarded will continue for many years until, either by a process of evolution or by conclusive research findings, the value of special education for these individuals is either confirmed and sustained or refuted and abolished.

The Right to an Education

All states have within their constitutions some provision for required school attendance. Unfortunately many of these constitutional provisions provide for excusing a child who, because of a mental or physical handicap, cannot profit from school attendance. The problem that inevitably arises is the determination of who can and who cannot "profit" from an education. The arbitrary decisions of the past to exclude or suspend handicapped children from public school programs, thereby denying them an equal opportunity to an education, has recently been rectified.

In two court actions, entitled *Pennsylvania Association for Retarded Children* vs. *Commonwealth of Pennsylvania* and *Mills* vs. *Board of Education of the District of Columbia*, precedent was established to protect the rights of handicapped children. The *Pennsylvania* case, decided in 1971 by a federal district court, required that all retarded children in Pennsylvania be offered the opportunity for free public education appropriate to their learning capabilities. The *Mills* case, decided in 1972, ordered the District of Columbia to offer all retarded children educational opportunities and required the school system to establish hearings before any child could be suspended from school for more than two days.

Federal legislation for the mentally retarded over the last decade has certainly been of considerable importance in helping the retarded to progress toward optimum life circumstances. Perhaps one of the most important pieces of recent federal legislation, passed by an overwhelming majority of the U.S. Congress and signed into law on November 29, 1975, by President Ford, was Public Law 94-142, known as the *Education for All Handicapped Children Act of 1975.*

The law provides that the federal government will furnish financial help to meet the educational needs of handicapped children ranging in ages from three to twenty-one. The law also set forth assurance that the constitutional rights of both handicapped children and their parents would be protected.

In brief, the law provides that the federal government will pay to each state an increasing amount of money for each handicapped student based on the per capita amount of money on all students in public schools. The amount of support will also be influenced by the number of handicapped children who are served by the school systems. The federal government will provide 5 percent of the cost of educating a handicapped child in 1978, 10 percent in 1979, 20 percent in 1980, 30 percent in 1981, and 40 percent in 1982 and all years to follow. The law also provides that federal money will be split 50-50 between state and local programs in 1978, but in 1979 and thereafter, in any one state, the state education agency will receive one-fourth of the money from the federal government and local school systems will get three-fourths of the money.

In order for either state or local education programs to be eligible for federal money under this law, they must provide assurances that handicapped children are given fair treatment by the law. There must also be provisions for regular parent consultation with the parents of the handicapped child. The state and local education systems must also assure that the handicapped child is being provided with the least restrictive program of education that is reasonable and possible for that child. In addition, the state and local education authorities must assure that children are not being given tests which are discriminatory in nature or that the evaluations of children are not biased. The law provides that no federal money will be made available to any state or locality that violates confidentiality or releases information improperly about a handicapped child. Last, but by no means of least importance, is the fact that each child's educational program must be written down and reviewed at least once a year to make sure that every handicapped child is getting the best possible service to meet his individual needs. Thus Public Law 94-142 may be viewed as a way to help all handicapped children receive the best education possible without being discriminated against, as has occurred so often in the past.

PROVIDING SPECIAL EDUCATION FOR THE
TRAINABLE RETARDED IN PUBLIC SCHOOLS

In any sizeable group of school-aged children representing an un-selected sample of their own community, it is probable that approximately two- or three-tenths of one percent generally will fall into the moderately retarded or, specifically, into the *trainable* group. The term "trainable" is used by educators and generally defines a range used by the American Association on Mental Deficiency (AAMD) to describe those who fall into the upper levels of the severe classification and all of the moderately retarded individuals.

Unless a very special program is provided, many of the trainable level retarded usually will not be found in classrooms of regular public schools. In some communities, one special facility may be used for all trainable-level children rather than having these children in special classrooms in the regular public school buildings.

The trainable retarded child's ability to profit from public school training has been the subject of controversy among educators in the field of special education for many years. The unwillingness of some educators to assume the responsibility for the jurisdiction of the trainable child is due, in many instances, to their feelings that these programs place the schools in an indefensible position. A special program in which basic academic skills are not stressed cannot, from their point of view, enhance the status of the schools. The value placed on intelligence and achievement in American society and the pressure by parents' groups have been so onerous that educators who do not initiate programs for these children often offer such excuses as the lack of classroom space or the unavailability of well-trained, special-education teachers. Unfortunately, it seems that only a limited number of educational administrators have developed a rationale for the inclusion of trainable children in the school that is consistent with their general philosophy of education.

There is a dearth of information on the development of trainable retarded children which can be utilized as a basis for school planning. The developmental expectations of "normal" children and the achievement areas for them in general are relatively clear and do not present major problems in regard to evaluating pupil growth. The goals in terms of citizenship, leadership, and social and economic contribution are seldom challenged. In contrast, the relevancy of the goals for the trainable child to the goals of general education has not been formulated explicitly. Consequently, reliable means of assessing the development of trainable children have been conspicuously lacking.

Divergent philosophical orientations in regard to the definition of education have been major deterrents to the development of a consistent approach toward the place of trainable children in the public schools. There are basically two philosophical points of view.

1. Those educators opposing programs for the trainable retarded in public schools who envision education as leading to complete independence of the individual and to his active participation in societal affairs.

2. Those educators favoring placement of the trainable-level child in the public school who define education as a systematic process through which positive behavioral changes are fostered that are consistent with the individual's abilities and who feel it is the right of every child to have the opportunity to be able to attend public school programs which are geared to meet his specific educational needs.

Research regarding the effectiveness of educating the trainable retarded in public schools has been summarized by Kirk (1964) and by Goldstein, Moss, and Jordan (1964). Research on the merits of special education for those at the trainable level has had many shortcomings in addition to the same problems cited for the research on the educable retarded. These additional shortcomings include:

1. A dearth of studies which have been of sufficient longitudinal nature. With few exceptions, the studies undertaken in the area of special education for the trainable have all been of relatively short duration. It is not reasonable to assume that short-term studies can obtain a true assessment of the trainable retarded child whose development is relatively slow and who generally will not show much change in a short period of time—even with rather intensive attention.

2. The insufficiency of the evaluation instruments, including the intelligence tests. Most well-standardized instruments have been devised primarily for school-aged children over the mental age of five. Many of the trainable children have mental ages (MA) under five years, and this fact considerably reduces the validity of tests, even those using well-standardized instruments.

3. The problem with sampling—one almost insurmountable problem in studying the trainable retarded and one which plagues the studies on this group—is the fact that these individuals are usually found in small numbers in the community and that, therefore, it is difficult to really obtain an adequate sample.

THE CONCEPT OF NORMALIZATION
IN SPECIAL EDUCATION

Recent professional opinions have held that living conditions and learning circumstances for the retarded should be as normal as possible. The theory underlying this concept is that it is not reasonable to expect the development of "normal" behavior in any individual if that person is living in abnormal surroundings such as an isolated school program or an institution. Until the 1960s, most educational programs segregated the retarded child from those who were considered "normal." The retarded were either separated in special schools or placed into self-contained classrooms which were located within regular school buildings. Until recently, almost 90 percent of all retarded students in the United States were educated in self-contained classrooms in which they were isolated from contact with other students. The term *normalization*, as applied to education for the retarded, represents an attempt to integrate the retarded child with others through an educational program where he or she learns by doing and where social competence is an important goal of the educational program. Thus retarded persons should be provided with normal life experiences inside as well as outside the classroom where they have an opportunity to observe others and interact with them in normal surroundings.

Similarly, the retarded child of the past was seldom allowed to participate in or make his own decisions. Because parents of retarded children need to be actively involved in helping their children to develop decision-making skills, a program of normalization requires a close linkage between the school and the home. Teachers have an important responsibility in assuring success of the normalization effort for the growing child. In so doing, however, teachers and schools must deal with some basic questions which inevitably have to be answered if the retarded are to follow normal life activities. There are still unresolved questions which cause anxiety on the part of many parents. Some of these questions are: To what extent is it reasonable for the retarded to travel alone? To what extent is it reasonable for the adult retarded person to consume alcoholic beverages? How about marriage and a family for the retarded? These are difficult issues that have arisen. Previous misconceptions about treatment of the retarded may need to be reconsidered if normalization is to be meaningfully applied to the real life experiences of the retarded.

MAINSTREAMING FOR THE MILDLY RETARDED

Mainstreaming generally refers to the socio-educational integration of retarded children into regular educational programs with their intellectually normal peers. Keeping any child in the mainstream of educational programming ideally requires a periodic assessment of the educational needs of the child in order to assure that either regular or special education, or some combination of each, is being appropriately provided. Children who have been placed into mainstream programs should be enrolled in regular classes for at least half of the time that they are in school. Any label such as "educable" or "mildly retarded" should be removed.

The strong interest recently generated within education groups concerning mainstreaming of mildly retarded children has created an emphasis on integration of retarded children into regular education programs. The mainstreaming concept, however, has not been without its problems. Some have said that mainstreaming does very little except to remove the retarded label from a child and return him/her to a regular classroom. Others counter by arguing that perhaps this action in and of itself is beneficial since mainstreaming, which is really a strategy for normalization, offers the child an opportunity to begin life without the stigma of a retardation label. The mainstreaming issue is an important one in today's educational programs, and educators will no doubt argue the pros and cons of this idea for many years to come. Mainstreaming can be a very important and beneficial plan for some retarded children but it should not be held out as a panacea.

Most professional articles which have been written about the subject of mainstreaming are not based upon hard research data confirming or refuting the merits of mainstreaming. Rather, writers have tended to be primarily philosophical in their approaches, either exhorting their readers to be in opposition or in favor of mainstreaming on the basis of their opinions or personal viewpoints. Much more research is needed to answer important questions about the concept.

In summary, mainstreaming usually means giving each retarded child the best opportunity to learn in the least restricted environment. It means that, instead of using classification labels, educational programs should closely scrutinize the child's educational needs and then meet these needs. Mainstreaming also connotes that if retarded children are to be placed in regular classes, educators must be diligent in the use of as many creative approaches as possible to help the retarded child overcome his learning and adaptive behavior problems. It means combining the resources, skills, and talents of general educators in order to maximize the educational opportunities for the retarded child.

Mainstreaming, however, can be misused. Some persons may view mainstreaming as a way to close up special classes or to stop providing ancillary or supportive services which the retarded child may need. Mainstreaming should not be used as a way of cutting costs by depriving children of services to meet special educational needs which cannot be adequately met in the regular classroom.

When you have completed this lesson, you should be able to perform the following:

1. Explain or identify the major adverse effect and the major consequence of attempting to educate everyone in the country through the public school system.

2. State or identify the three major considerations that were most often cited in the past as reasons for not requiring the establishment of educational programs for retarded children in the public schools.

3. Given a description of educational programs for retarded children and a list of decades, identify the period in which each program was used.

4. Given a description of the content of a court action or law related to the right to education for the retarded, identify the court action or law.

5. State or identify the approximate percentage of the school-age population that can be considered educable and/or trainable retarded.

6. Given a description of a viewpoint regarding special education classes for the educable retarded, explain or identify the reason or reasons professional educators give for holding this viewpoint.

7. Given an educator's viewpoint, state whether this individual is in favor or opposed to public education for the trainable retarded.

8. Identify or explain at least two shortcomings of the research on special education for the educable and/or trainable retarded child.

9. Explain or identify the best index for ascertaining whether a special-education program has been successful.

10. Explain the meaning of the term *normalization* as it applies to educating the mentally retarded.

11. Define, in your own words, the term *mainstreaming* as it applies to the mentally retarded.

12. Given descriptions of different uses of mainstreaming, identify those which are helpful for the retarded.

QUESTIONS

Please answer each of the following questions carefully. After each possible answer, you will be referred to a frame in the section beginning on p. 312 where you will be told whether or not your choice is correct. If the alternative you have selected is correct, you will be told in the answer frame which frame in the "Questions" section to turn to next. If your choice is incorrect, your answer will tell you to return to the question frame you have just answered to review and to try again. Please note that you will always be given your instructions according to frame number. Frames designated with "Q" indicate a frame in the "Questions" section (e.g., "Q-1, Q-2"). Frames designated with an "A" indicate answers. Only occasionally will you be given a page number to which to turn. It is most important that you follow the instructions for *each individual question or answer frame* most carefully.

THE EFFECTS AND CONSEQUENCES OF ATTEMPTING TO EDUCATE EVERYONE IN PUBLIC SCHOOLS

Educating the retarded has always been a problem. Particularly since it has been difficult enough for public schools to fulfill their responsibility of educating the mass of so-called "normal" children, the additional problem of educating the retarded has been viewed by many with a great deal of pessimism. The major approach to solving this problem has been the establishment of special-education classes within the public schools. These classes are considered "special" since different teaching methods and a different, far less difficult curriculum is employed in them than is used in classes for the "normal" child.

This lesson will focus on the education provided by our society for the educable and trainable retarded and will point out the results and shortcomings of the research which has aimed at discovering whether or not these individuals should be taught in the public schools.

In our society, one of the most important and desirable attributes that anyone can possess is to be "educated." The value of education has become so important that we assume that every American has the right and, indeed, the obligation to become educated—or at least to attend school until he has reached sixteen years of age. Although in most states everyone is required by law to attend school until reaching the age of sixteen, taking school attendance for granted does not insure school quality. The question of whether public schools can educate everyone, including the handicapped as is required by all state constitutions, has yet to be satisfactorily answered.

Mass education in America has created a major problem. In attempting to educate the largest group, the focus, of necessity, has been placed on the average or "normal" student. Those who are "different"—either in terms of having a physical handicap or in terms of having an above or below average mentality—have had to suffer most of the negative consequences of this attempt at mass education. The gifted individual in the regular classroom may be affected adversely because he suffers boredom, as school is often too easy to give him an incentive or challenge.

However, it is the individual of below average intelligence—the mentally retarded—who, until recently, has suffered the most from this sytem. Even in the recent past, there was inadequate provision in many public school systems for these individuals to obtain the skills necessary for self-sufficiency in adult life. Indeed, for various reasons, many educators believe that the trainable retarded should not be allowed to attend public school at all.

Test yourself with the following question.

One of the major consequences of attempting to educate the entire population of the country has been that:

a. The gifted person benefits at the expense
of the normal or handicapped.   Turn to A-37.
b. The average or normal person suffers more
than any other.   Turn to A-6.
c. The normal person benefits from the public
school system more than do those who are
retarded or gifted.   Turn to A-22.

Adverse Effects on the Retarded and His Family

Q-2   Since so much emphasis is placed on education in our society and since the retarded child often has not had the opportunity to obtain a proper education (in some cases, he even has been blocked from entering public schools at all), the child's family members experience damaging psychological effects just as he does. The devaluation and lowering of regard for the child because of his handicap and "differences" may have adverse effects on members of the entire family.

Test yourself with the following question.

Because the importance placed in our society on education is so great, when a retarded child is not allowed to enter school or is forced to drop out of school, he:

a. Is usually relieved and suffers no
   adverse effects.   Turn to A-14.
b. And his family often experience a
   psychologically damaging feeling of lowered
   self-esteem.   Turn to A-3.
c. Alone experiences a sense of lowered self-
   esteem.   Turn to A-27.

WHY HAVE PUBLIC SCHOOL EDUCATORS
BEEN RELUCTANT TO DEVELOP EDUCATIONAL
PROGRAMS FOR THE RETARDED?

Public school administrators have been reluctant to develop educational programs for the retarded for many reasons. Three reasons that seem to have been paramount include:

1. Educators' defensiveness regarding the adequacy of school programs for the "normal" children and their feelings that programs for the retarded might jeopardize or take away from the classes for the normal which have already been established.

2. A lack of information regarding:
   a. The development of retarded children.
   b. How to design a school program that will best serve the needs of the retarded child.

3. Divergent philosophical orientations of educators regarding the definitions and goals of education.

Test yourself with the following question.

Circle below the letters which correspond to those reasons most often cited for the shortage of public school education programs for the retarded; then turn to A-18 to check your answers.

a. A lack of interest in the normal child.
b. A lack of information about the development of the retarded person.
c. Conflicting viewpoints concerning the need for educating the retarded.
d. Inadequate information concerning how best to design a school program for the retarded.
e. Conflicting viewpoints among educators concerning the goals of education.
f. A defensive attitude among educators regarding the adequacy of educational programs for "normal" children and a feeling that programs for the retarded may jeopardize existing programs.
g. A belief, held by many educators, that all the retarded can only be educated in institutions.

HISTORY OF EDUCATION FOR THE EDUCABLE
RETARDED IN THE UNITED STATES

Q-4   The first special-education program for the retarded was established in this country before 1900. By the 1920s, the educable
retarded were being placed in "subnormal" classrooms. The emphasis here was on the development of useful skills, such as sewing,
cooking, and simple carpentry. In the great majority of these
classes, there was little or no academic curriculum.

During the 1930s, the conviction spread that retarded children
could be taught to read; consequently, a few academic skills especially reading skills, were stressed in classrooms for the educable
retarded. The use of "nonoral" reading methods and individual
work materials became the norm in these classes.

Test yourself with the following question.

The first special-education program for the retarded in the United
States was established:

a. Before the turn of the century.   Turn to A-25.
b. In the 1920s.   Turn to A-8.
c. In the 1930s.   Turn to A-29.

Q-5   Circle the letters below which correspond to the significant events
that occurred in the 1930s in the development of education for
the educable retarded; then turn to A-17 to check your answers.

a. Nonoral reading methods were widely used.
b. Reading skills development was not included in the curriculum.
c. Individualized instruction was widely used.
d. The first special-education program was established.
e. No academic curriculum was present in most public schools.

Beginning in the 1940s, a broader education program for the educable retarded was stressed, with many different activities occurring simultaneously in the special-education classroom. Since the 1940s, the educational curriculum in these classes has included such subjects as oral language, social studies, science, physical education, music, art reading, writing, and arithmetric.

Special-education classes for the older educable retarded person include the teaching of skills related to independent living, such as prevocational skills, citizenship, homemaking skills, preparation for community living, and understanding of problems of family living and job adjustment.

Test yourself with the following question.

Circle below the letters which correspond to the statements that apply to special-education classes for the educable retarded; then turn to A-13 to check your answers.

a. During the 1920s, the major emphasis was on simple skill learning.
b. During the 1940s, the major stress was placed on nonoral reading methods.
c. During the 1930s, individual instruction was the norm.
d. Beginning in the 1940s, a broad program of studies stressing many different types of classroom activities began.
e. For the most part, educable retarded children are now taught independent living skills, such as prevocational skills, citizenship, and homemaking skills.

Q-7 Two recent court actions, one in Pennsylvania and one in the District of Columbia, and a very important piece of federal legislation have contributed greatly to assuring that the retarded are provided with educational opportunities. The Pennsylvania case, entitled *Pennsylvania Association for Retarded Children* vs. *Commonwealth of Pennsylvania*, required that all retarded children in Pennsylvania be offered the opportunity to obtain free public education appropriate to their learning capabilities.

The other court case, *Mills* vs. *Board of Education of the District of Columbia*, required the state to offer all retarded children educational opportunities and also required the school system to establish hearings which would be required before any child could be suspended from school for more than two days.

In 1975 Congress passed a very important piece of legislation, Public Law 94-142, known as the *Education for All Handicapped Children Act of 1975*. This law not only provided federal assistance to the states to help meet the educational needs of handicapped children ages three to twenty-one, but also set forth that the constitutional rights of both handicapped children and their parents would be protected.

In this action the rights of the retarded to an education were provided increased protection.

a. Public Law 94-142. Turn to A-10.

b. *Pennsylvania Association for Retarded Children* vs. *Commonwealth of Pennsylvania*. Turn to A-2.

c. *Mills* vs. *Board of Education of the District of Columbia*. Turn to A-19.

d. b and c above. Turn to A-26.

e. a, b, and c above. Turn to A-35.

State the name of the legislation which provides that the federal government will provide financial assistance to states to help meet the educational needs of handicapped children ages three to twenty-one and then turn to A-38.

_____

_____

_____

PERCENTAGE OF SCHOOL-AGED
POPULATION RETARDED

Q-9   As was noted earlier, the retarded have been separated by special educators into three major groupings—educable, trainable, and custodial—for educational purposes. In this lesson, we are focusing for the most part on the educable, or the mildly retarded, and the trainable, or the moderately retarded, since the custodial, or severely and profoundly retarded individual is unable to benefit from public school-based academic training. Some types of training programs that have been developed recently are being offered in institutions and private agencies to help some of the more severely retarded children perform very simple self-help skills, but the public schools usually are not now and may never be able to offer useful training to these children.

Of the total school population in the United States, approximately 2 percent are educable retardates, while about 0.3 percent are trainable retardates. Since 1956, almost all states have either permitted or required special facilities for the education of these individuals. Therefore, there has been a steady increase in the number of special classes during the last two decades. For example, in the years from 1952-53 to 1964-65, there was a 250 percent increase in the number of educable retarded children in public schools in the United States and an 850 percent increase in trainable-level children in public schools.

If there were 100,000 children of school age in your hometown, approximately how many of these children would be educable retardates? How many would be trainable retardates? Circle below the two correct answers; then turn to A-20 to check your answer.

Educable	Trainable
1,000	100
10,000	1,000
2,000	600
20,000	2,000
3,000	300
30,000	3,000

THE PROBLEM OF PROVIDING EDUCATIONAL
FACILITIES FOR THE EDUCABLE RETARDED

A major problem faced by educators and school personnel is how Q-10 to provide education in the public schools for the educable retarded child without penalizing the other children in the schools.

Even if there are no special services for the retarded children, the problem is still there; these children will not disappear if there are no programs and they will still need education and training.

The major problem from the educator's point of view regarding education for the educable retarded child is:

a. Whether or not this individual should
   be educated in public school.   Turn to A-28.
b. How to educate this individual without
   penalizing other children.   Turn to A-39.
c. How to distinguish between educable and
   normal children.   Turn to A-23.

*Divergent Points of View among Educators
concerning Education for the Educable
Retarded Child in Public Schools*

There are two opposing points of view among educators regarding Q-11 the problem of educating the educable retarded in public schools. These viewpoints are:

1. That the educable retarded child needs individual attention and should be placed in small, special classes (i.e., special-education classes).
2. That special-education classes should not be used for teaching these children for two major reasons. First, educable retarded children learn best in regular classrooms because they are exposed to the stimulation of brighter children. Second, when special classes are used, the educable child develops feelings of inferiority and rejection as a result of being segregated in special classes.

One study (Johnson and Kirk in 1950) showed that when educable retarded children are placed in regular classes, they are rejected by their normal peers because of their inability to learn as quickly as the other children.

The results of the Johnson and Kirk study tend to substantiate which point of view regarding the education of the retarded child?

a. Special-education classes should be
   provided in the public schools.   Turn to A-16.
b. All children should be taught in regular
   classrooms in the public schools.   Turn to A-9.

Q-12   Explain in the space provided below which point of view you would take regarding the education of the educable retarded child and explain your reasons for positing this view; then turn to A-40 to check your answers.

_____

_____

_____

Q-13   RESULTS AND SHORTCOMINGS OF THE RESEARCH ON SPECIAL EDUCATION FOR THE EDUCABLE RETARDED

The research which compares the effectiveness of special-education classes for the retarded with programs where the educable retarded are taught in regular classes has yielded no positive results. According to these studies, there appears to be no difference between the two types of programs as far as the achievement of the children is concerned.

However, the majority of these studies can be seriously challenged on the basis of the following factors:

1. An *automatic sample bias* exists because the majority of the special-education children used in these studies had already "failed" from regular classes into these special classes. These children tended to be the lowest achievers or the greatest behavior problems of all of the educable retarded. The top groups of educable retarded would still be in the regular classes.
2. A *conceptual bias* exists because there is disagreement as to what is meant by special class (i.e., what constitutes such a class and what skills are needed by special-education teachers.).
3. An *instrumental bias* results from the lack of validity and reliability in the majority of the instruments used in the various research efforts.

Test yourself with the following question.

The results of the research regarding the effectiveness of education for the educable retarded in public schools has shown that:

a. Regular classes are superior to special-education classes in working with the educable retarded.   Turn to A-36.
b. Special-education classes are superior to regular classes in working with the educable retarded.   Turn to A-4.
c. No superiority has been proven for either special-education classes or regular classes in educating the educable retarded.   Turn to A-30.

Q-14   Much of the research done to compare the achievement of the educable retarded in special and regular classes has not been valid due to specific biases. Circle the letters below which indicate the three main biases; then turn to A-21 to check your answers.

  a. A conceptual bias.
  b. A maturation bias.
  c. An instrumental bias.
  d. A sample bias.
  e. A historical bias.
  f. A regression bias.

THE PROBLEM OF PROVIDING EDUCATION FOR THE TRAINABLE CHILD

Q-15   One major philosophical problem in providing educational programs for the trainable child has been the unresolved conflict among educators regarding whether or not these individuals can profit from public school training.

In essence, this conflict is due to the fact that some educators have been able to develop what they consider to be a reasonable rationale for excluding trainable retarded children from the public school system. They argue that a special program in which basic academic skills are not stressed will devalue the status of the public schools. In addition, the relevance of the goals of education for the trainable child to the goals of general education has yet to be explicitly formulated.

The major philosophical problem which educators have yet to resolve among themselves regarding the education of the trainable child in public schools is:

  a. How these individuals can be educated.   Turn to A-12.
  b. Whether or not these persons can profit
     from a public-school education.   Turn to A-5.
  c. How these individuals can be
     educated without withdrawing
     educational resources from other
     children.   Turn to A-31.

DIVERGENT PHILOSOPHICAL ORIENTATIONS REGARDING THE DEFINITION OF EDUCATION

A major deterrent to the admission of trainable retarded children to the public schools has been the divergent philosophical orientations regarding the definition of education.

Q-16

There are basically two philosophical orientations to this definition. The first is that education should lead to complete independence of the individual and to his active participation in societal affairs. Those educators who accept this orientation are opposed to placing programs for the trainable retarded in public schools. Those who hold the second orientation define education as a systematic process through which positive behavioral changes consistent with the child's abilities are fostered. In addition, these educators argue that all children have the right to be given an opportunity for public-school education. Those who hold this viewpoint favor placement of the trainable child in the public school.

If an educator envisions education as leading to complete independence of the person and to his active participation in societal affairs, he would probably be _____ placement of the trainable child in a public school.

a. In favor of.   Turn to A-15.
b. Opposed to.   Turn to A-1.

SHORTCOMINGS OF THE RESEARCH ON THE EDUCATION OF THE TRAINABLE CHILD IN PUBLIC SCHOOLS

The divergent philosophical orientations regarding the definition of education held by educators have resulted in an unwillingness on the part of some administrators to develop public school programs that would benefit the trainable child.

Q-17

Not unlike the results of research regarding the educable retarded, the research on the effectiveness of public school education for the trainable retarded has shown few positive results; once again, this research has many shortcomings.

A review of the educational research on the trainable-level child shows that there are two bias-creating factors which result in the same problems as the research difficulties found in studies on the educable-level child. In addition, there is another bias which is somewhat different. These three shortcomings are:

1. A *longitudinal bias* exists because most studies on the trainable groups have been of relatively short duration. Studies of the trainable retarded, whose development is slow, should be of a relatively long duration; otherwise little, if any, change will be evidenced.
2. A *sample bias* exists because there are so few trainable retarded that it is extremely difficult to obtain an adequate sample of these individuals in a proper manner.
3. An *instrumental bias* exists because evaluation instruments are insufficient. Most standardized instruments are devised for children who have a mental age (MA) of over five years; the MA of most of the trainable retarded is under five years.

Circle the letters below which correspond to the reasons that the studies regarding the effectiveness of public school education for the trainable retarded are of questionable validity; then turn to A-24 to check your answer.

a. Sample bias.
b. Instrumental bias.
c. Maturation bias.
d. Longitudinal bias.
e. Experimental mortality bias.
f. Conceptual bias.
g. Regression bias.

HOW TO EVALUATE THE SUCCESS OF A
SPECIAL-EDUCATION PROGRAM

Since the basic purpose of special-education programs is to help the individual to be as productive as he possibly can in later life, there is at least one index for determining whether or not a special-education program has been successful. Such an index enables researchers to view the work productivity of those who previously have been involved in special-education programs. If the members of the special classes become economically productive and contributing citizens in their communities, then the special-education classes they attended might be said to have been of value and beneficial to them.

A number of studies have been carried out on the post-school adjustment of the mentally retarded. You might want to read some of these studies which are listed in the Selected Readings in the last section of this lesson. Some of the authors of studies in this area are Fairbanks, Baller, and Charles, and reading their studies will provide you with a more comprehensive understanding of the material. Again, as with other studies, there were many inherent problems in the research efforts of these men. Their studies still provide no clear-cut answers as to what types of training programs for the retarded are best. More research is needed before definitive answers can be obtained.

One of the ways to assess whether or not a special-education program has been successful is to use:

a. Intelligence tests.   Turn to A-11.
b. Work productivity.   Turn to A-7.
c. Attitude scales.   Turn to A-32.

Q-18

Q-19   One of the most effective ways in which to fulfill the purpose of special education programs is to help the retarded individual function with all other individuals with and without handicaps. This includes making the educational environment and the educational objectives conducive to the development of skills which will be useful in life and will help the retarded individual function as normally as possible in any environment. Normalization represents an attempt to accomplish this by integrating the retarded individual into normal school life and helping him or her learn to perform useful skills in order to become socially competent. The present trend toward competency-based and performance-based educational programs could be readily applied in this attempt at normalization for the retarded. Including the parents in their child's learning process is another method that has great potential.

In most cases, retarded individuals have more potential for competent functioning than most of us realize. When our expectations are raised, they usually tend to meet them, especially when they are rewarded for their efforts.

In the space below, briefly explain what is meant by normalization as it applies to special education and then turn to A-33.

MAINSTREAMING

Q-20   The term *mainstreaming* as it applies to the mentally retarded refers to the integration of retarded children into regular educational programs rather than separating or isolating them with others who have similar handicaps. Mainstreaming is one of the major strategies for helping normalize the lives of the retarded.

There is a great deal of argument regarding the implementation of this process. The most effective implementation requires the following:

1. Removal of any labels, such as "educable" or "mildly retarded."
2. Periodic assessment of the educational needs of each child.
3. Provision of either regular and/or special classes as dictated by the child's needs.
4. Avoiding placing any child in a special class for more than half of the time they are in school.

5. The development and use of creative instructional approaches by all educators.
6. Avoiding the temptation to cut costs by stopping ancillary and supportive services needed by the retarded child.

In the space below, describe, in your own words, the meaning of mainstreaming as it applies to the retarded child and then turn to A-34.

_____

_____

_____

_____

_____

_____

_____

_____

Place a checkmark in the spaces provided beside those descriptions of the application of the mainstreaming concept which would be helpful for the retarded child and turn to A-41.   Q-21

a. ____ Use labels to distinguish the retarded from their normal intellectual peers.
b. ____ Periodic assessment of the educational needs of each child.
c. ____ Place the retarded child in a special class most of the time.
d. ____ Place the retarded child in a regular or a special class according to his educational needs of the moment, based on periodic assessments.
e. ____ Use of traditional instructional strategies and methods.
f. ____ Development and liberal use of innovative instructional strategies and methods.
g. ____ Eliminate supportive services for the retarded.
h. ____ Avoid labeling the retarded child.

ANSWERS

Please follow the same instructions as those you were given on page 294 in working this section. It is most important that you remember to follow the individual instructions in each answer frame.

A-1   You are correct. The educator who envisions education as leading to complete independence of the individual and his active participation in societal affairs probably would be opposed to placing programs for the trainable retarded child in the public schools. Continue now with Q-17.

A-2   This is correct but there are other actions listed in Q-7 which also contributed to enhancing the retarded person's right to an education. Return to Q-7 and select the best answer.

A-3   Right. Both the retarded child and his family usually experience the psychologically damaging effects of the rejection of the child if he is not permitted to enter or allowed to attend school. Continue now with Q-3.

A-4   Achievement of educable retarded students in special classes has not been shown to be superior to that of similar students in regular classes in public schools. Return to page 305 for a brief review before answering Q-13 correctly.

Exactly. The major philosophical problem lies in trying to decide   A-5
whether or not trainable children can profit from public school
education. Educators agree that the educable child can profit from
education, but there is not full agreement that the trainable can
also profit. Continue now with Q-16.

The normal person usually benefits to the greatest extent from our   A-6
present system of mass education, which is focused mainly on his
needs. He even profits at the expense of the handicapped and
gifted. Since you have missed the point here, return to Q-1 for a
brief review.

You have chosen the correct answer. An index of economic or work   A-7
productivity would indicate whether or not an individual is a
productive and contributing citizen in his community. If he is
shown to be productive, it can be assumed that the special education classes he attended were beneficial. Good Work! Turn now to
Q-19.

The first special-education program for the retarded was established   A-8
before 1900, rather than in the 1920s. By 1920 there had been
only modest improvements in public school education for the retarded. The major emphasis was on learning simple skills, and skill
development was tied to a meager academic curriculum, if, in some
classes, any curriculum at all existed. Return to Q-4 and answer
the question correctly.

A-9   Since the results of this study showed that the educable retarded child in the regular class was ridiculed, this study could be viewed as substantiation of the view that these children should be placed in special classes. Return to pages 303-4 for a brief review before answering Q-11 correctly.

A-10   Yes, this law requires the federal government to provide funds for educating handicapped children, thereby protecting the rights of retarded children to an education, but other actions listed in Q-7 also provided protection of this right. Return to Q-7 and select the best answer.

A-11   An intelligence test would tell you the intelligence of an individual compared with other individuals who had taken the same test. Such tests would not be of practical value in telling you whether or not a program had been a success. Return to page 309 for a brief review to answer Q-18 correctly.

A-12   Although figuring out how trainable retarded individuals can be educated is a problem for educators, this is not the major philosophical problem at present.

Return to page 306 for a review and then answer the question presented in Q-15 correctly.

You should have circled letters a, c, d, and e

Continue now with Q-7 if you feel that you have a firm grasp of the broad changes that have occurred in the history of special-education classes in the United States. If not, you should review the lesson before going on to Q-7.

This is rarely, if ever, the case. The retarded child, like all other   children faced with rejection or failure, often experiences a psychologically damaging sense of lowered self-esteem. For most retarded children, this problem only adds to their feelings of inferiority.

Return to Q-2 for a brief review of the damaging effect on the child that results from a lack of educational opportunities; then return and answer this question correctly.

You would have selected "opposed to" if you had read this lesson   carefully. The educator who envisions education as leading to complete independence of the individual and to his active participation in societal affairs will probably be opposed to establishing programs for the trainable child in public schools. Continue now with Q-17.

The results of this study are contrary to the conviction of those   educators who believe that the educable retarded child should be taught in regular classes. Therefore, these results could be used to substantiate the view that some type of special classes should be provided for the educable retarded child. You have chosen the correct answer. Continue now with Q-12.

A-17   The letters corresponding to the events occurring during the 1930s are "a" and "c." Nonoral reading methods and individual instruction made up the norm in special-education classes for the educable retarded during this period in history. Go right on to Q-6 if you answered this question correctly. If not, go back to Q-4 for a brief review before going to Q-6.

A-18   You should have circled the letters "b," "d," "e," and "f." Educators have been reluctant to develop programs for the retarded since they have had divergent views concerning the meaning and goals of education as well as the fear that developing programs for the retarded might in some way jeopardize the existing general education programs. More specifically, educators have been handicapped by a lack of information regarding the education and development of the retarded. Continue now with Q-4.

A-19   This answer is only partially correct. There are other actions listed in Q-7 which provided further protection of the rights of the retarded to an education. Return to Q-7 and select the best answer.

A-20   Of a school-aged population of 100,000 children, about 2 percent, or 2,000, would be educable retarded and about 0.3 percent, or 300, would be trainable retarded. With education and training, most of these individuals, especially the educable retarded, could be helped to become independent adults; without education and training, these 2,300 individuals could place a tremendous psychological and financial burden on the community in which they live.

Continue now with Q-10.

The letters you should have circled include "a," "c," and "d."   **A-21**
The research biases include conceptual, instrumental, and sample biases.

Continue now with Q-15.

Yes. The normal individual benefits to a greater extent than do the   **A-22** handicapped and the gifted who do not fall within the norm. The gifted child may suffer boredom due to lack of incentive; however, most gifted children manage to make it through school and in some cases are given the incentive they need to excell. It is the retarded child who probably suffers the most as a result of his slow learning pace.

Continue now with Q-2.

This is not one of the present problems of educators in regard to   **A-23** the education of the educable retarded. Diagnostic tools have been improved steadily, and it is now possible, in most cases, to distinguish among educable, trainable, and normal children.

Return to Q-10 for a review and then answer this question correctly.

The letters you should have circled are "a," "b," and "d."   **A-24**

Did you get all of these correct? If so, go right on to Q-18. If not, return to page 307 - 8 for a review before going on to Q-18.

A-25   Yes. The establishment of the first special-education program for the retarded occurred before the beginning of the twentieth century. Continue now with Q-5.

A-26   Yes, these two court actions provided increased protection for the retarded person's right to an education, but so did Public Law 94-142. Return to Q-7 and select the best answer.

A-27   Although the child experiences a psychologically damaging sense of lowered self-esteem when he is denied an education, he is not alone in this feeling. Usually his entire family is adversely affected by this rejection. Your answer was not correct. Return to Q-2 and answer the question correctly.

As will be discussed later, this is the major problem regarding the   A-28
trainable retarded child; however, most educators believe that the
educable retardate should be educated in public school.

Return to Q-10 for a brief review; then answer Q-10 correctly.

No, the first special-education program for the retarded was estab-   A-29
lished before the end of the Nineteenth Century rather than during
the 1930s.

Return to Q-4 for a brief review before answering this question correctly.

This, indeed, has been the result of the research on this topic. The   A-30
achievement of educable pupils has not been found to be superior
in either special classes or regular classes.

Continue now with Q-14.

Although this is a problem with regard to trainable children just as   A-31
it is with the educable retarded, it is not the major philosophical
problem.

Return to Q-15 and answer the question correctly.

A-32   Although an attitude scale may be helpful in revealing how a retarded person might feel about a subject, it will not help you ascertain whether the program is a success or not in terms of achievement. Return to the material in Q-18 and then answer Q-18 correctly.

A-33   Normalization, as it relates to special education, refers to the integration of the retarded individual with other individuals in educational programs in which they learn by doing (performance-based programs) and where one important goal of the program is the learning of social competence.

How close was your explanation to the one presented above? If you had any difficulty, return to Q-19 for a review. If you are satisfied with your response then go on to Q-20.

A-34   Mainstreaming as it applies to the retarded refers to the integration, both social and educational, of retarded children into regular educational programs in which *their* educational needs are provided for just as effectively as those of their more normal intellectual peers.

If you wrote something similar to the above, give yourself a compliment and then move on to Q-21. If you had trouble defining this term, review Q-20 before moving on to Q-21.

A-35   Excellent! All three of these actions taken by the courts and the congress of the United States have contributed greatly to the retarded person's opportunity to receive an appropriate education. Well done, go on now to Q-8 and continue the lesson.

This has not been demonstrated. Regular classes have not been shown to be superior to special-education classes in helping the educable retarded. Return to pages 304 - 5 for a brief review of Q-13 before answering Q-13 correctly.

A-36

The focus of mass education has been placed on the "normal" student. As long as an individual falls within the mental and physical norm, he is not penalized by the present system, except for the fact that he will be given little motivation to progress beyond mediocrity. The tendency toward mediocrity penalizes the gifted person who usually suffers boredom as a result. Return to Q-1 for a brief review before answering this question correctly.

A-37

The legislation which provides the federal government financial assistance for education for handicapped children is Public Law 94-142 or the *Education for All Handicapped Children Act of 1975*. If you answered this correctly, well done, go on to Q-9. If not, review page 300 before going on to Q-8.

A-38

You have chosen the correct answer if you turned directly to this item. The major problem regarding education of the educable retarded child is how to educate this child in the best way in the public school without, at the same time, penalizing other children. Turn now to Q-11 to learn about the divergent points of view among educators regarding this problem.

A-39

No matter which point of view you agree with, you will be able to find experts who agree with you and other experts who disagree. However, there has been little adequate research accomplished to substantiate either point of view on this subject. Your opinion may be just as strongly biased as any expert's! Continue now with Q-13.

A-41   The best answers are "b", "d," "f," and "h."

How well did you do? If you had any trouble, return to Q-20 for a review. If you identified the four best answers, congratulations, you have completed the programmed portion of this lesson. Move on to the conclusion presented on the next page before finishing this lesson.

CONCLUSION

You should now understand the history and the problems involved in educating the retarded in the United States. The need is great for improved methods which will teach the retarded most effectively and thereby help them to reach their maximum potential.

You have now completed this lesson, but before moving on to Lesson Sixteen, answer the questions on the following pages.

Questions

Circle the letter corresponding to the answer of each of the following questions.

1. In the past, most public school programs had an attitude about education for the retarded which can best be described by one of the following words:

    a. Eagerness.
    b. Willingness.
    c. Hesitancy.
    d. Total rejection.

2. Special education for the retarded in the United States was started:

    a. Before 1900.
    b. From 1930-1933.
    c. From 1940-1960.
    d. None of the above.

3. The earliest special-education programs for the retarded in the United States stressed:

    a. Reading.
    b. Writing and arithmetic.
    c. Developing useful vocational skills.
    d. Music and drama.

4. Educators have been hesitant to develop educational programs for the mentally retarded primarily because of which of the following factors?

    a. Inadequate information on the retarded.
    b. A belief among educators that the retarded should be educated in institutions for the retarded rather than in public schools.
    c. Conflicting viewpoints concerning the goals of education.
    d. a and c above.
    e. a, b, and c above.

5. Which of the following provided protection for the rights of the retarded to an education?

    a. Public Law 94-142.
    b. *Mills* vs. *Board of Education of the District of Columbia.*

    c. *Pennsylvania Association for Retarded Children* vs. *Common-wealth of Pennsylvania.*
    d. b and c above.
    e. a, b, and c above.

6. Current special-education programs for the older educable retarded individual do *not* emphasize which of the following skills?

    a. Preparation for institutional living.
    b. Citizenship.
    c. Homemaking skills.
    d. Prevocational skills.

7. In any sizeable group of school-aged children, one would be likely to find which of the following approximate percentages of educable retarded children?

    a. 1 percent.
    b. 2 percent.
    c. 3 percent.
    d. 4 percent.

8. The largest group of retarded children found in the public schools would be called, in educators' terminology:

    a. Trainable.
    b. Educable.
    c. Classroom Type A.
    d. Custodial.

9. Which of the following are apt to suffer the consequences of a lack of educational programs for the mentally retarded?

    a. The retarded child.
    b. The family of the retarded child.
    c. The entire community.
    d. a and b above.
    e. a, b, and c above.

10. Which of the following statements is most correct?

    a. Educators are still in disagreement about the value and effectiveness of special-education classes for educable retarded children.
    b. Educators are in general agreement as to the merits of special-education classes for the trainable retarded.
    c. Most educators feel that the educable retarded should be educated in state institutions for the retarded.

d. Most educators feel that the educable retarded should be dropped from the public-school programs because they cannot profit from the education which they receive there.

11. At the present time, there is research evidence that _____ the value of special education for the educable retarded as opposed to regular classroom education.

   a. Confirms.
   b. Refutes.
   c. Neither confirms nor refutes.
   d. This question cannot be answered because there has been no research in this area.

12. Which of the following terms would most likely be used by those in the field of special education?

   a. Mild, moderate, severe, profound.
   b. Subnormal, mentally retarded, mentally deficient.
   c. High grade, middle grade, low grade.
   d. Educable, trainable, severely retarded (custodial).

13. Research regarding the merits of special education for the trainable level child:

   a. Has been inconclusive.
   b. Has had shortcomings.
   c. Has not used well-validated instruments.
   d. All of the above.

14. One of the better methods used for trying to determine whether or not a special-education program has been successful is:

   a. Asking the special-education teachers.
   b. Asking the children in the special classes.
   c. Using work productivity as an index of the success of the education program.
   d. Administering an achievement test to the special-class students.

15. If an educator envisions education as a systematic process through which positive behavioral changes consistent with an individual's abilities are fostered, he would be:

    a. In favor of placement of a trainable-level child in an institution for the mentally retarded.
    b. In favor of placement of a trainable-level child in the public school.
    c. Opposed to placement of a trainable-level child in the public school.
    d. a and c above.

16. As applied to special education, normalization refers to which of the following?

    a. Placing retarded students in classes with nonretarded students.
    b. Isolating retarded students in classes with other students with similar handicaps.
    c. Helping retarded students attain competence in social skills using methods where they learn by doing.
    d. a and c above.
    e. b and c above.

17. Mainstreaming as applied to retarded children refers to which of the following?

    a. A normalization strategy.
    b. Integrating retarded children in regular educational programs.
    c. A panacea for assuming that all retarded children will attain their maximum educational level.
    d. a and b above.
    e. a, b, and c above.

Answers

The answers to the questions on the preceding pages are:

1. c.
2. a.
3. c.
4. d.
5. e.
6. a.
7. b.
8. b.
9. e.
10. a.
11. c.
12. d.
13. d.
14. c.
15. b.
16. d.
17. d.

Ainsworth, S. H. "An Exploratory Study of Educational, Social, and Emotional Factors in the Education of Mentally Retarded Children in Georgia Public Schools." U.S. Office of Education Cooperative Research Program, Project No. 171 (6470). Athens: University of Georgia, 1959.

Baldwin, W. K. "The Social Position of the Educable Mentally Retarded Child in the Regular Grades in the Public Schools." *Exceptional Children* 25 (1958): 106-8;112.

Baller, W. R. "A Study of the Present Social Status of a Group of Adults Who, When They Were in Elementary School, Were Classified as Mentally Deficient." *Genetic Psychology Monographs* 18 (1936): 165-244.

Blatt, B. "The Physical, Personality, and Academic Status of Children Who Are Mentally Retarded Attending Special Classes as Compared with Children Who Are Mentally Retarded Attending Regular Classes." *American Journal of Mental Deficiency* 62 (1958): 810-18.

Bruininks, R. and Rynders, J. "Alternatives to Special Class Placement for Educable Mentally Retarded Children." *Focus on Exceptional Children* 3 (1971): 1-12.

Cain, L. F.; Cain L. S. et al. "A Study of the Effects of Community and Institutional School Classes for Trainable Mentally Retarded Children." U.S. Office of Education, Cooperative Research Branch, Contr. No. 589, SAE-8257, 1961.

Carriker, W. R. "A Comparison of Post-School Adjustments of Regular and Special-Class Retarded Individuals Served in Lincoln and Omaha, Nebraska Public Schools." Project No. 146. Washington, D.C.: U.S. Office of Education, 1959.

Cassidy, V. and Stanton, J. E. *An Investigation of Factors Involved in the Educational Placement of Mentally Retarded Children: A Study of Differences between Children in Special and Regular Classes in Ohio.* U.S. Office of Education Cooperative Research Program, Project No. 043. Columbus: Ohio State University, 1959.

Charles, D. C. "Ability and Accomplishment of Persons Earlier Judged Mentally Deficient." *Genetic Psychology Monograph* 47 (1953): 3-71.

Christoplos, F. and Reny, P. A. "A Critical Examination of Special Education Programs." *The Journal of Special Education* 3 (1969): 371-79.

Cruickshank, W. M. and Johnson, G. O., eds. *Education of Exceptional Children and Youth.* Englewood Cliffs, New Jersey: Prentice-Hall, 1958.

Deno, E. "Special Education as Developmental Capital." *Exceptional Children* 37 (1970): 229-37.

Dunn, L. M. "Special Education for the Mildly Retarded—Is Much of It Justifiable?" *Exceptional Children* 35 (1968): 5-22.

Dunn, L. M. and Capobianco, R. J. "Mental Retardation: A Review of Research." In Mental Retardation, edited by J. H. Rothstein, pp. 548-73. New York: Holt, Rinehart and Winston, 1965.

Elenbogen, M. L. "A Comparative Study of Some Aspects of Academic and Social Adjustment of Two Groups of Mentally Retarded Children in Special Classes and in Regular Grades." *Dissertation Abstracts* 17 (1957): 2497.

Gallagher, J. J. "Educational Methods with Brain-Damaged Children." In *Current Psychiatric Therapies*, vol. 2, pp. 48-55. New York: Grune and Stratton, 1962.

Goldberg, I. I. "Trainable But Noneducable, A Debate with W. M. Cruickshank." *National Education Association Journal* 47 (1958): 622-23.

Goldstein, H. "Report Number Two on Study Projects for Trainable Mentally Handicapped Children." Issued by V. L. Nickell, Superintendent of Public Instruction, Springfield, Illinois, 1956.

Goldstein, H.; Jordon, L.; and Moss, J. W. "Early School Development of Low IQ Children: A Study of Special Class Placement." U.S. Office of Education Cooperative Research Program, Project SAE 8204. Urbana: University of Illinois, Institute for Research of Exceptional Children, 1962.

Goldstein, H.; Moss, J. W.; and Jordon, L. J. *The Efficacy of Special Class Training on the Development of Mentally Retarded Children.* Institute for Research on Exceptional Children, Cooperative Research Project Number 619, 1964.

Guenther, R. J. "Final Report of the Michigan Demonstration Research Project for the Severely Retarded." Lansing, Michigan: Department of Public Instruction, 1956.

Hill, A. S. "The Forward Look: The Severely Retarded Child Goes to School." *U.S. Department of Health, Education and Welfare Bulletin* No. 11 (1952): 1-54.

Hottel, J. "An Evaluation of Tennessee's Day Class Program for Severely Mentally Retarded Trainable Children." Nashville, Tennessee: State Department of Education, 1958.

Hungerford, R. H.; DeProspo, C. J.; and Rosenzweig, L. E. "Education of the Mentally Handicapped in Childhood and Adolescence." *American Journal of Mental Deficiency* 57 (1952): 214-28.

_____. *The Nonacademic Pupil.* New York: Association of New York City Teachers of Special Education, 1948.

Ingram, C. P. *Education of the Slow-Learning Child*, 3rd ed. New York: Ronald, 1960.

Johnson, G. O. "Special Education for the Mentally Retarded—A Paradox." *Exceptional Children* 29 (1962): 62-69.

Johnson, G. O. and Kirk, S. A. "Are Mentally Handicapped Children Segregated in the Regular Grades?" *Exceptional Children* 17 (1950): 65-68; 87-88.

Kirk, S. A. *Educating Exceptional Children.* Boston: Houghton Mifflin, 1962.

_____. *Public School Provisions for Severely Retarded Children.* Albany: New York State Interdepartmental Health Resources Board, 1957.

_____. "Research in Education." In *Mental Retardation*, edited by H. A. Stevens and R. Heber, pp. 57-99. Chicago: University of Chicago Press, 1964.

Kirk, S. A. and Johnson, G. O. *Educating the Retarded Child.* Boston: Houghton Mifflin, 1951.

Lilly, M. S. "Special Education: A Teapot in a Tempest." *Exceptional Children* 37 (1971): 745-49.

Mackie, R. P.; Dunn, L. M.; and Cain, L. F. "Professional Preparation for Teachers of Exceptional Children: An Overview." *U.S. Department of Health, Education and Welfare Bulletin* No. 6 (1959): 1-139.

Mackie, R. P. and Robbins, P. P. "Exceptional Children in Local Public Schools." *School Life* 43 (1960): 15.

MacMillan, D. L.; Jones, R. L.; and Meyers, D. E. "Mainstreaming the mildly retarded; some questions, cautions and guidelines." *Mental Retardation* 14 (1976): 3-10.

Martin, E. W. "Some thoughts on mainstreaming." *Exceptional Children* 41 (1974): 150-53.

Montessori, M. *Montessori Method*, arranged by A. E. George. New York: Macmillan & Co., 1950.

Mullen, F. A. and Itkin, W. "Achievement and Adjustment of Educable Mentally Handicapped Children." U.S. Office of Education Cooperative Research Program. Project SAE 6529. Chicago: Board of Education, 1961.

Peck, J. R. and Sexton, C. L. "A Comparative Investigation of the Learning and Social Adjustment of Trainable Children in Public School Facilities, Segregated Community Centers, and State Residential Centers." U.S. Office of Education, Cooperative Research Program Project No. SAE 6430, 1960.

Quay, L. C. "Academic Skills." In *Handbook of Mental Deficiency*, edited by N. R. Ellis, pp. 664-90. New York: McGraw-Hill Book Co., 1963.

Sternlicht, M. and Deutsch, M. R. *Personality Development and Social Behavior in the Mentally Retarded.* Lexington, Massachusetts: Lexington Books, 1972.

Thurstone, T. G. "An Evaluation of Educating Mentally Handicapped Children in Special Classes and in Regular Classes." U.S. Office of Education, Cooperative Research Program. Project No. OE-SAE 6452. Chapel Hill: University of North Carolina, 1959.

Wallin, J. E. W. *Education of Mentally Handicapped Children.* New York: Harper & Row, 1955.

Wolfensberger, W. *The Principle of Normalization in Human Services.* Toronto, Canada: National Institute on Mental Retardation, 1972.

Wrightstone, J. W. et al. "A Comparison of Educational Outcomes under Single-Track and Two-Track Plans for Educable Mentally Retarded Children." U.S. Office of Education, Cooperative Research Program. Project No. 144. New York: New York Board of Education, 1959.

UNIT 4

LESSON SIXTEEN
Learning and Mental Retardation

Growth and learning are two ways in which changes can be expected to occur in the education of retarded children. Growth is a characteristic over which educators have little or no control since its development, in large measure, is indicated by genetic factors. On the other hand, teachers can have considerable impact on learning because it may include any one of a variety of conditions, such as developing certain types of insight, adopting certain behavior, perceiving new and different concepts, or wanting to learn and to progress.

Most educators agree that a child's success in an educational program is basically dependent on three important desires:

1. Desire and ability to achieve.
2. Desire to persevere in a task until he has learned it.
3. Desire to gain satisfactory rewards for himself by virtue of his own accomplishments.

Children who have these desires tend to be the achievers who want to learn and who usually continue to learn up to the maximum of their capabilities.
Although it is well known that children with the proper incentives learn better, there are still a great many questions about

learning in mental retardation which remain unanswered. There are many scientific researchers who have investigated the learning abilities of the mentally retarded. The problems they have encountered in doing such studies are exceedingly difficult to overcome. One such problem, concerned with motivation in children, is difficult to study because it differs from place to place and from time to time. Establishing a research setting to assess learning abilities in retarded children also has proven to be difficult because controlling as many variables as possible in order to experiment in learning is very difficult.

Despite the difficulties, a considerable amount of research has been accomplished and has resulted in common agreement among professional workers on at least one point regarding the differences between the learning of retarded and "normal" persons and partial agreement on several other points. First, almost all professional workers agree that the retarded individual learns more slowly than the normal individual of the same chronological age. Partial agreement has been reached on the following points:

1. The normal individual has much less difficulty than the retarded person in learning abstract concepts.
2. The retarded person achieves at a lower level of learning than does the normal person.
3. The retarded person learns less than the normal person.
4. The retarded mind is less capable of reasoning than is the normal mind.
5. The retarded are less capable of spontaneous learning than normal persons.

Researchers and learning theorists who have contributed significantly to an increased awareness and understanding of the learning capabilities of the retarded include, among others:

Gestalt Theory—Heinz Werner, Alfred Strauss, Kurt Lewin,
Wolfgang Kohler, and G. Wallach.

The theory: the inborn structure of the central nervous system in which learning takes place by an integration of material is emphasized. Learning according to this theory is influenced by earlier life experiences.

Theory of Brain Function—Donald O. Hebb

The theory: learning is built up in circuits of cell assemblies within the brain and nervous system. Learning is, therefore, neurological and may be hampered, as in the case of mental retardation, by damage to the cell assemblies which are not properly formed or may be disrupted in some way.

Theory of Intelligence—Jean Piaget

The theory: learning takes place by the adaptive interaction between a child and his environment and that the child spontaneously develops increasing abilities to learn during the various stages of his growth and development.

Operant Conditioning or Behavior Modification—B. F. Skinner

The theory: the frequency of the occurrence of a certain type of behavior is modifiable by the consequences of the behavior and that behavior can be brought under control by identifying and establishing reinforcements or consequences. Reinforcement can be either negative or positive, with negative reinforcement usually used to decrease the behavior and positive reinforcement used to increase the behavior.

Social Learning Theory—Julian Rotter

The theory: a specific reinforcement may carry different connotations to different individuals because of various past experiences. What the individual anticipates in terms of a reinforcement is based upon the rewards or punishments that he has had in the past.

Behavior Theory—Clark Hull

The theory: learning is influenced by biological needs which affect the individual's behavior. Drive results from unfilled needs which in turn develop within the individual a "habit-strength" or a means of learning how to solve a problem in order to fulfill an unmet need.

Stimulus Trace Theory—Norman R. Ellis

The theory: the traces or pathways stimulated in the brain by learning will not hold intact for the retarded for as long a period as they do for the normal. Thus, the retarded have poorer, short-term memories as compared to the normal.

Discrimination Learning Theory—David Zeaman and Betty J. House

The theory: the retarded have greater difficulty in distinguishing items than do normal individuals and, therefore, the retarded learn more slowly.

The theory: in learning about something over a period of time a person learns the material more easily as he spends more and more time on it.

Investigators have done most of their research in two major areas of learning—verbal learning and motor learning. The greatest amount of research has been done in the area of verbal learning, probably because language is considered to be such an important part of intellectual functioning. These studies generally have emphasized language skills as a part of the process in learning some task. Most of the studies on verbal learning show that those within the normal ranges of intelligence are able to label verbally materials more readily and easily than the mentally retarded can. This inability on the part of the retarded to make easy use of labeling terms makes it more difficult for them to learn. In order to compensate for the children's deficiency in efficiently and readily placing definitive labels on items, teachers of the retarded have to be more direct in supplying these labels and bringing about their effective use. It has been shown that retarded children who must name an item before discussing it will learn about that item better than if they are not required to do so. This procedure helps the retarded to use language to provide labels which, in turn, can be related to concepts.

Some work has been done on memory and verbal learning. Most of the research in this area seems to indicate that once the more mildly retarded person has learned something by means of verbal association, he is able to retain it almost as well as his normal counterpart.

Studies on motor capabilities are another major area of research in learning. Most mentally retarded persons have a lesser handicap in learning motor tasks than they have in other areas of learning. Motor learning is an important part of the educational experience for the mildly retarded because motor skills are needed to accomplish most work tasks. Although it has been found that the mildly retarded may do very poorly at the outset on tasks requiring motor skills, they tend to show a rapid rate of improvement with continued practice. If the task is not too difficult, they may even catch up with normal individuals.

It should be noted that no matter what type of learning is to be accomplished, there are two important aspects of the learning environment which must be provided. These aspects include:

1. Many different opportunities for achievement.
2. Sufficient time for the retarded person to stick to a task until he is able to master it.

One of the most effective methods yet devised for facilitating the learning of all retarded individuals, especially those profoundly and severely retarded, is behavior modification or operant conditioning. Behavior modification is a method of choosing a desired behavior and then developing a plan to reinforce this behavior.

The idea of changing behavior to accomplish some useful purpose had as a part of its origin a World War II experimental missile which was nicknamed "Pelican." In this experiment, B. F. Skinner, by using behavior modification techniques, trained a group of pigeons to guide the "Pelican" missile. Although the missile never did become operational, it did help to launch the idea of teaching desired behavior to children through reinforcements or rewards.

Behavior modification does not change the individual; on the contrary, what occurs is a change in the behavior of the individual in a direction which is desirable in terms of his functioning in society. The goal of behavior modification techniques is the eventual creation of a self-reinforcement process by which the individual directs his own behaviors through some form of inner controls.

The ideas behind behavior modification are not something new or mysterious. They have been used for years, though sometimes unknowingly, to attain desired results. At the present time, this method is used in business and industry where workers are rewarded and receive reinforcements for their efforts by getting increases in salary, receiving promotions, or gaining tenure. The worker is positively reinforced by a reward system to create an increasing amount of productivity. In addition, behavior modification is used in schools to improve the child's level of functioning by offering gold stars, good grades, and promotions to the next grade, or by telling the child that he is doing well. Behavior modification has also been used in institutions to help to develop self-help and social skills in those children who are severely and profoundly retarded. Behavior in these individuals has been modified and improved in such areas as toileting, speech, self-grooming, self-feeding, and other important self-care activities. The primary means by which their behavior has been influenced and modified is a reinforcement procedure.

Retarded children, like all others, are inherently neither bad nor good. Instead, the behaviors which they have learned may very well be either bad or good depending upon how these behaviors occur in society. According to the theory behind behavior modification, the retarded child, as well as the normal child, will continue to maintain behavior as long as it is rewarded. In other words, reinforced behavior will tend to be repeated and thus strengthened while behavior that is not reinforced is less likely to be continued and will eventually either be extinguished or at least diminished.

In summary, the retarded have more difficulty with verbal learning simply because of their limitations in being able to assign a descriptive identification of words to materials which they may be studying. In addition, those who are more mildly retarded tend to perform physical tasks almost as well as normal persons, although they may take more time to learn the tasks. In the area of behavior modifcation and its use with the retarded, it has been found that this approach is useful for all levels of retarded persons, including the severely and profoundly retarded where reinforcement can take place without the need for verbal communication. In addition, behavior modification has also been found to be useful in working with normal children.

OBJECTIVES

This lesson deals briefly with those areas of learning in which the majority of work has been done regarding the retarded individual. When you have completed this lesson, you will be able to accomplish the following tasks:

1. State or identify the three major desires upon which a child's success in any educational program is dependent.
2. Given statements regarding the differences between the learning processes of normal and retarded individuals, identify those statements upon which there is at least partial agreement among professional workers in the field of retardation.
3. Given the name of one of the prominent learning theorists or researchers, name, identify, and understand the theory for which this person is largely responsible.
4. Given the name of one of the two major areas of learning in which investigators have focused most of their attention, make or identify a statement comparing the ability of a retarded individual to a normal individual in that area.
5. Explain or identify a method which will help to improve the verbal learning ability of a retarded individual.
6. Define in your own words the meaning of verbal association and explain or identify its value in teaching the retarded.
7. Explain or identify two aspects of the learning environment that should be present to best facilitate the learning of a retarded individual.
8. Define in your own words the concepts of "operant conditioning," "behavior modification," "reinforcement," and "reinforcement procedure."
9. Explain or identify the ultimate goal of behavior modification.
10. Given a situation requiring the need for a change in behavior by a normal or retarded individual or group, identify an application of behavior modification that might be used to help change the individual's or group's behavior in the desired direction.

QUESTIONS

Please answer each of the following questions carefully. After each possible answer, you will be referred to a frame in the section beginning on p. 356 where you will be told whether or not your choice is correct. If the alternative you have selected is correct, you will be told in the answer frame which frame in the "Questions" section to turn to next. If your choice is incorrect, your answer will tell you to return to the question frame you have just answered to review and to try again. Please note that you will always be given your instructions according to frame number. Frames designated with "Q" indicate a frame in the "Questions" section (e.g., "Q-1, Q-2"). Frames designated with an "A" indicate answers. Only occasionally will you be given a page number to which to turn. It is most important that you follow the instructions for *each individual question or answer frame* most carefully.

INTRODUCTION

The behavior of all individuals, including the mentally retarded, changes in two major ways—through development (growth) and through learning. Although there is little, if anything, that can be done to control development or growth, which is dictated by genetic factors, there is a great deal of behavior that can be changed in a favorable direction through teaching. This fact applies to the retarded individual as well as to the normal person.

DESIRES UPON WHICH EDUCATIONAL
SUCCESS USUALLY DEPENDS

Q-1   To be successful in any educational program, a child must begin
        the program with three major desires. These include:

1. A desire to achieve.
2. A desire to persevere (i.e. to stick with a task until it has been
   learned).
3. A desire to gain satisfactory rewards for his own efforts and accomplishments.

If a child has these three major desires, he has the necessary
motivation to afford him an excellent chance of learning to the
maximum level of his capabilities.

Test yourself with the following question:

Circle below the letters corresponding to those desires a child must
have in order to learn to the maximum of his potential.

a. A desire to be happy.
b. A desire to persevere.
c. A desire to achieve.
d. A desire to please his friends.
e. A desire to gain rewards for his own accomplishments.
f. A desire to find the quickest and easiest way to a goal.

After circling your choices, turn to A-7.

THE RESULTS OF RESEARCH ON THE LEARNING
ABILITIES OF THE RETARDED COMPARED
WITH THE ABILITIES OF NORMAL STUDENTS

Q-2

Although researchers have encountered many difficulties in attempting to uncover the learning abilities of the retarded, they have arrived at a few areas of agreement as a result of this research.

Based on research results, almost all professional workers in the area of learning and the mentally retarded are in agreement that the retarded individual learns at a slower rate than his normal peers. In addition, professional workers have come to a partial agreement on the following differences between the retarded and normals:

1. The normal person has less difficulty than the retarded in learning abstract concepts.
2. The retarded mind is less capable of reasoning than the normal mind.
3. The retarded achieve at a lower level of learning.
4. The retarded learn less than their normal peers.
5. The retarded are less capable of spontaneous learning (i.e. non-structured, nonformal learning—learning through observation, socializing, the radio, and television).

Test yourself with the following question.

Circle below the letters corresponding to those statements upon which there is at least partial agreement among professional workers in the field of learning and the mentally retarded.

a. The normal child can deal only with the abstract.
b. The retarded person is unable to deal with the abstract.
c. The retarded person is less capable of dealing with the abstract than the normal person.
d. The retarded learn less than normals.
e. The retarded can achieve at the same level of learning as normals.
f. Both the retarded and normals are capable of formal learning.
g. The retarded are less capable of spontaneous learning than normals.

After circling your answers, turn to A-17.

Q-3 Almost all professional workers would agree on which of the following findings of the research on learning by the retarded?

a. The normal child can deal only with
concrete materials.   Turn to A-26.
b. The retarded learn at a slower
rate than normals of the same age.   Turn to A-11.
c. The retarded learn less than normals.   Turn to A-30.

LEARNING THEORISTS AND RESEARCHERS WHO HAVE CONTRIBUTED TO AN UNDERSTANDING OF RETARDED LEARNING ABILITIES

Q-4 There are many learning theorists and researchers who have made significant contributions to better understanding of the learning abilities of the retarded. The names and descriptions of some of the most significant theories along with those theorists or researchers who developed or contributed greatly to each theory are presented below. A very brief description of each theory is also presented on subsequent pages. The objective here is not for you to learn the details about the theories but just to give you a beginning awareness of them. You may learn more about these theories and theorists as you progress in your studies concerning the mentally retarded.

Theory	*Researchers and Theorists*
Gestalt Theory	Heinz Werner, Alfred Strauss, Kurt Lewin, Wolfgang Kohler, and G. Wallach
Theory of Brain Function	D. O. Hebb
Theory of Intelligence	Jean Piaget
Operant Conditioning or Behavior Modification Theory	B. F. Skinner
Social Learning Theory	Julian Rotter
Behavior Theory	Clark Hull
Stimulus Trace Theory	N. R. Ellis
Discrimination Learning Theory	D. Zeaman and B. J. House
Learning Set Theory	H. F. Harlow

Which of the following men developed the Theory of Intelligence?

a. Jean Piaget.   Turn to A-5.
b. D. O. Hebb.   Turn to A-23.
c. Julian Rotter.   Turn to A-34.

Clark Hull developed which of the following theories?   **Q-5**

a. Operant Conditioning or Behavior
   Modification.   Turn to A-14.
b. Behavior Theory.   Turn to A-39.
c. Gestalt Theory.   Turn to A-27.

BRIEF DESCRIPTIONS OF NINE LEARNING THEORIES RELEVANT TO MENTAL RETARDATION

Although the following descriptions are very brief, it is hoped that   **Q-6**
they will stimulate your desire for further understanding which
you can obtain by consulting the references cited at the end of
this lesson.

Gestalt Theory

The first theory mentioned is Gestalt Theory which was developed
and refined by such persons as Heinz Werner, Alfred Strauss, Kurt
Lewin, Wolfgang Kohler, and G. Wallach. This theory attempts to
explain learning as an integration of information acquired throughout life. Two important aspects of this theory include:

1. The inborn structure of the central nervous system.
2. Earlier life experiences.

Theory of Brain Function

The theory of Brain Function, developed by Donald O. Hebb, emphasizes the key role played by the nervous system in learning. In brief, it states that learning takes place and information is stored within circuits of cell assemblies in the brain *and* the central nervous system. According to this theory, learning is conceived as neurological and damage to or improper formation of these cell assemblies may result in mental retardation.

According to which of the following theories does learning take place within the central nervous system, and is it an integration of informational material acquired throughout life?

a. Theory of Brain Function.   Turn to A-47.
b. Gestalt Theory.   Turn to A-55.

Theory of Intelligence

Q-7   Jean Piaget's Theory of Intelligence postulates that learning, which he conceives as intellectual development, takes place through adaptation. As the child adapts to his environment throughout the various phases of intellectual development, he spontaneously develops increasing abilities to learn. Piaget identifies three major developmental periods and a number of stages within the periods. He also uses the terms subperiods and substages for further elaboration. A brief outline of his theory includes:

1. The period of *sensory-motor intelligence* (0-2 yrs.). Piaget identifies six major stages within this two-year period.
2. The period of preparation for and organization of *concrete operations* (2-11 yrs.). This period contains two important sub-periods: (a) pre-operational representations (2-7 yrs.) and (b) *concrete operations* (7-11 yrs.).
3. The period of *formal operations* (11-15 yrs.) is when the child moves into the world of hypotheses and abstractions and begins to test reality by means of these hypotheses rather than needing to manipulate concrete, specific objects.

Operant Conditioning or Behavior Modification

Burrhus F. Skinner, or B. F. Skinner as he is more commonly known, by basing his findings on animal research, discovered that behavior is modifiable by the consequences of the behavior. In addition, behavior can be controlled by identifying and establishing reinforcements or consequences. Such reinforcements may be positive (desired by the person being reinforced) or negative (disliked). The proper use of positive reinforcers results in a higher probability of reoccurrence of the behavior that is being reinforced (desired behavior), while the proper application of negative reinforcers tends to reduce the probability of reoccurrence. For humans, one of the most powerful negative reinforcers has been found to be indifference to an undesirable behavior.

According to the Behavior Modification Theory, desired behavior may be increased through the use of:

a. Positive reinforcers.   Turn to A-41.
b. Negative reinforcers.   Turn to A-44.
c. Indifference.   Turn to A-51.

Which theory postulates that learning takes place simultaneously as   Q-8
the individual adapts to his environment?

a. Gestalt Theory.   Turn to A-56.
b. Theory of Intelligence.   Turn to A-50.
c. Operant Conditioning.   Turn to A-42.

Social Learning Theory

Social Learning Theory, as developed by Julian Rotter, is similar   Q-9
to behavior modification in that it attempts to explain learning in terms of reinforcement. However, according to this theory, it is the learner who, based upon the rewards and punishments he has received in the past, controls his responses to stimulus reactions rather than some other person (controller). If the learner anticipates, based on his own past experiences, what will be a positive reinforcement for his efforts, he will attempt to respond to a situation. If past experiences with a stimulus situation have resulted in negative reinforcements, then he will avoid the situation.

Behavior Theory

Clark Hull has been the most instrumental in the development of Behavior Theory. This theory attempts to explain learning in terms of drives aimed at fulfilling biological needs that have not been met. According to this theory, unfulfilled biological needs cause the development of a drive within the individual, and this drive leads to the development of a "habit strength" or a means of learning how to solve a problem in order to fulfill the unfilled need.

According to _____ _____ Theory, behavior may be brought under control by an outside agent through the proper use

of reinforcement while _____ _____ Theory states that control of behavior is exercised within an individual based upon his past experiences.

In order of appearance, the answers which fill in the above blanks are:

a. Behavior Modification; Social Learning.   Turn to A-46.
b. Social Learning; Behavior Modification.   Turn to A-53.

Q-10   Behavior Theory attempts to describe learning as:

a. A neurological process.   Turn to A-48.
b. Resulting from proper reinforcements.   Turn to A-43.
c. A biological process.   Turn to A-54.

Stimulus Trace Theory

Q-11

This theory, which has been developed mainly by Norman R. Ellis, postulates that learning is a process whereby traces or pathways are stimulated in the brain as learning takes place. In order to account for the fact that the short-term memory of the retarded individual is poorer than that of normals, this theory states that these traces do not hold intact for the retarded for as long a duration as they do for normals.

Discrimination Learning Theory

David Zeaman and Betty J. House have been most involved in promulgating the recently developed theory of discrimination learning. Very simply stated, this theory attempts to explain the slow learning of retardates as being mainly attributable to their lack of facility in making distinctions between and among different items.

Learning Set Theory

This theory, developed by Harry Harlow, simply explains learning as a function of time. According to this theory, learning becomes easier and easier as time spent in learning is increased and a set for learning is created.

A discrimination learning theorist would explain that retarded individuals learn more slowly than normals because:

a. Their attention span is shorter.   Turn to A-49.
b. Memory traces do not hold intact
   as long for retarded individuals as for   Turn to A-45.
   normals.
c. They are less competent at making   Turn to A-52.
   decisions.

Q-12   Match the following theorists and theories by drawing an arrow
        from one to the other; then check your answers by turning to A-9.

                Theory   *Theorists*

        Theory of Brain Function   N. R. Ellis
        Stimulus Trace   D. Zeaman and B. H. House
        Discrimination Learning   B. F. Skinner
        Learning Set   D. O. Hebb
        Operant Conditioning or
            Behavior Modification   H. F. Harlow

MAJOR AREAS OF RESEARCH RELATED TO
LEARNING ABILITIES OF THE RETARDED

The two major areas upon which research in the learning abilities
of the retarded have been focused are verbal learning and motor
learning.

Verbal Learning

The greatest amount of research has been accomplished in the area
of verbal learning. The significant findings of these studies include
the following:

1. Individuals within the normal ranges of intelligence are able to
   label materials more readily and easily than the retarded. This
   fact means that it is more difficult for the retarded to learn
   because they have greater difficulty assigning labels and, therefore, have greater difficulty in learning about items they are
   studying.

2. Once the mildly retarded person learns something by means of
   verbal association, he is able to retain it almost as well as a
   person of normal intelligence.

   Verbal association is the act of naming an item before discussing
   it thereby creating a verbal association between the word representing an item and the item itself. This association facilitates
   the ability of the retarded individual to use language to provide
   labels which can then be related to concepts.

Q-13   Research on verbal learning ability of retardates has shown that
        one of the major reasons the retarded child has more difficulty
        with verbal learning than the child of normal intelligence is that:

a. He has a smaller brain.   Turn to A-21.
b. He does not pay attention.   Turn to A-32.
c. He is less able to label items.   Turn to A-16.

Which of the following teachers is facilitating the verbal learning   Q-14
of a retarded child in a manner found to be most effective?

a. Miss Directed who discusses items
   but does not name them.   Turn to A-37.
b. Miss Uptodate who supplies the names for
   each item before discussing them.   Turn to A-1.

When the mildly retarded child has learned something by means of   Q-15
verbal association, he probably will be able to:

a. Retain it forever in his long-term memory.   Turn to A-28.
b. Retain it almost as well as a normal person.   Turn to A-18.
c. Retain it for a very short time but will
   then forget it.   Turn to A-33.

Q-16   *Motor Learning*

Motor learning is the other major area of research in learning abilities of the retarded. It has been found that the retarded, as a group, have less difficulty with motor learning than with any other area of learning.

Although the mildly retarded are slow at first when learning motor skills, they tend to improve rapidly as they continue practicing and, in some cases, may even catch up with those who are within the normal ranges of intelligence.

Underline the words in parentheses below that will make the sentence agree with research findings; then turn to A-4.

The retarded person has (less/more) difficulty learning (motor/verbal) skills than (verbal/motor) skills.

Q-17   Regarding motor skills, the mildly retarded are:

a. Capable of learning these skills as well as
normal persons in some cases.   Turn to A-22.
b. Incapable of learning these skills as well
as normal persons.   Turn to A-29.
c. Capable of learning these skills quickly
at first but then peak and continued
practice is of no more benefit.   Turn to A-12.

ASPECTS OF THE LEARNING ENVIRONMENT REQUIRED FOR FACILITATION OF LEARNING BY THE RETARDED

Before going on to a discussion of operant conditioning or behavior modification, a very effective method by which all types of
learning can be facilitated, it is important to mention the two
major environmental factors that should be provided to facilitate
all types of learning by the retarded. These factors are:

Q-18

1. Providing the retarded child with many different opportunities
   for achievement.
2. Providing sufficient time to allow the retarded child to stay
   with a task until he has mastered it.

Which of the following would best provide the two important
environmental factors needed for facilitating learning by the retarded?

a. Large classrooms. Turn to A-38.
b. Individualized instruction. Turn to A-2.
c. A traditional, time-based
   system of education. Turn to A-40.

Operant conditioning, or behavior modification as it is more commonly called, grew out of experiments with animals conducted by B. F. Skinner and has become one of the better methods by which the learning can be facilitated for both retarded and normal individuals.

In essence, behavior modification is a method of choosing a specific desired behavior and then developing a systematic plan to reinforce that behavior in the learner. The goal is to change the behavior of an individual in a desired direction rather than to change the individual.

In rather simplified terms, behavior modification is applied in the following manner. The desired behavior is specified; then, when the individual evidences that behavior, a reinforcement procedure strengthens his response (i.e., the individual is given rewards which can range from candy to a pat on the back). When the behavior is not evidenced or when behavior that is counter to the desired behavior is evidenced, the individual may be ignored or ostracized until he begins to evidence the desired behavior. Once desired behavior is consistently achieved, the rewards are slowly withdrawn as the individual develops the capacity for self-reinforcement and is able to control his behavior internally.

Uses of Behavior Modification

Although behavior modification techniques have been and still are being used unknowingly by almost everyone in some form or another, they had not been operationalized and formalized until the advent of the theory of behavior modification.

Many people are now becoming more aware of the uses of this approach and of how to apply its techniques more effectively and efficiently. Some of the situations in which behavior modification is used and some of the specific reinforcers used are presented below. You may be able to think of additional uses and other reinforcers that could be used to help improve the desirable behavior of others.

Situation	Reinforcers	Use
Business and industry	Promotions; pay raise; praise	Increase productivity Improve morale
Schools		
1. Learner	Good grades; gold stars; promotion to the next grade; praise from peers or instructor	Improve learning performance; reduce disruptive behavior
2. Instructor	Promotions; praise from superiors and peers; inhanced professional status; pay raises	Improve instruction
3. Severely and profoundly retarded persons	Candy or other food; praise; warm responses	Improvement in self-help skills and social skills, i.e., self-grooming, toileting, feeding, socializing, and so forth

The theory behind behavior modification, therefore, is that behavior which is reinforced will tend to be repeated (strengthened) while behavior which is ignored will diminish and eventually disappear.

The goal of behavior modification is to:
a. Change animals.   Turn to A-20.
b. Change an individual.   Turn to A-35.
c. Change an individual's
   behavior.   Turn to A-8.

The major technique used in behavior modification which helps   Q-20
shape an individual's behavior is:

a. Trial-and-error reward system.   Turn to A-25.
b. Planned reinforcement.   Turn to A-15.
c. Group dynamics.   Turn to A-31.

Q-21   Which of the following statements are correct?

a. Reinforcements are withdrawn completely once
   the individual has developed his own inner
   controls.   Turn to A-10.
b. Reinforcement will always be needed if
   behavior modification is to work effectively.   Turn to A-3.
c. Reinforcement eliminates the need for
   self-controls.   Turn to A-36.

Q-22   Test yourself with the following question.

Circle the types of reinforcers below that could be used to help
improve the self-help and/or social skills of severely or profoundly
retarded youngsters.

a. Candy.
b. Promotions.
c. Enhanced status.
d. Praise.
e. Good grades.
f. Food.
g. Warm responses.
h. Money.

To check your answers turn to A-19.

Q-23   Behavior modification has been found to be useful in working
        with:

a. Retarded individuals only, especially the
   severely and profoundly retarded.   Turn to A-13.
b. Both retarded and normal individuals.   Turn to A-24.

According to behavior modification theory, behavior that is (ignored/reinforced) will be strengthened while behavior which is (ignored/reinforced) will tend to diminish.

Underline the proper words in parentheses above and turn to A-6 to check your answers.

ANSWERS

Please follow the same instructions as those you were given on page 339 in working with this section. It is most important that you remember to follow the individual instructions in each answer frame.

A-1   Yes, both you and this teacher are up-to-date on the research. When the teacher supplies the name of an item before discussing it and when the retarded child repeats the label, his learning will be facilitated through verbal association. In this manner, the ability of the retarded person to use language to provide labels is facilitated; these labels, in turn, can then be used to relate to concepts.

Continue now with Q-15.

A-2   If you chose this answer, you have succeeded in understanding the two vital environmental factors for the facilitation of learning. You also realize that individualized instruction can provide these factors if it is accompanied by other variables. Well done.

Move on to Q-19 for a brief presentation of operant conditioning or behavior modification.

A-3   No. This is not the case. The reinforcement procedure is only used until the individual has substituted his own internal controls for the behavior in question. When this occurs, outside reinforcement should no longer be necessary.

Return to Q-21 and select the correct answer.

There were two ways in which to answer this question. You could A-4
have underlined the words "less," "motor," and "verbal" or you
could have underlined "more," "verbal," and "motor." The majority of the retarded, it has been found, have less difficulty learning
motor skills than other skills, including verbal skills.

Continue with Q-17

The Theory of Intelligence, indeed, was developed by Jean Piaget A-5
who used his children as the subjects for his studies.

D. O. Hebb developed the Theory of Brain Function, and Julian
Rotter developed Social Learning Theory.

Continue now with Q-5.

You should have underlined the words "reinforced" and A-6
"ignored." Reinforced behavior tends to be repeated (strengthened) while behavior that is ignored tends to diminish. This is the
theory behind behavior modification.

Turn now to page 325.

If you circled letters a, d, and f, you are wrong on all three counts! A-7
However, if you circled letters b, c, and e, you are absolutely
correct. Motivation generally includes a desire to achieve, to persevere, and to gain rewards for one's own accomplishments.

Continue now with Q-2.

A-8   It is to be hoped that the behavior modifier is able to plan a schedule of reinforcement that will lead to a change in the behavior of an individual in a desired direction. You are correct in saying that the goal of this approach is to change the behavior of an individual rather than to change the individual.

Continue now with Q-20.

A-9   *Theories*   *Theorists and Researchers*

        Theory of Brain Function   D. O. Hebb
        Stimulus Trace Theory   N. R. Ellis
        Discrimination Learning Theory   D. Zeaman, B. J. House
        Learning Set Theory   H. F. Harlow
        Operant Conditioning or   B. F. Skinner
            Behavior Modification Theory

        If you were able to match each theory with each of the theorists move on to Q-13. If you had any trouble, return to Q-4 for a review and then match the names and theories again.

A-10   Yes. The behavior modifier feels that he has succeeded once the individual has substituted his own inner control of the behavior and the outside reinforcement has been completely withdrawn (i.e., the reinforcement procedure is no longer necessary).

        Since you have chosen the correct answer, you are ready to go on to Q-22.

A-11   That the retarded learn at a slower rate than normal persons of the same age is the one fact with which almost all professional workers would agree.

        This was the correct answer so you should now go on to Q-4.

This is not the case. In most cases, just the opposite is true so please return to Q-16 and review the material you have missed before answering Q-17 correctly.

A-12

Yes. This is true; behavior modification has been found to be very useful in facilitating changes in the behavior of mentally retarded persons, especially the severely and profoundly retarded. However, this method has also been found useful in changing the behavior of normal individuals.

A-13

Go back to Q-23 and correctly answer the question posed there.

Operant conditioning, or behavior modification as it is usually called, was developed mainly by B. F. Skinner rather than Clark Hull.

A-14

Return to page 342 for a review of the learning theories and their developers before answering Q-5 correctly.

Through planned reinforcement, the necessary rewards (reinforcers) will be identified for each individual and this should be done if possible in advance. Therefore, a planned approach can be used effectively to facilitate the change in behavior in a desired direction.

A-15

Since you have correctly identified this answer, go on to Q-21.

A-16   You are right. This is the major reason why the retarded have difficulty with verbal learning—they are less able to label items than the normal individual.

Continue now with Q-14 which, it is hoped, you will have no trouble answering.

A-17   You should have circled letters c, d, f, and g to identify those statements upon which there is partial agreement among professional workers.

If you answered this example correctly, turn to Q-3. If you missed any part of the answer, return to Q-2 for a brief review and then correctly answer item Q-2.

A-18   You have chosen the proper response. Learning by verbal association allows the mildly retarded child to retain what he has learned almost as well as normal children do.

Continue now with Q-16.

A-19   The proper reinforcers for profoundly and severely retarded youngsters would include such things as "a" or candy, "d" or praise, "f" or food and "g" providing warm responses. The remaining reinforcers would not be understood or desired by these individuals and, therefore, would be ineffective reinforcers.

How well did you do? If your answer included all four of the above and no more, turn now to Q-23 and duplicate your performance. If, however, you added any reinforcers or missed any, return to Q-19 for a brief review and then select the correct reinforcers for Q-22.

Behavior modification originated from experiments with animals   A-20
and is now also used with human beings. However, the goal is not to
change animals or people themselves but to change their behavior.

Although you are now able to answer Q-19 correctly, it may be
helpful to return to Q-18 and briefly review the material presented
there before moving on to Q-20.

Brain size has not been found to be the important determinant of   A-21
intelligence. The key may be how much of the brain is used rather
than how large it is.

Return to page 348 for a brief review of research findings before
answering Q-13 correctly.

Although they may be slow to learn motor skills at first, with   A-22
continued practice, the mildly retarded can in some cases learn
these skills as well as normal persons.

You have chosen the correct answer.

Now continue with Q-18.

D. O. Hebb developed the Theory of Brain Function, not the   A-23
Theory of Intelligence as you have said.

Return to page 342 for a brief review of learning theories and
their developers before answering Q-4 correctly.

A-24   You have selected the correct answer. Behavior modification has been found to be useful for changing the behavior of all individuals in a desired direction, although it has been especially useful in working with severely and profoundly retarded persons where reinforcement can take place without the need for verbal communication.

Turn now to Q-24 and correctly answer the question posed there.

A-25   The effective behavior modifier will try to determine to the extent possible those reinforcements that will strengthen specific desired behaviors and those which will weaken and, ultimately, extinguish undesirable behaviors. The necessity for trial and error in determining the most effective reinforcers should be reduced as much as possible before initiating a behavior modification program. Therefore, you have selected the wrong answer.

Return to Q-20 and select the correct answer.

A-26   The statement that normal children can deal only with the concrete is not correct. Normal persons, of course, can deal with the abstract as well as the concrete. Although they are not as capable, the retarded can also deal with both the abstract and the concrete.

Since you had trouble with this one, return to Q-2 for a brief review and then answer Q-3 correctly.

A-27   Gestalt Theory was developed and refined by many individuals, but Clark Hull was not among them as you have just stated.

Return to Q-4 for a review and then answer Q-5 correctly.

No. Verbal association is a useful learning tool, but permanent   A-28
retention may be too much to ask from any learning tool.

Return to page 348 for a quick review before answering Q-15
correctly.

Although it is true that in many cases the mildly retarded are   A-29
unable to perform motor skills as well as normal individuals, this is
not always true, especially when the skill is not overly difficult.

Return to Q-17 and select the proper answer.

Professional workers in the field tend to be in only partial agree-   A-30
ment that the retarded learn less than normal persons. Some believe that the retarded can learn just as much in certain areas if
given enough time and proper instruction.

Since you had trouble with this question, return to page 341 for a
brief review and then answer Q-3 correctly.

Group dynamics is not used by the behavior modifier to alter   A-31
behavior in the mentally retarded.

Since you had trouble with this question return to page 352 for a
review before answering Q-20 correctly.

A-32   A short attention span is a problem with the retarded and slow learners in general, but it is also a problem with the gifted and the normal individual. Attention span may be shorter for the retarded than for others, but this is not the major reason for the difficulty they have in learning.

The attention span of a gifted child may be short because he learns easily and then quickly becomes bored. For most children, the attention span may be greatly reduced if they are not at all interested in what they are asked to learn.

Return to page 348 for a brief review of the research findings before answering Q-13 correctly.

A-33   Although it is not known how long a mildly retarded child or any other child will retain something learned by any method, it is known that the mildly retarded child's memory will be almost as good as a normal child's when verbal association has been used properly in the learning process.

Please return to Q-13 on page 348 and then select the correct response to Q-15.

A-34   Julian Rotter was instrumental in the development of Social Learning Theory, not the Theory of Intelligence as you have just stated.

It may be helpful if you return to page 342 for a brief review before correctly answering Q-4.

A-35   The goal of behavior modification is not to change the individual but to change his behavior in a desirable direction.

Return to page 352 for a brief review before answering Q-19 correctly.

No. Reinforcement is needed only until some form of self-control   A-36
has been fully developed. Therefore, reinforcement does not eliminate the need for self-control but, rather, helps the individual to
attain self-control.

Return to page 352 for a review before correctly answering Q-21.

Sorry, but Miss Directed is not teaching the retarded in the best   A-37
possible manner. Items should first be named by the teacher and
then by the child before they are discussed. This method will best
facilitate the verbal learning of the retarded.

Since you had trouble with this, return to page 348 for a review
and then select the correct answer to Q-14.

Large classrooms normally provide few opportunities for achieve-   A-38
ment, and there is little individual assistance. Both the slow and
the fast learner may suffer in a large classroom which is usually
geared to the average learner.

Return to Q-18 and select the correct answer.

Indeed, Behavior Theory was developed to a great extent by Clark   A-39
Hull.

Since you had no trouble with this one go right on to Q-6.

A-40   The traditional time-based educational system is just that—time-based, not learner-based. If a student has not reached the average level of learning of his peers at the same time that the majority of these peers do, he may be pushed ahead anyway. Soon, he falls so far behind that it is impossible to catch up and he becomes just another statistic of the system—a dropout perhaps or maybe, if he tries to remain in the system, an object of ridicule. The traditional system, therefore, generally fails to supply either a variety of opportunities or sufficient time to learn for many of the learners in the system, especially the retarded learners.

Return to Q-18 and select the proper answer to this question.

A-41   This is correct. According to Behavior Modification Theory, the frequency of occurrence of any desirable behavior may be increased by using planned positive reinforcement. Conversely, some negative reinforcers, such as teacher indifference, may reduce the frequency of behavior occurrence. It should be noted, however, that some types of reinforcers may appear to be negative (shouting at a person to get him to stop some undesirable behavior) but are really positive reinforcers for the recipient since he was seeking attention and received it.

Continue now with Q-8.

A-42   This is incorrect. Operant Conditioning, or Behavior Modification as it is more commonly called, does not attempt to describe the process by which learning occurs but, rather, shows how the learning of desirable behavior can be improved through reinforcement. Learning is viewed by this theory as a reaction to a stimulus. When the proper reaction to a stimulus is reinforced, this will increase the probability that a proper repetition of the response will occur next time the stimulus is presented. Thus, learning of the desired response is facilitated.

Return to page 344 for a review; then answer Q-8 correctly.

No. Behavior Modification Theory as well as Social Learning   A-43
Theory views learning as resulting from reinforcement.

Return to page 346 for a brief review before trying to answer Q-10
again.

No. According to Behavior Modification Theory, negative re-   A-44
inforcers are not used to increase the frequency of occurrence of a
desired behavior but, rather, are used to decrease the occurrence
of an undesired behavior.

Return to page 344 for a review before answering Q-7.

No. A stimulus trace theorist would probably attribute the slow   A-45
learning ability of the retarded individual to the idea that most of
his memory traces seem to disappear from his short-term memory
faster than from the short-term memory of normals. Therefore,
most of the material that is placed in short-term memory by a
retarded individual is not transferred to long-term memory where
it would be stored for later recall. Learning is thereby greatly
impeded.

Return to Q-11 and select the correct answer.

Absolutely correct. Behavior can be controlled by an agent outside   A-46
an individual. According to Behavior Modification Theory, this
agent is called a behavior modifier. The Social Learning Theory
explains that control of behavior comes from within the individual
and is based on his past experiences.

Continue now with Q-10.

A-47   This is not true. Hebb's Theory of Brain Function attributes learning to a neurological cell circuitry type of functioning of the brain and nervous system. Hebb's Theory places emphasis on learning as a neurological process rather than learning by means of the acquisition and integration into the nervous system of life reference data.

Return to page 344 for a review before answering Q-6.

A-48   This is incorrect. Hebb's Theory of Brain Function attempts to explain learning as a neurological process.

Return to page 344 for a brief review and then select the correct answer for Q-10.

A-49   No. A discrimination learning theorist would not attribute the slower learning of retardates to their short attention spans but, rather, would see the source of their difficulty as being in the inability to distinguish items.

Return to page 347 for a brief review of the last three theories before answering Q-11 correctly.

A-50   This is correct. Piaget's Theory of Intelligence attempts to explain learning (intellectual development) as a spontaneous process of adaptation to the environment which occurs in five developmental phases from birth to fifteen years of age. Piaget has not attempted to identify any additional intellectual developmental phases beyond the age of fifteen since, in his opinion, this is the average age at which the physiological brain has become fully developed.

Continue now with Q-9.

368   LEARNING AND MENTAL RETARDATION

No. According to Behavior Modification Theory, indifference to A-51
any type of behavior can be a powerful deterrent to that behavior's reoccurrence. It should be used to reduce the frequency of
occurrence of undesirable behavior.

Return to page 344 for a review; then answer Q-7.

Right you are. The discrimination learning theorist would attrib- A-52
ute the slower learning of retardates to the probability that they
are less competent than normals in making the distinctions between and among items required for learning, especially for the
learning of concepts.

Continue with Q-12.

No. You have them reversed. A-53

Return to page 345 for a review before answering Q-9 correctly.

This is correct. According to Hull's Behavior Theory, learning is A-54
influenced mainly by biological needs which have not been met
and which lead to the development of drives to solve problems
related to the fulfillment of these needs.

Continue now with Q-11.

A-55   Precisely. According to Gestalt Theory, learning takes place by an integration of material within the central nervous system. Learning, therefore, is based on and grows through an individual's life experiences.

Continue now with Q-7.

A-56   No. Gestalt Theory attempts to explain learning as an integrative process of the central nervous sytem rather than as a spontaneous process of adaptation.

Return to page 343 for a review; then try to answer Q-8 again.

CONCLUSION

You have now reached the end of this lesson. Once you have correctly answered the review questions on the following pages, you will have successfully completed this instructional text.

REVIEW QUESTIONS—LESSON SIXTEEN

Questions

1. Which item below does not belong in the following list and is not generally agreed upon by educators as a characteristic for educational success?

   a. The desire to be destructive for which there must be compensation.
   b. The desire and ability to achieve.
   c. The desire to persevere until the task is learned.
   d. The desire to be rewarded on the basis of accomplishment.

2. Almost all professional workers agree that the retarded learn _____ other children of the same age.

   a. Faster than.
   b. Slower than.
   c. At approximately the same rate as.
   d. None of the above since retarded children do not learn; they must be trained.

3. There is partial agreement among educators that:

   a. The retarded child has less difficulty learning abstract concepts than the normal child.
   b. The retarded child learns less than the normal child.
   c. The retarded child is less capable of spontaneous learning than the normal child.
   d. a and c above.
   e. b and c above.

4. In general, researchers have found that the retarded learn _____ skills better than any other skills.

   a. Motor.
   b. Verbal.
   c. Abstract.
   d. Visual.

5. Clark Hull was instrumental in the formulation of:

   a. Gestalt Theory.
   b. The Theory of Intelligence.
   c. Behavior Theory.
   d. Social Learning Theory.

6. B. F. Skinner is well known for his beginning work in:

    a. Operant conditioning.
    b. Gestalt Theory.
    c. Learning set.
    d. Social Learning Theory.

7. One of the major reasons the retarded have trouble in verbal learning is that they have difficulty:

    a. Manipulating their tongues.
    b. Assigning labels to materials they are studying.
    c. Seeing the items accurately.
    d. Paying attention.

8. In order to improve the verbal learning ability of the retarded child, teachers should:

    a. Find new methods for making these children pay attention.
    b. Punish these children for not learning.
    c. Ask each child to name items before they are discussed.
    d. Discuss items and then have each child label the items.

9. Which of the following situations should be present to facilitate the learning of retardates no matter what type of learning is to be accomplished?

    a. Sufficient time for mastery of the skill to be learned.
    b. A variety of opportunities for achievement.
    c. A strict, authoritative atmosphere.
    d. a and b above.
    e. b and c above.

10. Behavior modification is a method which tries to change:

    a. The individual.
    b. The environment.
    c. The individual's behavior.
    d. The individual's mentality.

11. In behavior modification, the term "reinforcement" means:

    a. Trial-and-error behavior.
    b. Behavior not observable.
    c. Strengthening the ego.
    d. Rewarding desired behavior.

12. The eventual goal of behavior modification is:

   a. Self-direction by some form of inner control.
   b. Direction by an authority figure.
   c. Self-direction to improve the intellect.
   d. Direction by means of group pressure.

13. Behavior modification techniques have been used with the severely and profoundly retarded primarily to develop which of the following skills?

   a. Self-help skills.
   b. Reading and writing skills.
   c. Social skills.
   d. a and c above.
   e. a, b, and c above.

14. The basic component of the learning theory developed by Donald O. Hebb is best described in which of the following statements:

   a. Learning takes place by reinforcement.
   b. Learning is facilitated by the need to satisfy drives.
   c. Learning results from adaptive interaction with the environment.
   d. Learning is a process in which information is stored by means of cell assemblies within the brain and nervous system.

15. The theory of learning which states that learning stimulates pathways in the brain is called the:

   a. Discrimination Learning Theory.
   b. Behavior Modification Theory.
   c. Stimulus Trace Theory.
   d. Behavior Theory.

Answers

1. a.
2. b.
3. e.
4. a.
5. c.
6. a.
7. b.
8. c.
9. d.
10. c.
11. d.
12. a.
13. a.
14. d.
15. c.

SELECTED READINGS

Altman, R. and Talkington, L. W. "Modeling: An Alternative Behavior Modification Approach for Retardates." *Mental Retardation* 9 (1971): 20-33.

Baumeister, A. A. "Learning Abilities of the Mentally Retarded." In A. A. Baumeister, ed. *Mental Retardation.* Chicago: Aldine Publishing Co., 1967.

Benoit, E. P. "Relevance of Hebb's Theory of the Organiz tion of Behavior to Educational Research on the Mentally Retarded." *American Journal of Mental Deficiency* 61 (1957): 497-507.

Cantor, G. N. "Hull-Spence Behavior Theory and Mental Deficiency." In *Handbook of Mental Deficiency*, edited by N. R. Ellis, pp. 92-133. New York: McGraw-Hill, 1963.

Cantor, G. N., and Stacey, C. L. "Manipulative Dexterity in Mental Defectives." *American Journal of Mental Deficiency* 56 (1951): 401-10.

Cartwright, D. "Lewinian Theory as a Contemporary Systematic Framework." In *Psychology: A Study of Science*, Volume 2, edited by S. Kock, pp. 7-91. New York: McGraw-Hill, 1958.

Eisman, B. S. L. "Paired Associate Learning, Generalization, and Retention as Functions of Intelligence." *American Journal of Mental Deficiency* 63 (1958): 481-89.

Ellis, N. R. "Amount of Reward and Operant Behavior in Mental Defectives." *American Journal of Mental Deficiency* 66 (1962): 595-99.

Ellis, N. R., editor. *Handbook of Mental Deficiency.* New York: McGraw-Hill, 1963.

Ellis, N. R.; Pryer, M. W.; and Barnett, C. D. "Motor Learning and Retention in Normals and Defectives." *Perceptual Motor Skills* 10 (1960): 83-91.

Ellis, N. R.; Pryer, R. S.; Distefano, M. K.; and Pryer, M. W. "Learning in Mental Defective, Normal, and Superior Subjects." *American Journal of Mental Deficiency* 64 (1960): 725-34.

Estes, W. K. *Learning Theory and Mental Development.* New York: Academic Press, 1970.

Flavell, J. H. *The Developmental Psychology of Jean Piaget.* Princeton: Van Nostrand, 1963.

Gardner, J. M.; Selinger, S.; Watson, L. S.; Saposnet, D. T.; and Gardner, G. M. "Research on Learning with the Mentally Retarded: A Comprehensive Bibliography." *Mental Retardation Abstracts* 7 (1970): 417-53.

Hall, C. S., and Lindzey, G. *Theories of Personality.* New York: Wiley and Sons, 1957.

Harlow, H. "The Formation of Learning Sets." *Psychological Review* 56 (1949): 51-65.

Hebb, D. O. *The Organization of Behavior.* New York: Wiley and Sons, 1949.

Hilgard, E. R. *Theories of Learning*, 2d ed. New York: Appleton-Century-Crofts, 1956.

Hill, M. *The Retarded Child Gets Ready for School.* Public Affairs Pamphlet No. 349, September 1963.

House, B. J., and Zeaman, D. "Visual Discrimination Learning in Imbeciles." *American Journal of Mental Deficiency* 63 (1958): 447-52.

_____. "A Comparison of Discrimination Learning in Normal and Mentally Defective Children." *Child Development* 29 (1958b): 411-16.

Kohler, W. *Gestalt Psychology.* New York: Liveright, 1929.

Kohler, W., and Wallack, G. "Figural After-Effects: An Investigation of Visual Processes." *Proceedings of the American Philosophical Society* 88 (1944): 269-357.

Lewin, K. *A Dynamic Theory of Personality.* New York: McGraw-Hill, 1935.

_____. *Field Theory in Social Science: Selected Theoretical Papers,* edited by D. Cartwright. New York: Harper and Row, 1951.

McCulloch, T. L.; Reswick, J.; and Roy, I. "Studies of Word Learning in Mental Defectives: I. Effects of Mental Level and Age." *American Journal of Mental Deficiency* 60 (1955): 133-39.

Montessori, Maria. *Montessori Method,* trans. by A. E. George. New York: Stokes, 1912.

Piaget, J. *The Growth of Logical Thinking in the Child.* New York: Basic Books, 1958.

_____. *The Origins of Intelligence in Children,* 2d ed. New York: International Universities Press, 1952.

Prehm, H. and Altman, R. *Improving Instruction Through Classroom Research.* Denver: Love Publishing, 1976.

Rotter, J. B. *Social Learning and Clinical Psychology.* Englewood Cliffs, New Jersey: Prentice-Hall, 1954.

Sapir, S. G. and Nitzburg, A. C., eds. *Children with Learning Problems.* New York: Brunner-Mazel, 1973.

Skinner, B. F. "Are Theories of Learning Necessary?" *Psychological Review* 57 (1950): 193-216.

_____. *The Behavior of Organisms.* New York: Appleton-Century-Crofts, 1938.

Sloan, W. "Motor Proficiency and Intelligence." *American Journal of Mental Deficiency* 55 (1951): 394-406.

Sloan, W., and Berg, I. "A Comparison of Two Types of Learning in Mental Defectives." *American Journal of Mental Deficiency* 61 (1957): 556-66.

Stevenson, H. W., and Knights, R. M. "Effect of Visual Reinforcement on the Performance of Normal and Retarded Children." *Perceptual Motor Skills* 13 (1961): 119-26.

Weatherwax, J., and Benoit, E. P. "Concrete and Abstract Thinking in Organic and Nonorganic Mentally Retarded Children." *American Journal of Mental Deficiency* 62 (1957): 548-53.

Werner, H. "Perceptual Behavior of Brain-Injured, Mentally Defective Children: An Experimental Study by Means of the Rorschach Technique." *Genetic Psychological Monograph* 31 (1945): 51-100.

Werner, H., and Strauss, A. A. "Impairment in Thought Processes of Brain-Injured Children." *American Journal of Mental Deficiency* 47 (1943): 291-95.

Zigler, E. "The Retarded Child as a Whole Person." In, Adams, H. E. and Boardman, W. K., eds. *Advances in Experimental Clinical Psychology.* New York: Pergamon Press, 1971.

Index

379

Ellis, Norman R., 334, 343, 347
Employment, 64, 226, 243, 247, 262
Environment, 18, 20, 27, 62, 65, 67, 68, 104, 109, 130, 131, 134, 135, 137, 141, 147-63, 181, 188, 212, 228, 253, 291, 310, 334, 335, 351
Estabrook, Arthur, 147, 148, 152, 159
Evaluation, 235, 236, 243, 245
  work, 254, 262-3, 270
Expectations, 288, 310
Expenses, 178, 183, 203
Experience, 32, 74, 129, 130, 148, 160, 226, 281, 290, 333, 334, 343, 367, 370

Faber, Bernard, 168
Facilities, 20, 21, 303
Fairbanks, Baller and Charles, 309
Family, 21, 95, 104, 110, 128, 129, 149, 164-87, 262, 281, 282, 296
Fear, 165, 171, 172, 190, 228
Feedback, 194, 195, 196, 197, 200, 202, 203
Feelings, 129, 167, 168, 189, 190, 193, 284
Filler, J. W., Jr., 42
Fitz-Herbert, Sir Anthony, 17, 24, 25, 29, 30
Frustration, 166, 227
Future, 129, 167

Galton, Sir Francis, 147
Genes, 134, 141
Goals, 28, 59, 130, 136, 191, 197, 202, 229, 233, 252, 288
Goddard, Dr. Henry, 147, 148, 152, 153, 155, 156, 159
Goldstein, Moss and Jordan, 284, 289
Goodwill Industries, 236
Grossman, H. J., 56, 57, 58, 105, 106, 115, 119
Groupings, 104, 107, 120
Growth, 7, 108, 166, 175, 214, 217, 222, 288, 332, 334, 339
  abnormal, 113, 122
Guggenbuhl, Dr. Johann Jakob, 19
Guidance, 59, 63, 64, 225, 228, 235, 236, 243, 245
Guilt, 167

Habilitation, 226, 228, 236, 245, 253
Habits, 57
  strength, 346
Handicap, 139, 212, 237, 286, 296, 310, 335
  physical, 59, 61, 227, 295
Harlow, Harry F., 335, 342, 347
Hebb, Donald O., 333, 342, 344, 357
Heber, R., 56
Heredity, 104, 109, 110, 121, 147-63
House, Betty J., 334, 342, 347
Howe, Dr. Samuel, 19, 26, 27, 30
Hull, Clark, 334, 342, 346, 369

Illness, 104
  mental, 73-88
Impairment, 3, 4, 5, 6, 8, 9, 11, 13, 57, 59, 60, 66, 68, 70, 78, 79
Improvement, 149, 335
Independence, 57, 59, 166, 171, 175, 226, 282, 289, 307, 312
Individuality, 174
Infections, 105, 111, 117, 118
Inferiority, 136, 141, 284
Injury, brain, 74, 79, 113
Institutionalization, 167, 229, 238
Integration, 291, 310, 320, 343
  family, 168, 175, 180, 183, 203
Intelligence, 2, 40-55, 58, 60, 66, 73, 134, 147, 149, 152-6, 288, 295, 344, 348, 350
Interaction, 66, 237
Intervention, 150, 154, 217, 218
Intoxications, 105, 111, 118
Itard, Dr. Jean, 18, 25, 26, 27

Jensen, Dr. Arthur, 149, 153, 156, 160
Jobs, 59, 64, 66, 235, 254, 262, 274
Johnson and Kirk, 304
Joint Commission on Accreditation of Hospitals, 20
Jukes family, 147, 152

Kallikak, Martin, 147, 152
Kennedy, John F., 20
Kirk, 284, 289
Knowledge, 164, 190
Kohler, Wolfgang, 333, 342, 343
Kuhlman-Binet test, 40